Modern Advertising and the Market for Audience Attention

Modern advertising was created in the US between 1870 and 1920 when advertisers and the increasingly specialized advertising industry that served them crafted means of reliable access to and knowledge of audiences.

This highly original and accessible book re-centers the story of the invention of modern advertising on the question of how access to audiences was streamlined and standardized. Drawing from late-nineteenth and early-twentieth-century materials, especially from the advertising industry's professional journals and the business press, chapters on the development of print media, billboard, and direct mail advertising illustrate the struggles amongst advertisers, intermediaries, audience-sellers, and often-resistant audiences themselves. Over time, the maturing advertising industry transformed the haphazard business of getting advertisements before the eyes of the public into a market in which audience attention could be traded as a commodity.

This book applies economic theory with historical narrative to explain market participants' ongoing quests to expand the reach of the market and to increase the efficiency of attention-harvesting operations. It will be of interest to scholars of contemporary American advertising, the history of advertising more generally, and also of economic history and theory.

Zoe Sherman is Assistant Professor of Economics at Merrimack College. Her scholarly writing has appeared in *Rethinking Marxism, Forum for Social Economics,* and other peer reviewed publications. Her popular writing appears regularly in *Dollars & Sense* magazine.

Routledge Explorations in Economic History
Edited by Lars Magnusson, *Uppsala University, Sweden*

For more information about this series, please visit www.routledge.com/series/SE0347

Modern Advertising and the Market for Audience Attention

The US Advertising Industry's Turn-of-the-Twentieth-Century Transition

Zoe Sherman

Routledge
Taylor & Francis Group

LONDON AND NEW YORK

First published 2020
by Routledge
2 Park Square, Milton Park, Abingdon, Oxon OX14 4RN

and by Routledge
605 Third Avenue, New York, NY 10017

First issued in paperback 2021

Routledge is an imprint of the Taylor & Francis Group, an informa business

Publisher's Note
The publisher has gone to great lengths to ensure the quality of this reprint but points out that some imperfections in the original copies may be apparent.

British Library Cataloguing-in-Publication Data
A catalogue record for this book is available from the British Library

Library of Congress Cataloging-in-Publication Data
Names: Sherman, Zoe, author.
Title: Modern advertising and the market : the US advertising industry
    from the 19th century to the present / Zoe Sherman.
Description: Milton Park, Abingdon, Oxon ; New York, NY : Routledge,
    2020. | Series: Routledge explorations in economic history | Includes
    bibliographical references and index.
Identifiers: LCCN 2019040705 | ISBN 9781138201545 (hardback) |
    ISBN 9781315511573 (ebook)
Subjects: LCSH: Advertising—United States—History—19th century. |
    Advertising—United States—History—20th century. | Advertising—
    United States—History—21st century.
Classification: LCC HF5813.U6 S535 2020 | DDC 659.10973—dc23
LC record available at https://lccn.loc.gov/2019040705

ISBN 13: 978−1−03−208335−3 (pbk)
ISBN 13: 978−1−138−20154−5 (hbk)

Typeset in Bembo
by Apex CoVantage LLC

Contents

Preface

When I first began to develop this project early in the 2010s, I did not foresee how prominent the issues of attention and personal data would become over the course of the decade. Most of the analysis is focused on digital platforms for the trade in attention. Facebook's parade of scandals (selling users' personal data to Cambridge Analytica, selling users' attention to fraudulent political operatives, and so on) keep bringing us back to the question of whether each scandal is a corruption of a basically OK business or whether, instead, a business based on mining information and attention resources from users' lives is irredeemable. Presidential candidates (some of them, forcefully) and regulators (tentatively) have raised the question of Facebook, Google, and Amazon's monopoly power in digital attention markets.

Meanwhile, self-reflective people who are the objects of attention mining find themselves pondering – and trying to articulate – what the subjective experience of attention depletion *feels* like. When Ford Prefect described the sensation of traveling through hyperspace as "unpleasantly like being drunk," Arthur Dent wanted to know what was so bad about being drunk. "Ask a glass of water," replied Ford. (*Hitchhiker's Guide to the Galaxy* fans know what I'm talking about.) Perhaps we could apply Ford's metaphor to the contemporary experience of attention depletion: like the water's experience of being drunk, we the attention- and data-mined feel an inner turbulence set in motion by being consumed from outside.

Decades ago, Mary Oliver concluded her poem "Yes! No!" with the lines "To pay attention, this is our endless/and proper work." But how do we do the work of paying attention when claims on our attention outstrip our capacities? Books on the topic are being written and published in such quick succession that they are often handled in group book review essays. (For example, just in April of 2019: Jia Tolentino wrote about Cal Newport's *Digital Minimalism: Choosing a Focused Life in a Noisy World* and Jenny Odell's *How to Do Nothing: Resisting the Attention Economy* in the April 29 issue of *The New Yorker*. Casey Schwartz, too, wrote about Odell and Newport, and also included Joshua Cohen's *Attention: Dispatches from the Land of Distraction*, Chris Bailey's *Hyper Focus*, and Sam Lipsyte's *Hark*, a satirical fiction take on attention depletion, in her book review essay published in the *New York Times* on April 19.) Many of these works attempt not only to document and explain, but to propose means of resistance . . . or at least suggest some coping strategies. Being drunk like a glass of water *is* unpleasant. The simultaneous explosion of mindfulness and meditation practices into cultural currency strikes me as more than coincidence.

At this moment, writing a book about the history of US attention markets is an illustration of the principle that history is inescapably about the concerns of the moment in which it is written. What's past is prologue, and we write prologues to lead into the story we want to tell next. The story of attention- and data-mining is one of the major themes of the story of what it is like to live in the US now. (Although this is not a uniquely American story, I have focused on the American variant of the story.) This book is one version of the prologue for today.

Acknowledgments

This project began while I was a doctoral student in the economics department at the University of Massachusetts Amherst and delves into themes that I learned to ask questions about while a master's degree student in the American Studies department at the University of Massachusetts Boston, so I will begin by acknowledging the teachers I learned from in those places. Jerry Friedman read and commented on more drafts of more sections of this book than anyone else and is the closest thing I had to a midwife in this labor. Judy Smith and Michael Ash also supported the completion of the portions of this project that appeared in my dissertation. I have now had Steve Resnick as a ghost in my head longer than I had him as a flesh-and-blood person in my life, but I think often of the question he asked me when I first started proposing to explore the themes in this research and he agreed to work with me (which he did as long as he lived). "Will you still be interested in this question three years from now?" he asked me. Yes, Steve! I stayed interested longer than that, even, and I am so glad to have had you with me as I started out in this direction. Gratitude also to teachers whose classes bear on the intellectual directions and methods of this work: Rachel Rubin, Carol Heim, Randy Albelda, Lois Rudnick, and David Kotz. I hope I achieved a standard of scholarship that reflects the high standards of my mentors' own scholarship and teaching.

I changed status from student to faculty when I joined the economics department at Merrimack College in fall of 2014. Thanks to all of my colleagues in the department, across the School of Liberal Arts, and across the college as a whole. Thanks, also, to the colleagues from other institutions who wrote letters on my behalf to support my tenure and promotion application. All of these colleagues' caregiving labor supports my professional life. Jack Amariglio and Tony Laramie have worked especially hard on my behalf. Their continuing love and care mean so much to me.

Scholars' work depends on the intellectual and practical support of the custodians of the documents we depend on. I depended in particular on the librarians and archivists at the Hartman Center for Sales, Advertising, and Marketing History at Duke University; the Baker Library at Harvard Business School; the Boston Public Library; the McQuade Library at Merrimack College. Thank you to everyone who answered my questions in person, by phone, by email, taught me how to discover what you had in your collections and what I could borrow from elsewhere, and let me handle the treasures in your keeping.

I received much appreciated financial support for this project from the Hartman Center's Outdoor Advertising Fellowship, the Political Economy Research Institute's Dissertation Fellowship, and the Association for Social Economics' William Waters Grant. Financial support paid for travel to the archives and paid for time in which I could write (by funding a semester of graduate school without work as a teaching assistant and by funding summer camps for my daughter). It took me long enough as it is!

A portion of Chapter 3 was first published as "Pricing the Eyes of Passersby: The Commodification of Audience Attention in U.S. Public Spaces, 1890–1920" in the *Review of Radical Political Economics*, December 2014, 46 (4): 502–508.

My life, including this project but far beyond this project, was made possible in the first instance by my parents Joe and Janet Sherman and my brother Reid, and for the last almost-twenty years by my husband Chris Kendig. I can count the number of times I set foot in a supermarket in a typical year on my fingers. I kid you not. And yet the kitchen is always stocked with the staples and hot dinners emerge every evening, even those evenings – the vast majority – when I am not the one making them. And so I live to write another day.

My daughter, Matilda, is only a couple of years older than this research project. When she was in kindergarten she offered to help me with my research. She said she could work on surveys and data. (Surveys are when you write down the questions, she explained, and data is when you collect the answers.) Now that she is in sixth grade she's probably embarrassed to be reminded of this episode, but never mind. For all those hours when I needed to write (or teach or perform any other responsibilities) and Chris was also otherwise engaged, thanks are due to the amazing Boston Public School teachers, first at the Baldwin School and then at the Edison School, who have had Matilda in their care. And during those after school and school vacation times . . . Matilda, pulling me away from the book and involving me in other interests is also help!

For intellectual community: Thanks to the overlapping memberships of the Association for Economic and Social Analysis, the Union for Radical Political Economics, the Association for Social Economics, the Association for Institutional Thought, the Dollars & Sense Collective. Christine Ngo was a wonderful writing buddy to have in the summer of 2019 as we were both nearing completion of our first book manuscripts. Jeanne Winner, Chris Sturr, and Liz Henderson volunteered their expert editing eyes to help me clean up the manuscript.

For cheerleading and encouragement: Thanks to the extended family I was born into and the extended family I married into. Thanks to friends new and, especially, old. Margaret, Joan, Assia, Cathleen, Rob, Bev, Steph, Mike, Christine, Junko, Licia, Desiree, Cate, Julia . . . I'm so glad to have you in my life.

1   Introduction

Audience attention as commodity, commodification as historical process

Audience attention as commodity

Our eyes and ears are coveted commodities. They are coveted by advertisers who seek to put their messages where we will see or hear them. They are commodities by virtue of the fact that advertisers pay to reach us.

The results of the workings of the access-to-attention market are familiar to us. Magazine and newspaper advertisements surround the articles we read (and maybe we read the advertisements, too). Billboards pass through our field of vision as we walk or drive or ride along the road (and sometimes we notice what they show and say). Advertisements are dropped on our doorsteps and in our mailboxes. Advertisements interrupt or are woven into radio and television programs. Advertising arrives in our email inboxes. Advertising permeates the web.

The access-to-attention market operates in the background for most of us; the advertisements become part of the fabric of daily life, a set of shared cultural referents. If we investigate how advertisements reach our awareness, what we find is that the advertisements reach us because our eyes and ears are on the auction block. But we are not the ones who put our own sensory organs up for sale. Instead, those with access to an audience – and some degree of exclusivity – sell space in that audience's field of vision or range of hearing. Advertisers then gain access to their desired audiences by buying their way in. A billboard owner, for example, can assure advertisers that the billboard will be visible to anyone who passes by on the street and that the only way to make use of that visibility is to pay for the billboard display space. Passersby are not party to the exchange and, at the same time, passersby are the whole point of the exchange.

This analysis has become commonplace in media studies: what the media produce is an audience; the media's customers are the advertisers. The content of the TV show is merely the bait; the sales transaction takes place between the media outlet and the advertiser, and the content of *that* transaction is . . . well . . . us. If it looks like you are getting something for free, you are probably the product. (Even if it has become commonplace in the academic literature and is growing in prevalence in journalism and popular discussion of some advertising platforms, especially social media, it can still be a jolt for an individual to come to that realization.)

It is a mistake, however, to project contemporary media studies' persuasive conclusion that audiences *are* commodities backward to the nineteenth century. This book shows how audiences *became* commodities. How is it that access to our eyes and ears came to be the property of someone else? Furthermore, how did it come to be that those who hold property rights in our eyes and ears can sell them to yet another someone else?

Commodification as historical process

Anything that has the status of a commodity must have, at some time or another, gone through a process of commodification; that is, a process by which private property rights are asserted and a market exchange mechanism is constructed. The rights of private ownership may be a *de facto* social practice or they may be *de jure* rights recognized and enforced by governmental authority. The private property rights must be alienable: the initial owner may relinquish the right of ownership to another. And the property must be considered fungible: commensurable with and exchangeable for something else, namely money (Radin 1996).

The commodity status of things that have long been commodified and the structures and practices of market exchange come to seem natural and obvious to market participants. But the initial commodification of a good is generally a struggle. There is struggle over what should be privately owned and by whom. There is struggle over what should be alienable. There is struggle over what sorts of exchanges should be allowed. What is commensurable with what? Once the commodity status and market practices pass into the realm of normalized, unquestioned social practice, the story of market exchange can be told as a story of freely chosen (within the constraints of existing circumstance), mutually beneficial exchanges. But establishing private property rights and commensurability in the market always involves an exercise of power. The market for audience attention in commodity form emerged from a process of fierce struggle amongst advertisers, advertising agents, publishers, billposters, and often-resistant audiences themselves.

The first stumbling steps toward the construction of an organized market for the buying and selling of audiences in the United States came around 1870. In the late nineteenth and early twentieth centuries, advertisers and the advertising professionals[1] who served them successfully pushed the transformation of audience attention into a form of tradable property. At the beginning of this period, getting advertisements before the eyes of the public was a haphazard affair. By the end of the period, advertising in periodical media, outdoor advertising such as billboards, and direct mail marketing had all gone through a process of standardization, allowing advertisers to, with a reasonably high degree of specificity and confidence, purchase access to the attention of desired audiences.

The standardization emerged from the interaction of advertisers' and advertising professionals' desires. Advertisers wanted reliable access to audience attention for use in their own competitive strategies. While providing the reliable access to audiences that advertisers sought, advertising professionals wanted to capture a healthy share of those advertisers' selling costs. The business practices that developed in the decades around the turn of the twentieth century assured advertisers of the size of their audience and assured those selling advertising space of revenue. The placement of advertisements in print media, on outdoor billboards, and in mailboxes (or on doorsteps) took on their modern, still-familiar form when the maturing advertising industry was able to sell standardized access to audience attention. By 1920 the basic structure of the market was pretty well set. Space-sellers collected or intercepted audiences. Advertising agents, generally identifying as advocates for the advertisers' interests, mediated the purchase of those audiences. Advertisers filled those spaces with their sales pitches, confident that those pitches would be seen by the number and type of people they had bargained for. Newer media – radio, television, the internet – were later incorporated into the audience attention market. Each new medium reshaped the market, certainly, but did not generate a market *de novo*. The initial construction had already been done.

Audience attention as a fictitious commodity

Markets are always embedded in a society that also includes non-market realms; what happens within the market depends in part on what happens without (and vice versa). Karl Polanyi argued that ours is a market society in which the market realm has a tendency to expand into more and more areas of social life, but this process of market expansion runs into contradictions. The self-regulating market ideal requires that every element of industry must be treated as a commodity, "subject to the supply-and-demand mechanism interacting with price." However, industry's needs include land and labor, which are "no other than the human beings themselves of which every society consists and the natural surroundings in which it exists." That is, they are not produced for the purpose of market exchange, and yet they become subject to market exchange. Polanyi calls such items, those that are traded on markets although they are not produced specifically for sale on the market, "fictitious commodities." He identified three: land, labor, and money. The self-regulating market ideal can never be fully achieved both because the market would fail – these fictitious commodities will not respond appropriately to market signals – and because allowing "the market mechanism to be sole director of the fate of human beings and their natural environment . . . would result in the demolition of society" (Polanyi 1957 [1944], pp. 71–73).

Audience attention is not produced for the purpose of market exchange; like labor, it is inherent in the existence of a human population. Although, unlike labor, which is sold by those laboring, attention was not (and is not) sold by those attending; it was (and is) sold by third parties. By the late nineteenth century, access to audience attention became important to the functioning of industry and it remains so today. This need of industry created a pressure for audience attention to take on a commodity form and the advertising industry was born in response. A new market in audience attention arose, interconnected with all other markets in the larger market economy. In short, audience attention became a fictitious commodity.

Sectors of the audience attention market

The emerging market for audience attention had several sectors. Before 1920, there were three main avenues for the interception of audiences' field of vision outside of places that were already considered places of commerce. One was to gather audience attention in the virtual spaces of the mass media. The second was to gather audience attention in public spaces. The third was direct mail marketing and door-to-door distribution seeking to intercept people's attention in the private space of their homes.[2]

Mass media

In the late nineteenth and early twentieth centuries, mass media meant print (Laird 1998, p. 58). There were local daily and weekly newspapers, many with a small local readership numbering only in the hundreds, and there were monthly national magazines with readership in the thousands or tens of thousands or even, for a very few stand-out successes, by around 1900, hundreds of thousands to a million. In the late nineteenth century, however, information about publications and their readership was incomplete and inaccurate. Advertisers could and did pay publishers for advertising placements and the advertisers' payments could pretty reliably secure the application of ink to paper. But the ultimate purpose of the ad placement – intercepting the gaze of a reader – remained a vague and entirely unverifiable promise. Advertisers put little faith in the circulation claims of publishers (Rowell 1906; Fowler 1900 [1897]; Myers 1960).

The production of all forms of print media grew remarkably quickly in the decades after the Civil War. As the volume of print media grew, advertising agents took on a larger role in circulating information about available advertising space and in negotiating ad placements. Through their intermediation, the market for media ad placements integrated regionally and nationally. From the perspective of producers and retailers with national ambitions, this service from advertising agents meant that newspapers in New Haven, New York, Newport News, and New Orleans were now part of a single, readily accessible market for audience attention. Also, as the market grew and integrated, the nature of the exchange between publisher and advertiser – the relationship between size, page placement, *and circulation*, to rates – became increasingly standardized. There is a rich literature on print media advertising in the economic and cultural setting of the late nineteenth and early twentieth centuries. The core of this literature is a flurry of scholarship published in the fifteen years from Daniel Pope's *The Making of Modern Advertising* in 1983 to Pamela Walker Laird's *Advertising Progress* in 1998. Chapter 2 relies on the work of Pope, Laird, and others to retell the story of the development of print media advertising, re-centering the analysis on the question of quantifying audiences to develop print as a sector of the audience attention market.

Outdoor advertising

While greater volumes of print media were engaging the eyes of a larger and larger readership, city streets and major regional transportation routes were gathering together denser and denser spatial concentrations of people. The throngs of people funneled into major thoroughfares were of great interest to many advertisers. As with print media, however, advertisers in 1870 had only spotty access to these throngs. They could and did pay printers for posters, and those purchase orders were generally fulfilled. Advertisers could then pay billposters to paste the posters around the city, but that was a much iffier proposition. Billposters in the postbellum period were as little trusted as publishers, for good reason. They were sometimes caught burning or otherwise disposing of the posters they were paid to hang. Even if the billposter did earnestly paste every one of the posters in his charge, there was no inventory of display locations, nor was there protection or inspection of display spaces. The next billposter to walk by could paste over one advertiser's poster with a new poster before anyone read the first. The owner of the property to which the poster was affixed – or anyone else, for that matter – could tear it down (Associated Billposters Association of the United States and Canada December 1897, pp. 20–21).

Then some enterprising and innovative billposters introduced a new practice: billboards. Rather than pasting a poster to any surface they happened upon, they leased space, constructed specialized display surfaces, and pasted posters there. This new practice allowed advertisers to contract for particular display locations and verify that their posters were in fact hung as promised. Billboards rapidly proliferated and by 1900 billposters in every major city in the US could offer advertisers standardized billboard displays. With display now guaranteed, display pricing was negotiated on the basis of size, placement, *and number of passersby*. Rather than paying billposters for the service of affixing poster to wall, advertisers were now paying billposters for access to an audience's eyes. Billposting has not received nearly the volume of focused scholarly attention devoted to print media (or other elements of consumer culture such as retailing). Chapter 3 draws heavily on the Outdoor Advertising Association of America archives, held at Duke University's John W. Hartman Center for Sales, Advertising, and Marketing History, to tell the story of standardizing the field of outdoor advertising.

Direct mail

Advertising professionals of the late nineteenth century found another important venue in which they could intercept an audience's attention and offer it to advertisers: private homes. Advertisers made use of three main ways to enter people's homes. One was to distribute trade cards and other bits of advertising ephemera (calendars, rulers, paper fans, tins. . .) and hope that the targeted audience themselves would bring those items home. Late nineteenth century and early twentieth century scrapbooks show that this often worked (Laird 1998, pp. 219, 265; Banta 2013).

But advertisers did not necessarily want to wait for audiences to self-select into perusal of their promotions, nor did advertising professionals want to pass up an opportunity to mediate advertisers' contact with audiences. The result of both parties' discontent was two practices that delivered advertising to audiences' doors. One was door-to-door delivery: distributors (this was their standard job title) would take sacks of advertisers' materials and walk the streets, handing items to people they found at home, or tossing them through a window, or sliding them under a door, or leaving them on a porch. The advantages offered by distributors were that advertisers did not need a mailing list and could send out a wide variety of advertising materials such as product samples and items of nonstandard shapes and sizes that the Post Office would not handle, at least not at affordable postage rates (Associated Billposters and Distributors of the United States and Canada 1905–1908). However, distribution suffered from the same principal-agent problem as early billposting: there was no way to know whether or not distributors had fulfilled their side of the bargain.

Another option was direct mail marketing sent through the United States Post Office, which first began home delivery in select urban areas in the 1860s and began delivering mail to all households, even in rural areas, by 1902 (Gallagher 2016, p. 190; Henkin 2006, pp. 86–90). Direct mail limited the types of material that could be delivered (only paper of fairly standard sizes and weights) and required that advertisers already know the names and addresses of those they wanted to reach. But in compensation, advertisers had a high degree of confidence that the items were delivered and the individual addressing allowed them to track contacts with individual targets and run detailed studies of responses. Modern commercial data mining can trace its roots to the businesses that compiled and sold mailing lists beginning as early as the 1880s and entered a period of rapid growth after 1900. (Data mining can also be traced to the consumer credit reporting that arose around the same time (Lauer 2017).) Like billposting, direct mail has attracted less scholarly attention than print. Relying largely on primary source material, much of which I accessed at Harvard Business School's Baker Library, Chapter 4 tells the direct mail story.

The dramatis personae

Pamela Walker Laird suggests that we think of the process of advertising in five steps: decide to advertise, conceive the message, produce the material that encodes the message, distribute the material, and pay for it. Advertisers themselves must do the first and last, but the middle steps "devolved to specialists at different rates over the years" (Laird 1998, p. 39). Laird's central purpose in her book *Advertising Progress* was to explore the emergence of the second and third steps, conceiving of the message and producing the material that encodes it, as specialized professional tasks. The purpose of this study is to explore the transformation of the fourth step as distribution of advertising came to be accomplished through the purchase of access to audiences. To understand the conversion of audience attention into a purchasable commodity, we need as context some understanding of the advertisers' decision to advertise.

Who were the advertisers? Why did their sales practices change?

The scale and style of advertising developed in the closing decades of the nineteenth century differed in kind from earlier advertising. The most familiar and non-suspect form of advertising prior to the Civil War came from merchants alerting the local public to recent shipments. Few items, especially items transported from afar, were consistently stocked. The implicit assumption behind such early advertisements was that buyers generally knew what they wanted to buy (a bolt of cloth, a porcelain tea set, a slave) and were keeping half an eye out for when the items they wanted reached a merchant in their area (Laird 1998, pp. 23–24; Strasser 1989). Such advertising was modest and generally limited to merchants. Aggressive advertising or advertising undertaken by manufacturers was considered highly untrustworthy. Only the disreputable or the desperate would undertake a large-scale advertising campaign. If a business had to advertise, it was taken as a sign of weakness; bankers were likely to conclude that the business was in trouble and decline to offer credit (Fox 1997, p. 15). The suspicion harbored toward businesses that advertised made some sense. Even if the people at the beginning of the supply chain did not know the ultimate consumers, the links between them were constituted by a sequence of personal connections. Whatever buyers and sellers at each intermediate link needed to know about one another, they could communicate without advertising as an intermediary (Strasser 1989).

Now, of course, advertising is an accepted and expected part of almost any business plan. Indeed, a hundred years ago it was already so accepted and expected that beginning in 1917 the federal government recognized advertising as a fully deductible business expense; money spent on advertising would not be subject to the excess profits tax. Prior to 1917, the Internal Revenue Service considered expenditures on advertising a choice a business might make about its use of retained profits (Olney 1991, p. 169). What led to this about-face in the status of advertising?

Earlier in the nineteenth century, there were already some manufacturers with large enough outputs or diffuse enough customer bases that they needed to sell to strangers across geographic distance. In these cases, the distance between producers and ultimate buyers was closed by market intermediaries. Middlemen specialized in information; they developed broad knowledge of manufacturers' product lines and retailers' inventory needs. They most often purchased on their own account, then divided their inventory into lots appropriate to the size of the retailers they dealt with and resold the goods at a markup covering their transportation and storage costs . . . and a profit (Porter and Livesay 1971, pp. 162–163). Indeed, the biggest pre-Civil War personal fortunes, at least in the North, were usually built from mercantile activity (Pope 1983, pp. 78–79). Later in the nineteenth century, the scale of the individual enterprises and the extent of the markets in which they operated ballooned. Even greater distances opened up between those directing production decisions and those ultimately consuming the goods produced – geographic distance, often social distance, and layers of bureaucratic and market intermediation. The greater distance posed a different selling problem than that faced by earlier, smaller-scale enterprises. Consumers needed new ways to make meaning in their material culture and producers wanted to intervene in this altered process of meaning-making in profitable ways, but those at the opposite extremes of the distribution chain were not personally known to one another and did not communicate directly (Strasser 1989). The impetus to commodify commercial communications came from these emerging large-scale producers and sellers of the late nineteenth century.

Large-scale producers of the late nineteenth century were more capital-intensive than their predecessors. New technologies dramatically increased effi-ciency and lowered unit costs, but these technologies came with high fixed costs. These new technologies also were most efficiently employed with steady through-put of materials. Manufacturers thus wielded unprecedented produc-tive powers and, as these productive powers only worked at large scale, used these powers to produce unprecedented volumes of goods, but without any guarantee of finding buyers (Chandler 2002 [1977]). Production was bureau-cratically coordinated and largely predictable. Exchange on the market was anarchic and uncertain. There is nothing distinctive about the US in displaying this contradiction. It is a pattern common to industrial capitalism anywhere it manifests (Engels 1880). With massive productive powers and no guarantee of buyers, not just individual businesses or industries, but the entire economy reg-ularly overproduced. The period from 1873 to 1897 on the whole was a period of staggering growth, and yet fourteen of those twenty-five years were years of depression or recession as supply kept overshooting demand; increased output did not automatically generate increased profits (Ohmann 1996, p. 55). The US was experiencing recurrent outbreaks of "an epidemic that, in all earlier epochs, would have seemed an absurdity – the epidemic of over-production." The country suffered from "too much civilization, too much means of subsist-ence, too much industry, too much commerce" (Marx 1983 [1848], p. 210).

With production already so controlled and rationalized, manufacturers began working by the 1880s to "control and maximize the flow of their goods through distribution channels to the consumer," that is, to rationalize distribution. Demand, they began to realize, is not *only* cost driven, but can be managed through promo-tional communications (Laird 1998, p. 184). "Late-nineteenth-century capitalists," writes Richard Ohmann, "understood that they needed broad controls over their world, in order to continue amassing wealth peacefully." They attempted various forms of cooperation amongst themselves (trade associations, cartels, trusts), but attempts to pace production in keeping with profitable prices were

fragile and succeeded only for short periods. They also didn't succeed in sta-
bilizing labor relations: they relied largely on force, which succeeded only
temporarily and undermined their legitimacy (Ohmann 1996, p. 56). Their
most successful strategy proved to be managing demand through branding and
advertising.

At the same time that manufacturers and even retailers, especially in cities,
were all engaged in similar efforts to manage consumer demand over growing
distances, they were also engaged in a fierce struggle amongst themselves. Their
drive to assert some control over their business environment encompassed not
just final consumers, but also competitors and distributors. Advertising was a
critical component of manufacturers' competitive strategies, both in horizontal
competition against other sellers of similar goods and in vertical competition
against others in the consumer good distribution chain. In vertical competition,
advertising was a tool used to try to capture the largest possible share of the
difference between the final retail price and the manufacturer's cost of producing the goods – that pool of surplus out of which everyone in the distribution
chain must carve their profits. In horizontal competition, advertising was a tool
used to pursue high market share at steady, profitable retail prices (Chandler
2002 [1977]; Laird 1998; Strasser 1989). While nineteenth-century middlemen
had been necessary to the smaller manufacturers whose product lines they handled so profitably, in the last few decades of the century they came to seem an
obstacle and a constraint for manufacturers implementing the dynamic transformations of the industrial revolution. Through their personal contact with
consumers, retailers were in the habit of steering their customers' consumption; retailers pushed the product lines that were most profitable to themselves
and those that had been most persuasively promoted to them by the jobbers
(McGovern 2006, p. 81; Porter and Livesay 1971). Manufacturers could not
achieve their growth and profit ambitions while remaining so dependent on
these intermediate links in the supply chain to make their case to consumers.

Sellers of newly invented or newly abundant goods could only sell their output if consumption patterns changed. To get a push from jobbers and retailers,
manufacturers would have to accept a smaller share of the surplus and let the
middlemen continue to amass the fortunes. So, instead of relying on jobbers and
retailers to push their products through distribution channels, manufacturers
looked to communicate directly to consumers. "The masters of production . . .
could, and did, turn the same kind of attention and energy that had made an
agricultural society into an industrial one toward marketing." The better they
could stimulate and anticipate final sales, the better they could plan production.
Not only could they plan the production process from beginning to end – raw
materials, to factory equipped with machinery and staffed by workers, to distribution network – but they could plan backwards, starting with "confident
expectations about sales" (Ohmann 1996, pp. 57–58). Furthermore, if consumers could be persuaded to request a product, the retailer would be pressured to
stock it and the jobbers would be pressured to distribute it, even if the manufacturer kept a larger share of the surplus and the distributors got squeezed. This

is known as pull marketing; rather than suppliers pushing products through the distribution chain, consumer requests pull the products through to their final buyers (Chandler 2002 [1977]; Laird 1998, pp. 30–34; Strasser 1989, pp. 18–20). To a large extent, manufacturers succeeded. Profit margins for wholesale and retail merchants narrowed; profit margins for manufacturers grew.

In addition to wrestling with jobbers and retailers, manufacturers were also competing against one another. The larger scale of manufacturing meant just a few producers could saturate the market, so each one had to fight for market share to sell their output. Reducing output, given the new capital-intensive techniques, would raise unit costs, so that was not a viable strategy and would be particularly fatal for a firm that reduced output unilaterally while competitors did not. Meanwhile, price competition was ruinous. If each high-volume manufacturer tried to find buyers for their output by underselling the competition, they would all end up selling at a loss until the most financially fragile firms failed (Lamoreaux 1985). (This was not a rare occurrence.) Interpreting their own experience and explaining themselves to the wider public, producers developed economic theories that characterized competition, especially price competition, as a destructive force. Rather than pushing their goods through distribution channels by means of low prices and the intercession of jobbers and retailers, producers sought to avoid ruinous price competition and dispose of their vastly increased output enabled by new technology through pull marketing. Manufacturers sought to be price setters, and in highly concentrated industries they could be. Producers with a significant market share could treat price as part of the "marketing mix," rather than an uncontrollable, market-determined datum driving one's fate (Strasser pp. 27–28, 57).

With the overall inability of inter-firm coordination through cartels and pricing pools to evade ruinous price competition, many firms merged during the "great merger movement" around the turn of the twentieth century. What could *not* be managed through inter-firm agreements *could* be managed through intra-firm managerial control. In an industry with fewer firms, each with a larger market share, those firms could more successfully choose the pace and scale of investment in new capital, the size of production runs, and the pricing strategies that would keep them in business. The horizontal mergers swept through the US economy in a particularly fast-moving wave. Over a somewhat longer and overlapping period, many firms also pursued backward and forward integration, acquiring their raw materials suppliers and/or their distributors, reducing the ranks of independent middlemen (Chandler 2002 [1977]; Lamoreaux 1985). Marketing needs of firms with these new internal and industrial structures changed, and ads changed to fit with these new needs (Laird 1998, pp. 184–185).

It might seem reasonable for a highly oligopolistic industry to reduce advertising expenditures; with so few sellers, most potential buyers already know what their options are. However, producers found that those who established a recognizable brand identity through consistent advertising were most successful. Heavy advertisers of branded goods weathered the pre-merger movement

Great Depression of 1893 better than those who advertised little. Holding a trademark proved to be better protection against price declines than price-agreement pools formed with others in the industry. After mergers, those who tried economizing on the advertising budget were often displeased with the results and quickly returned to advertising-intensive sales strategies (Laird 1998, p. 190; Lamoreaux 1985, pp. 18, 45).

Growth, through merger or other means, could even introduce new reasons to advertise. Consolidation of many small firms into a few large ones was expected to decrease advertising, wrote Herbert Casson in 1911, but monopolies *have* to advertise. "As soon as any corporation masters its competitors and controls its output, the public is afraid of it. All the irresponsible writers and talkers in the country begin at once to abuse and torment it. To save its life, it has to be sociable and friendly." Advertising is the sociable, friendly, favor-seeking face of big business (Casson 1911, pp. 140–141). Advertising could also help keep the industry concentrated: a market dominated by a few large, brand-name firms would be resistant to new entrants, making the business environment more stable (Ohmann 1996, p. 58).

Reality was, of course, messier than the story just sketched. Manufacturers of national brand-name goods *were* the most dynamic force in the transformation of advertising and, on the whole, they *did* gain control over distribution at the expense of jobbers and retailers. But other types of advertisers and other advertising practices did not disappear. The new national brand-name advertising didn't so much displace already-established practices as it overwhelmed them by its faster growth rate. Retailers still listed their current inventories in newspaper columns, manufacturers with only regional reach still worked to maintain a niche in the face of national brands (Laird 1998, p. 7). The new goods and new marketing coexisted and conflicted with the old systems. Manufacturers' efforts to engage consumers as allies against the retailers were only partially successful. The new, advertising-instigated symbolic relationships of consumers with brands and corporate identities limited retailers' power, to be sure, but at the same time the ongoing personal relationships of customers with local retailers limited the manufacturers' power (McGovern 2006, p. 81; Strasser 1989, p. 28). Even branding could be deployed as either a push or a pull strategy. Before manufacturers deployed brands to sway consumer loyalties to themselves over the retailer, manufacturers used brands to make their goods attractive for retailers to stock. Susan Strasser illustrates the principle with the case of Schilling tea, which "explicitly offered store-keepers freedom in price-setting" and made sure the labeling did not indicate the quality of the tea inside the can, making it difficult for customers to comparison shop between merchants carrying different Schilling brands. "Schilling used its brands not to identify itself to the consumer but to convince retailers that tea bought from this company would not have to confront competition in price or quality" (Strasser 1989, p. 38).

Influencing consumption patterns by participating in the meaning-making of popular material culture on a scale appropriate to the scale of production required mass producers and mass retailers to develop a mass communications strategy. As manufacturers gained power and pursued new strategies, they instigated changes in advertising practices and spurred newly specialized service providers in the emerging advertising industry. Other advertisers then, too, adapted their practices to the new circumstances and took advantage of the new advertising industry services. Readily available, predictable, measurable access to audience attention was a necessary prerequisite for advertisers to carry out their marketing strategies, emphasizing, as they did, continuous communication with consumers. The solution that took shape was for large-scale firms to buy advertising space that gave them access to consumers' attention, which then allowed market incentives to spur attention sellers to gain and sell access to the audiences that advertisers wanted. To best reap the benefits of access to advertising space, after 1900 advertisers often also paid for the service of professionals to prepare advertising content that attracted and held consumers' attention. Furthermore, the access to audiences' attention through advertising space and the engagement of audiences' attention through content could benefit advertisers most if they captured any stimulated sales themselves, rather than unintentionally sending customers their competitors' way. Manufacturers and their allies in the field of advertising lobbied for, and beginning in the 1880s got, legislation establishing strong property rights in trademarks. Trademark protection better enabled an advertiser to prevent imitators from free-riding on their advertising campaigns. A firm could even, by purchasing a trademark, buy the effects of someone else's past advertising (Strasser 1989, pp. 43–52). (When Henry L. Pierce bought Baker's chocolate in the 1880s, he paid Walter Baker's widow $10,000 per year for use of Baker's name and trademark (Laird 1998, p. 192).)

The advertisers' willingness, even eagerness, to purchase audience attention spurred a market response from those who could collect or attract and sell (or resell) it: periodical publishers and billboard owners, advertising copywriters and illustrators, advertising agents and solicitors.

Who were the advertising professionals? What were their business practices?

Space sellers

If we trace the supply chain from the raw material of the audience to the advertiser who ultimately purchases the audience's attention, the first step in the process is to intercept the audience's field of vision. (Aside from street crying, a marketing practice which was in decline for most products, late nineteenth and early twentieth century advertising media were visual. Radio came later.)

Newspaper and magazine publishers intercepted audiences' field of vision by printing content that readers wanted to see. Readers, in fact, wanted to see the content enough that they often paid to receive it. For most of the nineteenth century, most publishers made a majority of their income from the readers themselves. But publishers also knew that their readers' attention was valuable to those wanting to sell something and even the earliest American newspapers sold advertising space. As the nineteenth century progressed, publishers became more focused on cultivating advertising revenue. Editorial content was still needed to attract readers' eyes but readers came to be more valuable as product than as customer. Publishers found they could sell the readers' eyes to advertisers for more money than they could sell the content to readers. The first publishers to pursue an advertising-centered business strategy were publishers of the urban daily newspapers collectively known as the penny press, named for the below-production-cost price they charged to readers beginning in the 1830s. It was not until the 1890s, when modern magazines had only recently emerged and more newspapers found it possible to attract enough advertising dollars, that the publishing industry in the aggregate flipped from being mostly subscription-financed to mostly advertising-financed. In the 1910s, publishers began submitting to independent verification of their circulation, making reliable information about the audiences they sold available to purchasers (Fox 1997; Myers 1960; Ohmann 1996; Pope 1983; Wu 2016).

Billposters intercepted audiences' field of vision by securing access to locations that were visible from heavily traveled streets. Early billposting relied on unpaid appropriation of space: billposters would glue broadsides to any surface they happened upon. But modernizing and standardizing access to passersby required a more systematic claim to publicly visible space and so billposters developed a distinctive sort of real estate component to their business. They would lease space, which could be in an otherwise empty lot but could also be on the wall or roof of a building. On that space or wall or roof, they would construct a display surface. Once they had property rights in a dedicated display space, they could sell not only the service of gluing the advertiser's poster, but also a rental fee for the surface to which they glued it. During the 1890s, the same years that magazines were transforming most dramatically, billposting also underwent a rapid change. An aggressive drive to organize the industry secured a high degree of cooperation among large-scale billposting operations in noncompeting territories and squeezed out more marginal billposting operations. By 1900, most cities' outdoor advertising came under the control of a local monopolist and many of those local monopolists belonged to the same national association, the Associated Billposters Association. With monopoly control of their local territory and the organizational support of the national association to maintain price floors, billposters were able to evade price competition and keep the rental component of their income up. The larger the local population, the higher the price floor for billboard space, and the larger the share of their income derived from rental fees for access to an audience's eyes, rather than fees for the work of affixing posters (Associated Billposters Association of the United States and Canada 1897–1898, 1899–1904; Associated Billposters and Distributors of the United States and Canada 1905–1908, 1906; Sherman 1900).

Direct-mail marketers intercepted audiences' field of vision by entering homes via the intercession of the United States Postal Service. The Post Office, as a function of the federal government, was subject to a broader range of interests than were the purely profit-oriented publishers or billposters. Unlike other audience interceptors, the Post Office did not choose "making audiences accessible to advertisers" as an explicitly stated goal or primary objective. Nevertheless, mail delivery was a potential route to reach desired audiences and some advertisers made use of it. The indispensable starting point for this strategy was a mailing list. In order to intercept an audience by mail, an advertiser or an advertising professional acting on the advertiser's behalf had to have name and address data for every individual member of that audience. Some advertisers compiled mailing lists for themselves from a variety of sources, but other advertisers outsourced that task to businesses that constructed lists for the purpose of selling the data. Rather than acquire advertising space in places where audiences were likely to go (the virtual space of the media or the physical space of the heavily trafficked street), direct mail marketers delivered advertisers' messages to audiences where they lived by mining data, though the information processing demands of direct mail were daunting in a pre-digital age. This route to audiences developed slowly and fitfully. Direct mail marketers were less powerful than publishers in influencing postal policy, so had to react to changes in institutional circumstance more than they could drive such change. Direct mail specialists did not develop a professional organization to pursue their distinct interests until 1915. The national brand-name manufacturers whose influence was such a dynamic force in print media and billboard advertising had no urgent need to assemble a narrowly-targeted consumer advertising campaign through direct mail (though they did sometimes use direct mail to discipline those farther along the distribution chains that connected them to their final consumers). Instead, the direct-mail strategy was most attractive to makers of producer goods selling to manufacturers, to lesser-known manufacturers selling to jobbers, to jobbers selling to retailers, and to local retailers selling to a local consumer base. In short, direct mail was best suited to exactly those advertisers who seemed least progressive in their use of other media. And yet, direct mail was the medium that brought us data mining, which has proved to be an even more profound transformation in the alienation of audiences from property rights over themselves than the commodification of their attention in aggregate packages (Direct Mail Advertising Association 1916; Harder 1958; Kielbowicz 1989).

Agents and solicitors

Those who intercepted audiences' attention could sometimes sell their services directly to the ultimate users of that attention. Often, however, attention interceptors, like manufacturers, worked through distribution channel intermediaries. The geographic range of ambitious advertisers often exceeded the geographic range of the advertising space sellers. The national brand-name manufacturers wanted to sell their goods everywhere, but any given newspaper publisher or billposter could only sell the eyes of those in their city. (By choosing attention bait other than local news and sending their materials through the

Post Office, both magazines and direct mail were able to transcend the place-based boundaries on newspaper publishers' and billposters' attention harvests.) Often, a middleman could save an advertiser a lot of time and effort by collecting information on all the available advertising venues and negotiating many placements (Pope 1983).

In the print media field, the middlemen were called advertising agents. The first of them in the US set up shop in the 1840s and were closely identified with the publishers; their role was to push sales of newspaper advertising space. In the 1870s, a growing number of advertising agents reoriented themselves toward the interests of the advertisers and acted more as procurement agents for attention buyers than as sales agents for attention sellers. "Still," Pamela Walker Laird writes, "the ambiguities of the agents' loyalties remained at issue for decades. Advertising agents thus carved a niche within the expanding marketplace at the point where the needs of advertisers and publishers intersected, and both sets of clients gradually, grudgingly accepted the agents' brokerage functions" (Laird 1998, p. 157). Even as their uncertain loyalties and opaque business practices bred mistrust, advertising agents' ability to compile information and lower coordination costs facilitated both the integration and the expansion of the nascent attention market. (The number of agents also multiplied. The Trow Business Directory of New York listed 42 of them in 1869 and listed 288 in 1892 (Laird 1998, p. 157).) In time, as agents became more deeply allied to advertisers and more antagonistic toward publishers, they became somewhat more transparent themselves and brokered agreements between publishers and advertisers regarding the transparency of publishers' business practices in the attention market. Several advertising agents attempted to offer critical assessments of publishers' circulation beginning as early as the 1870s. Though the agents' own limited ability to carry out credible circulation estimates eventually ended those efforts, the mediation of advertising agents was critical to, in 1914, establishing the independent circulation audits that allowed advertisers to be more certain of how many eyes they were buying. Agents' increasing identification with advertisers also, after 1900, manifested as a greater role in speaking for advertisers. Advertising agencies became employers of creative workers who prepared advertising copy, art, and layout (Laird 1998, p. 183).

Billposters, too, relied on intermediaries for some of their business. The advertising agents who dealt in print media advertising space did not initially expand into mediation of billboard placements. Instead, the billboard placement intermediaries were a separate roster of middlemen, known by the title of solicitors. To a significant degree, the basic information problem that advertising agents solved for the medium of print – who had advertising space for sale and how could they be contacted? – was solved for billposters by their own national organization. The redundantly-named Associated Billposters' Association, formed in 1891, published lists of their extensive membership. Most of their members were in a strong monopoly position, often a pure monopolist, in their local billboard market. (The Association Billposters' Association was a reorganization of the International Billposters Association of North America, which had been established in 1872 (Fisk undated).) For a coordinated national poster campaign, there were no good substitutes for the Associated Billposters' Association's member list. Still, even with the information problem solved, transaction costs remained and it was often convenient for an advertiser who wanted to advertise in dozens or even hundreds of cities and towns to work with a single solicitor who then negotiated the large number of placements. The Association kept a list of approved solicitors with whom they would do business. Some billposters transcended the geographic boundaries of the billboards under their direct control by also acting as solicitors to place their clients' posters elsewhere, thus occupying multiple positions in the supply chain simultaneously.

Business practices for direct mail marketing remained less standardized than the other sectors of the attention market. This sector did not develop a set of dedicated intermediaries between attention buyers and the list brokers who had the information needed to access that attention. (Unless we consider the brokers themselves to be intermediaries between attention buyers and the Post Office, but the Post Office was not primarily or intentionally an attention interceptor in existence only to be of service of advertisers, so it is more useful to think of the list brokers, not the Post Office, as the attention interceptors. The Post Office shaped the circumstances of the interception, like city planners and road builders shaped the circumstances of billposters' interception of audiences.) The direct mail medium needed intermediaries less than the print media advertising or the billboard sectors with their agents and solicitors did. Direct mail was inherently less place-bound than billboards or local newspapers. For an advertiser, contracting with one direct-mail-marketing provider could give access to audiences anywhere in the country, so there was no need to place attention orders with dozens of different providers in different cities. Also, direct mail was often used in conjunction with other media; advertising agencies identified with print media might take on a direct mail operation as a complement to a print media advertising campaign.

As advertising agencies that had started out as print-media advertising space brokers evolved into advertiser-oriented professional service providers, they branched out into other sectors of the attention market. After trying and failing to suppress billboards as an alternative advertising medium, advertising agents tried instead to enter the billboard market, securing recognition as approved solicitors with the Associated Billposters Association and offering to design integrated multimedia advertising strategies for their clients. Just as there were dedicated billboard advertising solicitors and also advertising agencies that offered to mediate both print and billboards, there were dedicated direct-mail marketing service providers and also advertising agencies that could provide both print and direct-mail services. While adding billboards to a print-media advertising campaign could simply replicate and reinforce the images and slogans put before audiences, adding direct mail could allow advertisers to test audience responses and differentiate their engagement with different consumers based on their individual responses. Some advertisers would run their own direct-mail follow-up operation, but others would outsource the direct mail follow up to the same agency that designed and placed their print ads. From their mid-nineteenth-century beginnings as geographic integrators of the print media sector of the audience attention market, advertising agencies with their roots in print grew into inter-sectoral integrators of the attention market, promising to broker access to audiences' eyes almost anywhere by almost any means (Associated Billposters Association of the United States and Canada March 1902, p. 3; Bates 1896; Cruikshank and Schultz 2010, p. 63; Laird 1998, pp. 158–159).

Who were the consumers?

There never was household autarky; Americans had always purchased some of the items they consumed. One long historical trend, beginning before the period of this study and continuing to the present, is an expansion in the range of items purchased and a reduction in the degree of post-purchase household production needed to transform items into the forms in which they are ultimately consumed.[3] Even within a continuous trend, there can be a period of qualitative change, and the decades around the turn of the twentieth century were such a period. As manufacturers took on a greater share of the physical production of goods, they also took on a new role in the creation of symbolic meanings associated with goods. The relationships between consumers and manufacturing corporations, as they were transformed late in the nineteenth century, created a consumer culture. "Since that time," wrote Susan Strasser in 1989, consumer-corporation relations "have flourished at the boundaries between public and private life, the theoretical boundaries of the marketplace and the literal ones of the supermarket parking lot where the products of corporate decision-making are transformed into intimate objects that people use daily" (Strasser 1989, p. 28).

Before the emergence of a modern consumer culture, much of the buying that people did in the course of provisioning their households took place in face-to-face interactions with sellers who were known personally to the buyers. The terms of the exchange between retailer and customer – quality, quantity, and price of goods – could be negotiated; the retailer would carry on similar negotiations with jobbers, and jobbers with manufacturers. In a self-service retail store carrying branded products at marked prices, the consumer provisioning their household faced take-it-or-leave-it choices. Consumers retained the right not to buy but had less scope to negotiate the terms on which they would buy (Strasser 1989, pp. 25–26). Even as the terms of exchanges came to be more fixed from afar by people not personally known to the consumer, the number of yes-no purchase decisions proliferated. In this context, a "common sense" emerged that the role of consumer is central to American identity (McGovern 2006, p. 3) even as the unequal social relationships between consumer and producer became masked behind the point-of-purchase performance of seemingly sovereign consumer choice (Strasser 1989, pp. 25–26).

An emphasis on consumer identity also helped to mask, or at least distract from, the relations of production. Consumer goods were the output of a production process permeated by capitalist relations of production. At the same time, an expanding share of households became increasingly dependent on wage labor to earn the income they used to make consumer purchases – if indeed they found sufficient employment. Efforts by workers to challenge the terms on which they sold their time were risky; strikes were often put down with violence. Strasser writes, "Everybody could join the 'class' of consumers in the marketplace, a new arena for individuals' relationships with corporations that promised salvation from the strife of the turn-of-the-century workplace" (Strasser 1989, p. 26). Capitalist employers, wanting unchecked top-down control of their workforce, hoped that workers would identify with a vision of the good life centered on intensive commodity consumption. If they did, perhaps consumerism could moderate class antagonism in the workplace (Ohmann 1996, p. 58). Probably, promoting consumerism helped capitalists' cause. During the Progressive era, even some of those staunchly on the side of labor took up the language of consumerism. However, even if an orientation toward consumption made it harder to talk about the quality of life on the job, it also offered a language for making distributional demands, pressing for incomes high enough to let workers buy the commodities constituting a consumerist good life while off the company clock (Currarino 2011). In 1919, President Wilson identified "the labor question," with its constituent parts of the question of distributional outcomes and the question of worker voice in the workplace, as the central issue confronting the US at the close of World War I (Lichtenstein 2002).

Of course, distributional questions were contentious because distribution was unequal and many people did not have household budgets that allowed for extensive engagement in consumer culture. In general, advertisers' interest in consumers was proportional to their disposable income. Living within the shocking inequalities of the distribution of income prevailing from the Gilded Age through the Roaring Twenties, there were populations of newly urbanized, not-yet-Americanized immigrants, edge-of-subsistence farmers (whether immigrant or American-born), and one-generation-after-emancipation, pre-Great Migration African Americans who were simply beneath advertisers' notice. Such groups could not possibly spend enough for it to be worth spending money to attract them (Marchand 1985, p. 64). They were also beneath notice because they fell outside the social experience and imagination of the vast majority of advertising professionals, who were uniformly white, disproportionately American-born, small-town, often Midwestern men – often, interestingly, sired by ministers (Pope 1983, pp. 177–179). But there were also growing ranks of independent professionals and salaried managers and relatively better paid workers who were worth advertising to. If their consumer desires could be stimulated, they would have the disposable income to act on those desires. Richard Ohmann characterizes the target audience of the successful magazines as an "audience that is not hereditarily affluent or elite, but that is getting on well enough, and that has cultural aspirations" (Ohmann 1996,

p. 25). In the aggregate, the magazines reached millions. Such an audience was out there. Production kept outrunning demand and triggering recessions and depressions, yes, but enough households captured enough income that demand kept catching up, allowing for lurching economic expansion.

The drama

Conflicting and complementary interests

Both the horizontal and vertical competitive struggles taking place amongst the advertising industry's clients had analogs within the advertising industry. Newspaper and magazine publishers competed horizontally against other publishers for advertisers' business. They competed with one another for readers whose attention they could sell. They sought preferential treatment from advertising agents. They competed on price for advertising placements. They competed on their own name recognition and perceived quality (Laird 1998; Pope 1983). Likewise, billposters competed against other billposters for advertisers' business, which involved competing for the most visible billboard locations and attracting advertisers' notice through intermediaries, name recognition, and perceived quality of service. To a great extent, billposters suppressed horizontal competition over the long term by securing local monopolies, but the process of securing local monopoly was a cutthroat affair: aggressive space acquisitions and predatory pricing sustained until the weaker combatant failed (Associated Billposters and Distributors of the United States and Canada 1906; Sherman 1900). Mailing list data sellers competed against one another, each claiming greater list accuracy than their competitors, each putting pricing pressure on one another.

Horizontal competition spilled across sectors: publishers, billposters, and mailing list businesses competed over their respective shares of sellers' advertising appropriations. Billposters argued that their price per pair of eyes could not be matched in any other medium: a large poster at a busy intersection was, in truth, the most efficient means of intercepting a mass audience. Publishers, however, argued that most of the thousands intercepted by a billboard were "waste circulation," audiences who simply could not be induced to buy the advertised product no matter how often they saw the poster. The jumbling and jostling together of people on city streets, they said, mixed in a lot of the wrong sort of people for whatever it was an advertiser was attempting to sell. But a newspaper or a magazine, they continued, could assemble an audience based on shared interest and sort on income. A savvy print media purchase could align the advertisement's intended audience with an appropriate readership. Direct mail, meanwhile, could not claim any advantages on the basis of unit price. Each set of eyes reached by mail cost more even than eyes reached by newspaper or magazine, which in turn cost more than eyes reached by billboard. But direct mail, skillfully deployed, promised to cut waste circulation more than any other medium. The price-per-interception might be higher, but the selling cost, direct-mail service providers insisted, would be less in the end.

Even as space sellers competed horizontally against one another, space sellers in a given sector shared an interest in gaining ground in their vertical competition along the distribution chain. Advertising agents and solicitors acted as intermediaries between the attention sellers and the advertisers who were the final buyers. In vertical competition, publishers and billposters struggled with the agents and solicitors over the size of those intermediaries' commissions. Publishers' industry associations, most prominently the American Newspaper Publishers Association, tried to mute destructive horizontal competition and present a united front in vertical competition, tamping down agents' commissions (Pope 1983, p. 157). The Associated Billposters Association supported members' aggressive pursuit of local monopoly, which allowed billposters to sidestep horizontal price competition and also allowed them to collaborate on disciplining solicitors.

Meanwhile, all space sellers and attention-market intermediaries shared an interest in persuading goods sellers to advertise expansively. They fought amongst themselves over the share each would receive of goods sellers' aggregate advertising spending, but they all agreed that they wanted aggregate advertising spending to grow rapidly so they would have a larger pie to carve up. All space sellers and attention-market intermediaries also shared an interest in cultivating consumers' receptiveness to advertising. They needed advertising to be a legitimate source material for consumers to use in constructing meaning in their cultural lives. Relatedly, they shared an interest in training audiences through repetition to become literate in the communicative codes of advertising (Ohmann 1996; Strasser 1989). While hoping to command a high price for the audience eyes they intercepted and sold, advertising professionals' longer-term survival depended on consumer spending outpacing the production and selling costs of the goods they bought. Though glad to capture as large a share of gross sales as they could command, advertising professionals' longer-term survival depended on sellers' profitability.

Engaging the state

Though the gains from the sale of any component of audience attention are privately enjoyed, the construction of attention as a salable good requires collective governance through industry trade groups and state action. Those within the advertising and related industries established standards of conduct and enforcement authorities. The state recognized and enforced contracts related to the trade in audience attention, thereby establishing new forms of property. The ability to buy and sell attention depends on establishing property rights in attention so that there is some*thing* to be traded, and on establishing rules for market engagement so that there is some *way* to carry out the trade. Advertisers and the suppliers of attention both enlisted the state in the definition and defense of the necessary new property rights. They struggled over how to carry out the exchanges and a new market infrastructure was forged in the heat of their battles.

As the role of manufacturers in advertising expanded, the purpose of manufacturers' advertising shifted from making potential buyers aware of what was available to inspiring consumer loyalty to a particular brand. It therefore became important to manufacturers that they be able to prevent masqueraders from capturing the purchase inspired by their publicity. Earlier legal perspectives treated customers' goodwill toward a firm as an attitude of the customers themselves, not something that could be owned by the firm. But in the 1880s, manufacturers and their allies in the advertising industry successfully lobbied for trademark legislation that constrained the ability of competitors to imitate a trademarked good, and hence allowed firms to capture goodwill as a form of intangible property recognized by law. Furthermore, the trademark and the goodwill it represented could be sold (Strasser 1989, pp. 43–44).

Print media space sellers and the advertising agents who mediated their sector of the advertising market also had a strong interest in postal policy, which is established by Congress. (The courts granted Post Office administrators some leeway in deciding how to implement policy but kept them tethered to policies decided by legislative action rather than administrative decree.) Some newspapers and most magazines depended heavily on the Post Office to deliver their publications to readers. The Post Office facilitated publishers' business through longstanding – though repeatedly challenged and occasionally adjusted – subsidies. These subsidies predated the decisive turn toward advertising as the primary source of publishers' revenues and were eventually weakened but not entirely dislodged (Gallagher 2016; Henkin 2006; Kielbowicz 1989). As advertisers and publishers battled one another over access to reliable information about circulation, Post Office policy made a gesture in favor of advertisers' interests, requiring sworn circulation statements for any publication receiving subsidized postal rates, but did not commit the resources to verify publishers' claims or penalize dissemblers. It ended up falling to advertisers, publishers, and agents themselves to institutionalize their own circulation-auditing practices (Pope 1983, pp. 171–173).

Conflicts arising from the ambiguities of the advertising agents' position sometimes made it into the courts, where judges were asked to decide whether agents owed their loyalties to the publishers whose space they sold, the advertisers on whose behalf they purchased, or whether they were entirely independent brokers. Judicial decisions did not reach a clear consensus on these questions, so appeals to the law did not, on this matter, resolve the ambiguities (Pope 1983, pp. 160–161).

While much of the governmental action of concern to print media space sellers took place at the federal level, billposters engaged more often at the municipal and state level. The term "zoning" was not yet in use, but local lawmakers were already experimenting with ways to manage urbanization through setting standards for use of privately-owned land and through construction of publicly maintained roads and public spaces such as parks. Billposters cared deeply about such matters and successfully resisted most substantive constraints on their ability to buy and sell access to the privately-owned locations that would be visible to audiences passing through public spaces. At the same time, established billposters welcomed land use or licensing standards that they could easily meet but which would serve as a barrier to new entrants.

Billposters also tangled with the state over the matter of pricing. The Associated Billposters Association set minimum rates that members were required to abide by if they were to remain members (Associated Billposters and Distributors of the United States and Canada 1906). (Unless they applied to the Association for temporary permission to engage in predatory pricing to vanquish a competitor and secure their monopoly.) The policy could easily be interpreted as a violation of anti-trust legislation, but for many years the government declined to act against the Association. By the time the billposters' price-fixing was successfully challenged in court, the position of the Association and its members was secure enough that taking away their publicly announced, binding price floor did not matter as much as it would have earlier. State inaction on the extra-legal pricing agreement among Association members, which billposters enforced within the organization, coupled with the usual state recognition of contracts between billposters and their clients, created the circumstances in which billboard advertising could be a profitable business.

Direct-mail marketing depended on intellectual property rights practices treating data as the property of those who collect it, not the property of those who are described by it. (This was true, too, of commercial and consumer credit reporting.) The law made no particular ruling on data ownership and so possession of data was sufficient to enable use of that data. Various government agencies collected their own data on citizens and residents; their record on participating in the commodification of that data is uneven. As automobiles proliferated, for example, almost all states began requiring cars to be registered with the state, so most states had fairly complete and accurate lists of the car owners residing within their borders. All treated these registrations as a matter of public record, so anyone could access the data by going to the relevant government office and requesting the records. Knowing that marketers would want this data, some states saw the opportunity for an extra source of revenue and would replicate and share the data for a fee. Other states would not. Postal policy adopted in 1902 forbade postmasters from selling or sharing the names and addresses of local residents, to direct mail marketers' chagrin. Postmasters were, though, permitted to check a list for accuracy, which could save direct mailers some waste circulation though they could not identify new prospects (Burdick 1916, p. 54). Direct mail marketers also cared about postage rates and the requirements that must be met to qualify for those rates. The Post Office permitted advertising materials to be sent; if they met the relevant requirements, they could even be sent at lower rates than first-class mail – and receive a lower level of service: no forwarding of mail whose intended recipient had moved; undeliverable mail would be discarded, not returned to the sender.

To sell attention is to offer those who pay the fee preferential access to the eyes of audiences. Despite some gaps and inconsistencies in the overall property rights regime, government did on the whole recognize and legitimate the collection and sale of audience attention and of personal data. The ability to sell preferential access to some depends on the ability to exclude others. State-sanctioned property rights in attention therefore represent a degree of state-sanctioned monopoly in the sense of the term used by Edward Chamberlin in *The Theory of Monopolistic Competition* (1962 [1933]) – every producer has a monopoly on their own individual output. No one had legal access to the advertising space in a publication except by paying the publisher, a fairly easy property right to defend as the printing was done out of reach of any but the publishers' employees. No one had legal access to the display space on a billboard except by paying the billposter, a more difficult property right to defend in practice, requiring continuous monitoring and frequent maintenance of display spaces outdoors along public roads. No one had legal access to a list-compiler's mailing list data except by paying for its use; replication was sufficiently cumbersome that list houses were able to maintain some control over their data. To the extent that any one particular seller's batch of attention-intercepting space was differentiated from others', they might also be able to achieve monopoly in the more traditional sense of the word. Billposting, for example, was dominated by local monopolists who controlled all the display spaces in the city. The attention of audiences, when not yet claimed, was treated as an open-access resource. There were few opportunities for populations to collectively disallow the treatment of their attention as an appropriable resource. (The most substantive attempts were probably some Progressive Era reformers' campaigns to restrict or even ban billboards, which they talked about both as an assertion of a right not to be sold to in particular spaces and as a matter of preserving scenic beauty. They may have won some minor battles here and there, but the billposters won the war.)

Growth

The eventual outcome of the shifting alliances and perpetual conflicts among private actors, along with the intercession and context-establishing action of the state, was a standardized attention market. Participants could buy and sell within a narrowed range of familiar, established types of transactions with greater certainty about what exactly it was they were buying and selling and what prices they could expect to pay or receive.

Along with its standardization, the attention market grew in scale and scope. Audiences, as the raw material of attention exchanges, faced greater draws on their attention. More people saw more ads. It is difficult to be more precise than that. How many ads did the average person see across all media in a day or a week or a year? What was the distribution around the mean? It seems likely that the most intensely advertising-exposed were the upper-middle class. Their income made them worth targeting; their activities left documentary traces from which mailing list assemblers could scrape their personal information; they disproportionately subscribed to the mass circulation lifestyle magazines; they were not rich enough to buy themselves expansive private living and leisure spaces out of sight of billboards or to hire a personal assistant to sort their mail (Marchand 1985; Ohmann 1996). It also seems likely that those living in rural poverty saw the fewest advertisements, but how few? As road infrastructure improved, billposters erected more billboards outside the cities. As postal service increased its reach, even the lowest density populations could get a newspaper or magazine or catalog and mail-order businesses like that of E.C. Allen made extensive use of this possibility (Popp Forthcoming).

The amount of money changing hands in the attention market also grew, though it is, again, difficult to be precise. A *Printers' Ink* article in 1953 claimed that from the Civil War to 1900 the total volume of advertising rose tenfold, from $50 million to $500 million and the share of ad expenditures in overall GNP rose more than fourfold, from 0.7 percent to 3.2 percent (quoted in Fox 1997, p. 39). But this may be an exaggeration. The best aggregate data are for the print-media sector, which grew from $39.1 million in advertising revenues in 1880 to $95.9 million in 1900. Rough but reasonable estimates judged print media advertising to constitute somewhat under half of all advertising expenditures, probably fluctuating in the neighborhood of 40 percent throughout the pre-radio era, generating Daniel Pope's calculations of total advertising spending across all media: $104 million in 1880, rising to $256 million in 1900. Pope also doubts the *Printers' Ink* claim that advertising rose substantially as a share of gross national product (GNP) – a doubly-uncertain retrospective estimation as GNP, after all, was not systematically calculated at the time, either (Waldron 1903, p. 158; Pope 1983, p. 26). Even keeping pace with overall economic growth during a period when overall growth was so rapid is notable. As the average cost of reaching each set of eyes fell, growth in aggregate spending only reinforces the conclusion that advertisings' draw on audience attention was greater.

Ultimately, the advertising industry thrived because its own successes served the needs of other industries. Advertising's qualitative and quantitative transformations especially depended on those industries that became oligopolies. In these industries, a small number of large players found pursuing market share through branding to be more effective than other marketing strategies. The advertising industry's transformations also depended on the fact that a large enough portion of the US population shared enough in economic growth that they could participate in consumer culture, making their attention worthwhile for advertisers to purchase. Those with the opportunity and ability to attract and hold audience attention found an expanding economic niche and increasing economic rewards.

Conclusion

Studies of the rise of mass consumer culture typically emphasize the development and integration of markets for the new consumer goods and the new producer goods used to make them. Such studies often attend carefully to the transportation and communications infrastructure – railroads, telegraphs and telephones, postal service – that made it possible. The then-new marketing practices are widely recognized and are seen as necessary corollaries of market development. This is true enough, but I argue in addition that the changes in marketing consumer goods were built on the development and integration of yet another new market: the market for audience attention. Manufacturers of branded goods, periodical publishers, billboard owners and billposters, advertising agents, and others, together with local, state, and federal government brought this new market into being.

We can form a richer understanding of the linkages among a variety of late-nineteenth- and early-twentieth-century marketing activities and their development over the period if we view them all as aspects of the incorporation of audience attention as a fictitious commodity into the orbit of market exchange. In this study, I trace the concrete historical process of converting audience attention into a commodity. Standardizing and streamlining the variety of business practices involved in advertising, such as accurate reporting of media circulation, standardized contracts between advertising agents and advertisers, standardized billboard display practices, and practices for collecting and protecting mailing lists as a form of property converted a wildly heterogeneous resource (people's attention) into a sorted, classified set of commodities with a market price.

The commodification of audience attention meant the creation of new forms of property and new arenas of market exchange. This expansion of the market realm was driven primarily by the large-scale advertisers. Their interests dominated the negotiation of new professional standards and practices in advertising, such as the Audit Bureau of Circulations. Advertisers wanted accurate circulation data; publishers would rather not share that information. Advertisers won. Reliable external circulation audits became the norm. Large-scale advertisers' influence shaped the government's updated definitions and defenses of property. Trademark laws were good for Coca-Cola, but not good for smaller-scale soft drink bottlers trying to ride along in Coke's cola-marketing wake. Again, large-scale advertisers won. With the cooperation of both the legislative and judicial branches of government, trademarks were defined and defended to brand-name manufacturers' benefit. Even so, Ohmann judges that in 1890, "a self-conscious and united ruling class . . . did not yet exist, and for all their power, businessmen had so far been unable to cope with the disorder they had created, while creating that power" (Ohmann 1996, p. 57). The economic developments at the turn of the twentieth century were swayed by the actions and interests of the large manufacturers and the large manufacturers disproportionately benefited from these developments, yet intra-class competition among industrial capitalists and conflict between industrial and merchant capitalists were as much a force as were capitalist class consciousness and cooperation about those matters on which they shared an agenda.

The activity of advertising has been carried out in some form as long as there has been trade, but in the years from 1865 to 1920 advertising became a new and distinct industry devoted to realizing the new economic value of audience attention. At the micro level, advertising professionals' interests could collide with the interests of their clients – the advertising agencies wanted to be paid as much as possible for their services while the advertisers wanted to pay them as little as possible. At the macro level, however, many advertising agents, and all of the most successful ones, understood that beyond the very short term, their economic fortunes depended on the success of their clients. Advertising agents such as George Rowell were behind the first systematic attempts to assess and publicize circulation figures. Advertising agents such as Artemas Ward heartily seconded the manufacturers' call for trademark protection, and the most vocal spokesmen for the advertising industry consistently extolled the virtues of brand-name goods sold at steady prices.

As the large advertisers and their allies successfully established a market exchange in audience attention, they found themselves facing the contradiction inherent in fictitious commodities – fictitious commodities are traded in the market, but, since they are not produced for the purpose of being traded, supply does not respond to the market mechanism (Polanyi 1957 [1944]). The number of people whose attention was of interest to advertisers could grow no faster than the number of people with disposable income. There was no corresponding limit to the advertisers' demand for this attention and there is good evidence that advertisers' attention demands strained audiences' capacities. Commentators from outside the advertising profession, especially those of higher socioeconomic status whose attention was most in demand and whose participation in the material culture of the day was least dependent on what they could glean at low or no cost, remarked despairingly on the sensory assault. They complained in particular about the proliferation of outdoor advertising degrading the landscape and the flood of junk mail infiltrating their homes and demanding at least enough attention to distinguish it from personal mail and discard it. (Though it's worth keeping in mind that advertisers and advertising professionals themselves considered approximately half the population to be too poor to be worth targeting (Marchand 1985, p. 64), and those with lower incomes published fewer opinion pieces in the *New York Times* and made greater use of advertising ephemera to decorate their living spaces, so the reaction to the explosion of advertising was certainly not univocal.)

Meanwhile, advertising practitioners commented on the difficulty of attracting attention to their message and developed theories and strategies regarding both placement and content to try to increase the effectiveness of their advertising efforts. Since the supply of the raw resource of audience attention was unresponsive to the market (though certainly growing for demographic reasons), all market-driven supply-side adjustments had to take place through efficiency improvements on the part of advertising professionals. Extensive strategies for accessing attention (e.g. more placements in more newspapers, more posters on more billboards) were soon complemented or even overshadowed by intensive strategies (e.g. carefully targeted placements and carefully market-tested content). By 1900, audience segmentation began in earnest and improved in accuracy as circulation data improved in accuracy when the Audit Bureau of

Circulations began performing audits in 1914 (Goodrum and Dalrymple 1990, p. 33). Targeted placements were soon paired with differentiated, targeted copy (Laird 1998, pp. 284–285). In 1898, *Printers' Ink* quoted a commentary first published in *Metropolitan Magazine* about the effects of the overwhelming volume of print media, including ephemera like trade cards and fliers along with the newspapers and magazines. The deluge of print made the "busy American loath to read. His eyes must be attracted, coaxed, cajoled." The attraction, coaxing, and cajoling were accomplished through graphic design as much as through copy. As a result, "to-day the advertising columns of high-class mediums are nearly as attractive from a literary and artistic point of view as the regular text and illustrations" (quoted in Laird 1998, p. 281). From the perspective of advertisers and the advertising industry, if the game became scarce, the solution was not catch limits, but more sophisticated hunting techniques (Scott 1910, pp. 131–132).

The struggles to shape the market and thrive in the market took place in a wider context of social struggle over the appropriate reach of the market. Billposters achieved sufficient excludability to secure monopoly rents on the sale of attention, but excludability extended only to the borders of the billboard. It was enough to create a market in a new form of property, but not enough to avert a tragedy of the commons.[4] For audiences, the clamor for attention could lead to sensory overload. In 1893, the advertising trade publication *Printers' Ink* ran an article about increased competition for audience attention (Laird 1998, p. 264). Similarly, the *Newark Evening News* asked "Has it come to this?" in bold headline type over an illustration of an intersection entirely overtaken by advertisements, with rooftop billboards doubling the height of buildings and banners stretched across the streets (October 11, 1911). Billposters would have been quick to point out the self-interest behind editorializing against billboards from a newspaper dependent on advertising revenues, but the question was – and remains – legitimate. Is it, in fact, acceptable for attention to be appropriated and sold anywhere and everywhere it can be intercepted? Advertisers resisted any claims to the contrary. They would, Ohmann observes, "colonize the leisure of most citizens, as they [already] dominated work time" (Ohmann 1996, p. 59).

This all had repercussions for the legions of consumers whose attention was so eagerly sought and actively traded. The users of branded goods were never passive in the process of meaning-making in their material culture, and manufacturers' best efforts to stoke demand did not always work as intended. Still, Strasser notes, "[a]s participants in the branded mass market, consumers entered mutually dependent but unequal relationships with large corporations." Especially when paired with rising purchasing power, consumer sovereignty looks like a kind of freedom but unequal power relations remain. Strasser is not the only one to note that identifying as a member of the "class" of consumers pushes considerations of class in the workplace to the background (Strasser 1989, pp. 25–26). But people now had a third economic role – not just producers and consumers but also, in part, products. Power was unequally distributed in the audience attention market, just as in the labor and goods markets. The economic value of audience attention was growing, but that value was realized by the suppliers of advertising, not by audiences. For advertisers, access to audiences was a weapon in their horizontal and vertical competitive struggles. For advertising professionals, access to audiences was the basis of profitability. For both, achieving their ends depended on securing a degree of monopoly control over audience attention. No matter how difficult advertisers found it to get their messages heard, that was nothing compared to the difficulty of trying to be heard without the ability to buy the attention of an audience.

Notes

1 A note on terminology: Advertisers are the sellers of advertised goods. I am using the term "advertising professionals" to refer to the array of people involved in providing advertising services, including characters such as advertising agents, copywriters and illustrators, billposters, lithographers, and distributors of advertising ephemera.
2 Though important, for purposes of this study, I'm leaving aside in-store displays and promotions. These practices changed in this period as the relationships between retailers, wholesalers, and manufacturers changed, but point-of-sale marketing was still within the range of merchant activities and did not represent a new form of economic activity centered around the exchange of commodified audience attention.
3 For example, in 1800 it was common for the spinning and weaving of cloth to take place in the household where the cloth would be used. In 1850 it was common for the spinning and weaving to take place in textile mills but for the sewing of clothing to take place in the household where the clothing would be worn. In the twentieth century, it became common for clothing to be purchased ready-made.
4 Audience attention in fact fits Garrett Hardin's classic model of the tragedy of the commons quite well (Hardin 1968). Attention is rival, but excludable to only a very limited degree, and each individual's efforts to appropriate attention increase the difficulty of accessing attention for all. For an individual advertiser, the benefit of advertising is at least as dependent on the advertiser's share of attention relative to competitors as on absolute volume. As a result many advertisers become locked in an arms race with competitors – to the great benefit and delight of advertising professionals (Mataja 1903).

Bibliography

Associated Billposters Association of the United States and Canada. 1897–1898 monthly. *Display Advertising*.
Associated Billposters Association of the United States and Canada. 1899–1904 monthly. *The Billposter-Display Advertising*.
Associated Billposters and Distributors of the United States and Canada. 1905–1908 monthly. *The Billposter and Distributor*.
Associated Billposters and Distributors of the United States and Canada. 1906. *Constitution and By-Laws*. OAAA collection box CB1, Hartman Center for Sales, Advertising, and Marketing History.
Banta, Melissa. 2013. *The Art of American Advertising, 1865–1910* (exhibition catalog). Cambridge, MA: Harvard Business School. www.library.hbs.edu/hc.artadv
Bates, Charles Austin. 1896. *Good Advertising and Where It Is Made*. New York: Bates.
Burdick, H. C. 1916. "How to Compile a Mailing List." In *Sales Promotion by Mail: How to Sell and How to Advertise*. New York: The Knickerbocker Press.
Casson, Herbert. 1911. *Advertisements and Sales: A Study of Advertising and Selling from the Standpoint of the New Principles of Scientific Management*. Chicago, IL: A. C. McClurg.

Chamberlin, Edward. 1962 [1933]. *The Theory of Monopolistic Competition*, 8th Edition. Cambridge, MA: Harvard University Press.

Chandler, Alfred. 2002 [1977]. *The Visible Hand: The Managerial Revolution in American Business*. Cambridge, MA: Belknap Press.

Cruikshank, Jeffrey L., and Arthur W. Schultz. 2010. *The Man Who Sold America: The Amazing (but True!) Story of Albert D. Lasker and the Creation of the Advertising Century*. Boston: Harvard Business Review Press.

Currarino, Rosanne. 2011. *The Labor Question in America: Economic Democracy in the Gilded Age*. Champagne: University of Illinois Press.

Direct Mail Advertising Association. 1916. "A New Movement and Its Meaning." *Postage* Volume 1 Number 1. January: 9–11.

Engels, Frederick. 1880. *Socialism: Utopian and Scientific*. www.marxists.org/archive/marx/works/1880/soc-utop/index.htm

Fisk, H. E. undated. *Organization in the Outdoor Medium – Industry*. OAAA collection box HI1, Hartman Center for Sales, Advertising, and Marketing History.

Fowler, Nathaniel C. 1900 [1897]. *Fowler's Publicity: An Encyclopedia of Advertising and Printing, and All That Pertains to the Public-Seeing Side of Business*. Boston: Publicity Publishing Company.

Fox, Stephen. 1997. *The Mirror Makers: A History of American Advertising and Its Creators*. Urbana and Chicago, IL: University of Illinois Press.

Gallagher, Winifred. 2016. *How the Post Office Created America*. New York: Penguin Press.

Goodrum, Charles, and Helen Dalrymple. 1990. *Advertising in America: The First 200 Years*. New York: Henry N. Abrams.

Harder, Virgil Eugene. 1958. *A History of Direct Mail Advertising* (Doctoral thesis), University of Illinois.

Hardin, Garrett. 1968. "The Tragedy of the Commons." *Science* Volume 162: 1243–1248.

Henkin, David M. 2006 *The Postal Age: The Emergence of Modern Communications in Nineteenth-Century America*. Chicago, IL: University of Chicago Press.

Kielbowicz, Richard B. 1989. *News in the Mail: The Press, Post Office, and Public Information, 1700–1860s*. New York: Greenwood Press.

Laird, Pamela Walker. 1998. *Advertising Progress: American Business and the Rise of Consumer Marketing*. Baltimore: The Johns Hopkins University Press.

Lamoreaux, Naomi. 1985. *The Great Merger Movement in American Business, 1895–1904*. Cambridge and New York: Cambridge University Press.

Lauer, Josh. 2017. *Creditworthy: A History of Consumer Surveillance and Financial Identity in America*. New York: Columbia University Press.

Lichtenstein, Nelson. 2002. *State of the Union: A Century of American Labor*. Princeton, NJ: Princeton University Press.

Marchand, Roland. 1985. *Advertising the American Dream: Making Way for Modernity*. Berkley, CA: University of California Press.

Marx, Karl. 1983 [1848]. "The Communist Manifesto." In *The Portable Karl Marx*, ed. Eugene Kamenka. New York: Penguin Books.

Mataja, Victor. 1903. "The Economic Value of Advertising." *International Quarterly* Volume 8: 379–398.

McGovern, Charles F. 2006. *Sold American: Consumption and Citizenship, 1890–1945*. Chapel Hill, NC: The University of North Carolina Press.

Myers, Kenneth. 1960. "ABC and SDRS: The Evolution of Two Specialized Advertising Services." *The Business History Review* Volume 34: 302–326.

The Newark Evening News. Editorial. October 11, 1911.

Ohmann, Richard. 1996. *Selling Culture: Magazines, Markets, and Class at the Turn of the Century*. London and New York: Verso.

Olney, Martha. 1991. *Buy Now, Pay Later: Advertising, Credit, and Consumer Durables in the 1920s*. Chapel Hill, NC and London: The University of North Carolina Press.

Polanyi, Karl. 1957 [1944]. *The Great Transformation*. New York: Farrar and Rinehart.

Pope, Daniel. 1983. *The Making of Modern Advertising*. New York: Basic Books.

Popp, Richard K. Forthcoming. "The Information Bazaar: Mail-Order Magazines and the Consumer Data Trade in Gilded Age America." In *Surveillance Capitalism in America: From Slavery to Social Media*, ed. Josh Lauer and Kenneth Lipartito. Philadelphia: University of Pennsylvania Press.

Porter, Glenn, and Harold C. Livesay. 1971. *Merchants and Manufacturers: Studies in the Changing Structure of Nineteenth-Century Marketing*. Baltimore: Johns Hopkins Press.

Radin, Margaret Jane. 1996. *Contested Commodities*. Cambridge, MA: Harvard University Press.

Rowell, George P. 1906. *Forty Years an Advertising Agent, 1865–1905*. New York: Printers' Ink Publishing Company.

Scott, Walter Dill. 1910. *The Psychology of Advertising: A Simple Exposition of the Principles of Psychology in Their Relation to Successful Advertising*, 2nd Edition. Boston: Small, Maynard & Company.

Sherman, Sidney. 1900. "Advertising in the United States." *Publication of the American Statistical Association* Volume 7 Number 52: 119–162.

Strasser, Susan. 1989. *Satisfaction Guaranteed: The Making of the American Mass Market*. New York: Pantheon Books.

Waldron, George B. 1903. "What America Spends in Advertising." *Chautauquan* Volume 38: 155–159.

Wu, Tim. 2016. *The Attention Merchants: The Epic Scramble to Get Inside Our Heads*. New York: Alfred A. Knopf.

2 Packaging readers

Newspaper and magazine
advertising

Introduction

Early in the twentieth century and late in his career, George Rowell remi-
nisced about his forty years in the advertising business and his several years of
employment with the Boston *Post* before that. While working as a bill collec-
tor for the *Post* immediately before and during the Civil War he found that,
"[A]dvertising space had at that time no recognized measure or standard of
value. Practically, within certain limits, it amounted to getting as much as possible and taking what one could get" (Rowell 1906, p. 30). When he left his job at
the newspaper and went into business for himself as an independent advertising
agent, he started a career that made him one of the pivotal figures in the maturation of the newspaper sector of the audience attention market. He is often
seen as a reformer who raised the ethical standards within the advertising profession and the reputation of advertising in the eyes of the general public. His
major achievements could indeed be characterized as (relatively) plain dealing
in the service of advertisers, but they can also be characterized as innovations
that provided a workable structure for the newspaper sector of the expanding
market for audience attention. Accompanying the maturation of newspaper
advertising, the magazine sector underwent an even more dramatic transformation to become a vehicle for audience attention sales. Placing advertisements in
print media dominated advertisers' collective advertising budgets for the entire
period of this study. Furthermore, print media publishers and the advertising
agents who handled print media advertising placements were the first to begin
the shift toward treating audience attention, rather than the intermediate good
of ink on paper, as a standardized commodity actively traded in an interconnected market (Laird 1998; Pope 1983).

Newspaper readers as an incompletely tapped resource

When Rowell started working for the *Boston Post* around 1860, newspapers
had long been operating in two markets simultaneously. They sold news to
readers and they sold readers to advertisers. Retailers and manufacturers were
expanding in number and often in scale as the nineteenth century progressed.

(At the close of the century, a wave of mergers reduced the number of manu-facturers in many industries while accelerating the growth in scale (Lamor-eaux 1985).) As manufacturers and merchants moved an increasing volume of products and struggled with one another – and with the layers of middlemen between them – over their shares of the pie, their interest in the intermediation of printers' ink to communicate to customers grew. Newspapers stood to profit if they responded to advertisers' demand for audiences. However, for much of the century, frictions resulting from a lack of information and a lack of mutual trust impeded the exchanges between advertisers and newspapers. At the time Rowell entered the newspaper business, most newspapers collected greater rev-enues from readers than from advertisers (Fox 1997, p. 14).

The exception proves (as in tests) the rule. Several decades before Row-ell began his career, the *New York Sun* had flipped the relative weights of sub-scription and advertising on its balance sheet and shown the feasibility of an advertising-centered model of newspaper financing. In 1833, the *Sun* charged customers one cent, prioritized attention-grabbing sensationalism in their con-tent, increased street and newsstand sales, and, as their readership surged, so did their advertising revenue. The publishers correctly calculated that their read-ers, once there were enough of them, were more valuable as product than as customer. Richard Ohmann writes, "Naturally, with the lower selling price of the papers, ads also paid a much greater share of costs. And, since the new edi-tors had hit on the idea of selling readers to advertisers, they also aggressively pursued new readers: most strikingly, they sent newsboys to hawk papers in the streets, whereas earlier editors had depended on subscriptions. The newspaper itself became part of the spectacle of city life" (Ohmann 1996, p. 20). The *Sun* served as proof of concept and attracted enough imitators that publishers adopt-ing the same business model earned a collective nickname: the penny press. Nevertheless, many potential imitators still faced barriers to adopting that same advertising-centered business model. Crucially, the *Sun* served New York City, a major metropolis where they could reach many readers, and the paper's ubiquity was highly visible to the large number of advertisers doing business in the city. The paper's value as an advertising medium was obvious to advertisers. Though the number of daily readers could not be precisely or verifiably quantified, it was a good bet that advertising in the *Sun* (and/or one of the two local competitors to follow on its heels) was the most effective way to reach a large share of the New York City population; similar assessments could be made in other large cities with penny press daily newspapers (Wu 2016, pp. 11–18; Ohmann 1996, p. 20). Even by the impressionistic accounting practices of the mid-nineteenth century, it was clear that a rural or small-town newspaper had fewer readers to sell. Furthermore, a rural or small-town paper was unlikely to be known to any potential advertisers beyond a handful of local retailers. So, even with the penny press playing a role, for the industry as a whole, advertising at midcentury still contributed only a third of newspapers' total revenues (Fox 1997, p. 14).

Urban concentration enabled the *Sun* to tap into advertisers' demand for audience attention, but in a country whose population was still majority non-urban, many newspaper readers' attention remained less thoroughly tapped. In 1840, the penny press reached an aggregate readership estimated at around 300,000, close to a fourfold increase over the previous decade, but a readership of 300,000 still meant that only one in fifty-seven Americans could be reached this way (Ohmann 1996, p. 20). Collectively, the smaller daily and weekly newspapers had plenty of readers, even though any one of them alone had only a few hundred or a few thousand. Those readers were a potential market for many advertisers' goods and so advertisers could potentially be interested in buying access to these readers' attention. But how were the two sides of the attention market to find one another? How were they to negotiate prices? How were they to judge which exchanges were worth their while and which were not? Newspapers had the latent potential to serve as intermediaries between advertisers' supply of goods and customers' demand for those goods. To realize this potential, newspaper publishers needed intermediaries of their own between themselves and the advertisers.

The early-nineteenth-century commercial scene was shrouded in ignorance. As Goodrum and Dalrymple note, "No one knew which all the papers were or where they were located. No one (including the major papers themselves) knew how many readers they had, and there were no set rates for commercial accounts – these were bargained over at each submission. It will come as no surprise then that this vacuum of unknowns produced the first advertising agents" (Goodrum and Dalrymple 1990, pp. 20–21). The first handful of advertising agencies opened in major eastern seaboard cities – Boston, New York, Philadelphia – in the 1840s (Fox 1997, p. 14, Goodrum and Dalrymple 1990, p. 21). The new figure of the advertising agent served as intermediary between the advertisers' demand for audience attention and the newspapers' supply of that attention. The information coordination task of the agents was already formidable and growing. A supply of advertising space could be found in something on the order of a thousand weekly newspapers (991 of them in 1838, according to Daniel Pope's sources) and several hundred dailies (254 of them in 1850). In the 1890s, the earliest decade for which we have a useful estimate, the number of advertisers with a potential demand for ad placements beyond their local area was approximately 4,000 (Pope 1983, p. 113).

Advertising agents were solving an information problem in a new market for audience attention, but this sort of information problem was not new. Most markets in the antebellum economy featured many producers and many buyers. Because of the large number of firms involved, market intermediaries were hugely important in nineteenth-century distribution channels. Buyers typically bought small amounts of a variety of different goods from a variety of different producers. It did not make economic sense for a manufacturer to employ their own sales force to handle many small transactions with many small retailers, or to operate their own transportation network to deliver the goods. Instead, middlemen, often known as jobbers, handled distribution. Jobbers placed large enough orders to be worth each manufacturer's while, saving those manufacturers the trouble of making hundreds or thousands of small transactions.

They assembled varied enough inventories to be worth the retailers' while, saving them the trouble of searching out and doing business with hundreds of manufacturers for thousands of different products. And final customers could then visit a modest number of retailers to meet most of their needs (Porter and Livesay 1971, p. 162).

The market for print-media readers' attention was similarly structured – many newspapers with a modest supply of readers' eyes to sell, many advertisers looking to place a modest order for eyes – so it is no surprise that this market adopted the same middleman solution to the coordination problem. "Advertising being a commodity that has the same commercial value as other articles of commerce, needs to have and does have its middlemen," advertising professional Nathaniel Fowler explained (Fowler 1900 [1897], p. 352). The first advertising agents functioned as advertising space jobbers: they purchased advertising placements in many newspapers on their own account, then resold the space to advertisers in lots assembled from multiple newspapers. Alternatively, advertising agents might take an order from an advertiser first and then procure the newspaper advertising space to fulfill it. Just as jobbers could do for groceries, advertising agents had a clear opportunity to lower transaction costs. One advertising agent collecting information about many newspapers could save much duplicated time, cost, and effort for advertisers who no longer had to track down newspaper publishers themselves. They could also save much duplicated time, cost, and effort for newspapers who didn't have to seek out and negotiate with multiple advertisers. Agents also reduced the publishers' risk – collecting on ad placements, especially from out-of-town advertisers, was iffy and it was common for publishers to find themselves unable to collect on a quarter of their advertising space sales. Agents were more likely to pay promptly, or even pay in advance; paying for space up front and then reselling it is how the two first advertising agents in the US, Volney Palmer and John L. Hooper, both began their businesses in the 1840s. About a quarter century later, early in his advertising career, Rowell offered advertisers packages of one column-inch-sized ad placements in 100 newspapers for $100 (Goodrum and Dalrymple 1990, p. 21; Laird 1998, p. 73; Myers 1960, p. 304; Pope 1983, pp. 114–118; Rowell 1906, pp. 63–69). By serving as a clearinghouse for advertising space and lowering search costs, advertising agents could in principle allow themselves, newspapers, and advertisers to all profit together. Dividing the spoils of these efficiency gains among all these actors was a matter of continuous struggle.

Middlemen in early-to-mid-nineteenth-century goods markets were in business for themselves and didn't necessarily see eye to eye with all of the producers whose goods they handled at all times. Still, their interests overlapped considerably; middlemen were more distribution agents for the producers than they were procurement agents for the buyers. Once they decided to handle the goods, they also served as salesmen for those goods, pushing them along the supply chain (Porter and Livesay 1971, p. 224). Similarly, the first advertising agents acted primarily as distribution agents for the newspapers. Most early agents entered the business with newspaper experience on their resume, whereas few had the manufacturing experience that would align their perspectives with advertisers. Agencies clustered geographically around the offices of major newspapers in major cities (Pope 1983, pp. 119–120).

Despite the opportunity for mutual benefit among publisher, agent, and advertiser, the advertising agents also, just as clearly, had an opportunity to exploit information asymmetries to profit most, especially at the expense of advertisers. As Daniel Pope notes, "Since agents dealt with publishers on their own and did not reveal to advertisers the terms on which they acquired space, advertisers might well wonder whether they were the beneficiaries or the victims of agents' negotiating skills" (Pope 1983, p. 127). Whether or not the advertising space they sold served advertisers well was not the agents' immediate concern. At least in the short run, an agent could best serve his own interest by encouraging advertisers to place their advertisements in the media where the agent had the largest margin, not necessarily the media best suited to the advertisers' needs. The agents' obvious conflict of interest damaged credibility with the advertisers who bought their services (Pope 1983, p. 127). In principle, the same conflict of interest could undermine any buyers' trust in the seller of any product, but most products could at least be examined by the buyer. Not so when the product is readers' attention. Advertisers had no way of knowing whether the audience attention they contracted for was in fact delivered. They could submit their advertising copy to the publisher, they could pay for it to be printed in the newspaper, they could even examine a copy of the newspaper to see that the column space they paid for did indeed include their advertising copy. (In a large-scale campaign with placements in many newspapers in many places, this last step could become unwieldy, but it was not in principle impossible.) But the advertising space was only an intermediate good. As Rowell coyly put it, "Evidently it is not the space he occupies that an advertiser pays for, but an indefinite something the exact value of which neither the man who buys nor the man who sells quite understands" (Rowell 1906, p. 31). We can be more definite about the something advertisers pay for: space in the readers' field of vision was the final good. What advertisers could not do, however, was ascertain how many readers actually read the paper and saw their advertisement. They had good reason to mistrust whatever claims the advertising agents and publishers made.

George Rowell and some of his forward-thinking peers saw the advertisers' justifiable mistrust as a drag on their business. Advertisers seeking reliable access to desired audiences were dissatisfied with the take-what-you-can-get situation Rowell described as prevailing in the 1860s. He couldn't solve his sales problem, which was also the newspapers' sales problem, without establishing credibility with the advertisers who were his potential buyers. He was among the first advertising agents to pursue an alliance with advertisers, presenting himself more as a procuring agent for advertisers than as a sales agent for newspapers. Francis Wayland Ayer[1] aligned his practices even more definitively in the buyers' interests (Laird 1998, pp. 164–167). Despite the potential for more trusting advertisers to buy more advertising space from newspapers, when Ayer, Rowell, and those of their ilk changed their allegiance, it often meant entering into greater conflict with publishers. Publishers felt that agents charged an unfairly steep rate for solving the information/coordination problem, forcing publishers to drastically discount their advertising space for agents who purchased in bulk. Publishers called such hard-bargaining agents "scalpers." The profit margins and quick growth enjoyed by the big successes among early advertising agencies suggest that agents did indeed gain an edge in market power over the publishers whose advertising space they handled. At least in his own telling, Rowell's advertising space packages earned him a profit of $10,000 on $27,000 worth of placements in 1865, and within a few years his agency was handling a million dollars in business a year. The also-large N.W. Ayer and Son agency enjoyed a profit rate of 15 percent in the mid-1870s. And all this was achieved while even the largest agencies ran their entire business with only about a half-dozen employees (Pope 1983, pp. 118–119, 127–128).

Disputes between agents and publishers involved, of course, the shares they would each keep of advertisers' outlays. Their disputes – and disputes *among* agents – also involved control over information. Control over information, after all, was one source of market power and hence claims on shares of the spoils. For advertisers, even finding out what newspapers existed in the mid-nineteenth century was daunting, never mind negotiating ad placements. Advertising agents did the work of compiling this information, and many of them considered their lists to be a key business asset. In 1866, Rowell, in a bid to cultivate goodwill and trust among advertisers, published a list of advertising media and aimed distribution of this publication at advertisers. Other agents were furious about the decision to pull back the curtain on the inner workings of their business. "It is true," wrote Rowell a few years later, "every Advertising Agency possessed lists more or less correct, but each one looked upon them rather as a part of the stock in trade than for public examination. They were and still are by many, guarded with great vigilance and care" (Rowell 1869, p. 3). In other words, agents fearful for their business prospects wondered why advertisers would use agents as intermediaries and pay a commission if a published list saved the search costs and allowed them to contact the newspaper publishers directly themselves. Advertisers, on the other hand, clamored for access to more detailed information about the newspaper publishing industry and Rowell responded with *Rowell's American Newspaper Directory*, first published in 1869. In the *Directory*, Rowell and his staff elaborated on the earlier lists that had simply recorded publication names and towns. The *Directory* included circulation data and other pertinent characteristics of the publications, such as type of content, political affiliation, frequency of publication, and characterization of readers. At least eight agencies published similar newspaper directories. Now publishers were furious, not least because the estimates of their circulation printed in the agencies' directories were often far below their own claims. (Some directories, such as the one published by S. M. Pettengill, did not include circulation data, however. Pettengill explained that without reliable, independent verification, citing circulation numbers was a disservice to honest publishers who would suffer by the comparison to the inflated circulation figures of liars.) Though Rowell published circulation data, he commented on the difficulty of verifying it. His assessment was that only about a quarter of publishers provided the circulation information he wanted and, whether for reasons of willful misrepresentation or accounting incompetence, only a quarter of those who did provide data were reasonably accurate. Furthermore, the directories were financed through advertising placed by publishers seeking to use the directories to attract advertisers. Rowell, for one, bartered with publishers, trading space for newspaper publishers to promote themselves in his *American Newspaper Directory* for space in newspapers his clients could fill with their advertisements. Many publishers accused Rowell of giving more generous circulation estimates to newspapers that purchased or bartered for advertising space in the *Directory* and penalizing those that did not. (Rowell denied the charges and though he was threatened with libel suits, the threats never reached court) (Myers 1960, pp. 315–319; Pope 1983, pp. 121–123, 167–170; Rowell 1869; Fox 1997, p. 20).

Though in conflict as they jockeyed over control of information and market power, the agents' and publishers' disputes over the newspaper directories established a consensus understanding that the market for advertising space was really a market for audience eyes. The format of Rowell's directory, published more or less annually from 1869 until 1909, leaves no doubt about the nature of the transactions the directory facilitated. It reads as a catalog of the size and character of the readership of each newspaper. The first edition lists newspapers first by town, then lists towns with population data pertinent to advertisers, then re-lists the newspapers ordered by circulation so that an advertiser may easily pick out the newspapers with the largest audiences, then re-lists the newspapers yet again by genre (religious, agricultural, etc.). Pricing information and instructions for advertisers on how to place an order with Rowell's agency for packages of advertising placements in selections of the newspapers listed are displayed throughout (Rowell 1869). In later editions, Rowell specially marked the listings of those newspapers boasting a large circulation of readers with higher-than-average disposable income with a bullseye symbol. Despite their resistance to external audits of circulation by Rowell or anyone else, the publishers did not really question the premise that they were selling audiences. They simply wished to retain control over the terms on which they sold this highly desirable resource. Publishers promoted their papers as advertising media by highlighting the virtues of their paper and the virtues of their readers. In the 1877 edition, for example, the publishers of the weekly *Milton* [Iowa] *Head-Light* took out an ad in the *Directory*, saying first, "The Head-Light is a first-class, nicely-printed, newsy newspaper," then adding that it, "has a large circulation in its own and adjacent counties" and "as an advertising medium, is unexcelled in this section of the country." The publishers of the *Truckee* [California] *Republican* promoted their paper as an advertising medium by describing their readers as "industrious" (Rowell 1877, pp. 391–392). At the end of the *Directory's* run, the 1909 listing prepared by Rowell's staff for the *Boston Daily*

Advertiser is followed by the publisher's paid announcement claiming a higher circulation than Rowell had given him credit for and asserting that the *Boston Daily Advertiser* is "a clean newspaper, and reaches the homes of the best families in Boston and suburbs – a most desirable medium for placing announcements before a large, intelligent and wealthy class of readers" (Rowell 1909, p. 446). Publishers, advertisers, and advertising agents were in full agreement on the nature of the transactions they wanted to complete: eyeball sales.

Advertising agent and prominent advertising industry booster Nathaniel Fowler, like Rowell, positioned himself as the advertisers' ally against the newspaper publishers. He wrote an encyclopedic guide to the business of advertising in the closing years of the nineteenth century, when the maturation of the print-media advertising market was underway but incomplete. Over and over throughout *Fowler's Publicity*, Fowler insisted that advertising space "is a commodity that has the same commercial value as other articles of commerce" (Fowler 1900 [1897], p. 352). The purpose of purchasing advertising space was to reach an audience. This being so, it struck him as a moral outrage that publishers would, as they were universally understood to do, dissemble about the circulation of their periodical publications (Fowler 1900 [1897], pp. 360–362). Fowler's insistence that advertising space is a commodity was a case of rhetoric running slightly ahead of reality – and helping to create the new reality he claimed. Accurate newspaper circulation numbers were essential to the standardization and quantification of the audience attention commodity, which was, in turn, a crucial component of the maturation of the audience attention market. Fowler wrote during a period when the institutions and practices necessary for an organized audience attention market were rapidly developing but hadn't yet solved the standardization and quantification problem. If publishers were assumed to be inflating their circulation numbers, which was often true, a publisher who told the truth about readership would be at a disadvantage. Furthermore, advertisers' justifiable mistrust would hamper advertising space sales for publishers with accurately and inaccurately reported circulations alike (Laird 1998, p. 162).

Rowell's American Newspaper Directory and some other agency-published directories were a gesture toward standardization and quantification. They lasted a few decades but were ultimately untenable as they couldn't entirely resolve their own contradictions. The innovative Gilded Age advertising agents such as Rowell and Ayer enjoyed their first-mover advantage, in the form of high profit rates, for a decade or so. Then the results of their success began to undermine their position. The directories, initially a successful way to diversify agency income streams, did indeed weaken agents' information monopoly and some advertisers used the directories to bypass the agencies and their commissions, instead placing orders directly with publishers. Meanwhile, with no significant barriers to entry, the number of advertising agencies rose exponentially. A New York City business directory listed forty-two agencies in 1869–1870, then the count doubled each decade until there were more than 400 in 1899. Some of these were minor operations, including individuals who were still sales agents for newspapers rather than modern advertiser-oriented agencies, but the trend still clearly points toward intensifying competition. Agents competing horizontally against one another were less able to overmatch publishers in negotiation over pricing for advertising space and agency profit rates fell. S. M. Pettengill and Co. of New York collapsed spectacularly in 1903 with "almost a million dollars in unpaid debts to publishers." This was not the only agency to fold (Pope 1983, pp. 129–130).

However imperfect, the stumbling steps toward standardization of the audience attention commodity were enough, in combination with other contributors, to facilitate explosive growth in the newspaper industry. In the 1860s, the attention of those who read newspapers was an incompletely tapped resource and large swaths of the population had not yet even become regular newspaper readers, but as advertising agents chipped away at the coordination and trust challenges in the attention market, newspapers more thoroughly monetized their readers and new attention-gathering ventures proliferated in the newspaper industry, turning more people into regular newspaper readers. Although there was no major change to the format of the publications or the business model of the publishers, the number of distinct newspaper publications and the total volume of newspaper production increased markedly. (See Table 2.1.)[2]

Increased production of newspapers meant increased production of audiences. Estimated readership of daily newspapers, still most common in cities, rose from 2,800,000 in 1870 to 24,200,000 in 1909. This increasing supply of readers was eagerly purchased by advertisers; the aggregate expenditure on newspaper advertising increased from $39 million in 1880 to $71 million in 1890 and then more than doubled to nearly $150 million in 1900 (Sherman 1900, pp. 119–120; Hofstadter 1972 [1955], p. 187). (Those figures are given in current dollars. Expenditures grew even faster in real terms than in nominal; the price level fell almost 18 percent over the twenty years from 1880 to 1900 (Officer and Williamson 2019)). Advertising revenues grew faster than other sources of publisher income to become the largest share of total revenues. (Not only did publishers lower the price to readers, but the political party-affiliated and party-subsidized newspapers faded from prominence (Hofstadter 1972

Table 2.1 Number of daily and weekly newspapers

Year	Daily newspapers	Weekly newspapers
1838		991[1]
1850	254[1]	
1870	574[2]	
1880		3,232[2]
1899	1,610[2]	7,600[2]
1900	2,226[1]	
1904		13,513[1]
1909	2,600[2]	

Sources: [1]Pope 1983, p. 113; [2]Hofstadter 1972 [1955], p. 187

[1955], p. 188).) With the intervention of advertising agents to serve as jobbers in the attention market, more and more papers could be like the *Sun*. The gain in bargaining power for publishers resulting from the proliferation of advertising agents may have helped keep more newspapers alive, too. Now content was primarily attention bait, the primary source of revenue was attention sales, and whatever the readers paid was a supplement to the income derived from the publishers' main customers, the advertisers.

As the volume of print media grew, the market for media ad placements integrated regionally and nationally. Pamela Walker Laird writes, "By the end of the [nineteenth] century, all types of businesspersons tried to reach consumers through newspapers, including brand-name manufacturers seeking national markets. Advertising filled three-fourths of some papers" (Laird 1998, p. 73). Rowell perceived those seeking to expand their business geographically as the primary patrons of advertising agencies (Laird 1998, p. 159). Advertising agents such as Rowell, and soon his imitators, were able to select from a national array of newspapers and coordinate purchases in many newspapers simultaneously, making advertising space in far-flung publications useful and attractive to large-scale brand-name manufacturers. From the perspective of producers and retailers with regional or national ambitions, this new coordinating function taken on by advertising agents meant that newspapers nationwide were now part of a single market for audience attention. The American Newspaper Publishers Association also worked for this national integration; the association was formed in 1887 for the purpose of helping newspapers to attract and negotiate with advertising agents, thereby improving their access to far-flung buyers of access to their readers' eyes. Advertisers took advantage of this market integration: the proportion of newspaper ads placed by advertisers based outside the newspapers' region, especially national brand-name manufacturers, increased (Sherman 1900, p. 120; Laird 1998, p. 221)).

Even as their advertising expenditures rose, advertisers remained troubled about the lack of reliable information about the audiences their newspaper placements might (or might not) reach. Rowell's staff produced purportedly independent estimates of newspapers' circulation – possibly, according to disgruntled publishers, biased in favor of those publishers who paid to advertise in the directory. The publication of the directory was financially dependent on publishers' paid advertisements, but publishers resisted playing Rowell's game; by 1898 nearly all the big-city newspapers had withdrawn their advertising from the *Directory*, cutting into Rowell's revenues and starving the project of the resources that would have been needed to investigate publications more thoroughly (Myers 1960, p. 320; Pope 1983, pp. 129–130). Advertisers polled in 1891 liked the idea of a circulation auditing association but were not confident it could be accomplished. In 1899, the American Advertisers Association (AAA) formed and began performing circulation audits, but they were not entirely clear about their standards. Circulation accounting, it turns out, has some gray areas. The number of subscribers is a good starting place for a count, but what of newspapers with high, but variable, individual-issue street sales? How are those to be assessed? What about free sample copies or issues that the publisher continues to send to lapsed subscribers? Or bulk purchases through clubs? Furthermore, successful audits required that publishers be forthcoming with information, and they weren't. Just as they resisted cooperation with agency-published directories, they resisted the AAA audits. "[P]ublisher resistance and an absence of organizational backing stymied efforts to find out circulations," explains Daniel Pope. Also, the AAA did battle with advertising agencies where interests conflicted, which hampered their ability to collaborate on the matter of audits, where their interests would seem to coincide. Also hurting their cause, patent medicine manufacturers were a big force in the AAA, but patent medicines were already falling into disrepute and not in a good position to be the standard-bearers for honesty in business dealings (Pope 1983, pp. 168–170).

The agency-published newspaper directories were eventually done in by their contradictions and conflicts of interest; *Rowell's American Newspaper Directory* published its last edition in 1909. The auditing efforts of the AAA were not fully satisfactory either. In 1912, Congress passed a postal bill with a rider that required publishers to supply sworn circulation statements twice a year. The law did not provide for independent verification or impose penalties for false statements, so it expressed an ideal that it could not enforce. But as trusted circulation data remained elusive, advertisers' demands for circulation data only intensified. A group of advertisers dissatisfied with the AAA's attempt at systematic circulation auditing established an alternative organization, the Association of National Advertising Managers (ANAM) in May of 1912. ANAM had better relations with advertising agents and some sympathetic publishers than the AAA had and in May of 1913, ANAM brought these groups – advertisers, advertising agents, and publishers – together at a meeting in New York to address the issue of circulation auditing. The plan approved by a majority at the meeting called for a Bureau of Verified Circulations, to be financed by publishers, who could influence the Bureau's practices. The AAA objected to the plan, mistrusting an audit bureau under a significant degree of publisher control; they preferred that advertisers finance and manage the audits. Cereal manufacturers C. W. Post and Emery Mapes financed a reorganization of the AAA as the Advertising Audit Association in the fall of 1913 and then redoubled their efforts to succeed at auditing. Publishers and agents could join the reorganized AAA, but advertisers would be the majority (Pope 1983, pp. 170–171; Myers 1960, pp. 309–312).

The Bureau of Verified Circulations and the Advertising Audit Association outwardly competed for primacy for several months. Meanwhile, advertising agents in the two associations were negotiating a merger. A plan for a new, merged organization was presented in January 1914. Advertisers affiliated with ANAM had some concerns, worrying that the AAA advertisers would dominate their own members. Pope writes, "By May, however, most doubts were assuaged; an amalgamated convention met in Chicago with 595 delegates attending, four-fifths whom represented media. Nevertheless, the Board of Directors reflected the national advertisers' authority. They held eleven of the twenty-one seats. The new organization adopted the title of Audit Bureau of

Circulations (ABC) and set to work" (Pope 1983, pp. 171–172; Myers 1960, pp. 309–312).

Publishers could no longer deny advertisers' demands for accurate circulation data. They knew they were packaging and selling access to audiences' eyes and they had to admit the legitimacy of advertisers' desire to know how many eyes were in the package. To continue resisting circulation audits would just arouse mistrust that would hinder their ability to sell advertising space. (Also, by the turn of the twentieth century other advertising media such as billboards were becoming standardized and available as an alternative to print.) The ABC's credibility became so widely recognized that a periodical publisher could not afford to decline an ABC audit; advertisers would not trust a publication's circulation claims without it (Myers 1960, pp. 310–312). Indeed, at first publishers signed on for audits faster than the Bureau could train auditors and fulfill the requests (Pope 1983, p. 172). From then on, when advertisers bought readers' eyes, they could be fairly sure of how many eyes they were buying. After working so long without any such certainty, participants in the attention market knew just how important a turning point this was. In a history of advertising published in 1929, just fifteen years after the formation of the ABC, Frank Presbrey wrote, "Organization of the Audit Bureau of Circulations was an epoch-making event" (Myers 1960, p. 312).

Magazines, mass culture, and the expanded production of audiences

Print was the only form of mass media in the late nineteenth and early twentieth centuries (Laird 1998, p. 58). Newspapers, however, were not the only form of print. The daily and weekly newspapers shared the media landscape with magazines. Newspapers, as we have seen, proliferated as advertising agents facilitated publishers' sales of their readers' attention. Magazines' metamorphosis into mass suppliers of audience attention after 1870, and even more so after 1890, transformed their genre and business model more dramatically than the newspapers had done. Goodrum and Dalrymple note of this transformation, "[T]he role of the publisher changed from being a seller of a product to consumers to being a gatherer of consumers for the advertisers" (Goodrum and Dalrymple 1990, p. 31).

Richard Ohmann casts magazine publishers as the protagonists in the creation of a national mass culture in the US: "[M]ass culture in societies like this one," he explains, "includes voluntary experiences, produced by a relatively small number of specialists, for millions across the nation to share, in similar or identical form, either simultaneously or nearly so; with dependable frequency; mass culture shapes habitual audiences, around common needs or interests, and it is made for profit" (Ohmann 1996, p. 14). Nothing before the national magazines put together all these components. Before the Civil War, magazines had not yet assembled all these components, either; they occupied a sleepy corner of the publishing world, focused on literary content, had modest circulations paid for by subscriptions, and carried little to no advertising. Beginning in the 1870s, four decades after the emergence of the penny press, then accelerating in the 1880s and beyond, magazines became a major sector of the publishing industry dominated by religious and lifestyle content and paid for largely by advertising revenues. In the 1890s the most successful monthly national magazines reached a readership in the thousands, sometimes tens of thousands – by 1900 the biggest few even reached circulations in the hundreds of thousands (Fox 1997; Goodrum and Dalrymple 1990; Laird 1998). The older print medium then imitated the newer. "[T]he newspaper became a channel of national mass culture about the same time [the 1890s] as did the magazine, in spite of a longer and richer evolution" (Ohmann 1996, p. 21).

An important early experiment with this new vision of what a magazine could be came not from an established publisher, but from an advertiser. F.G. Kinsman, a patent medicine bottler from Maine, wanted more advertising space than existing media could supply. He wanted more eyes over a wider geographic range than the newspapers with their primarily small and local circulations could effectively deliver. Existing magazines did not take advertisements, aside from notices of their own publishers' upcoming releases. To address this marketing challenge, Kinsman started his own attention-harvesting operation. He published Sunday School monthlies and weeklies, but the fact that he published for all Christian denominations indicates that he did not choose this genre out of any particular religious conviction. The religious content was the attention bait, not the message; he achieved wide circulation and ran his own patent medicine advertisements in all issues (Goodrum and Dalrymple 1990, p. 31).

Most patent medicine manufacturers did not follow Kinsman's move to become publishers in their own right, but patent medicine manufacturers were a driving force behind much of the early innovation in print media advertising. For the first forty years of the advertising agencies' operation, patent medicines accounted for more than half of the agencies' revenues, pressuring both agencies and newspapers to be responsive to patent medicine manufacturers' wishes. Furthermore, patent medicine manufacturers' intense demand for audiences spurred the invention of the modern magazine, even when the publishers were not themselves patent medicine manufacturers. Seeing the revenue opportunity demonstrated by the advertising orientation of the new magazines, even the grand old magazines started taking ads in the 1870s but continued to keep them segregated in special advertising sections. Four types of advertisements accounted for almost all of the magazines' placements: patent medicines, insurance, transportation (trains and steamships), and the same old announcements of new books (Goodrum and Dalrymple 1990, pp. 29–31).

In this early period, while many other manufacturers still hesitated to advertise, worrying that advertising was disreputable and so could hurt their image as much as help it or simply doubting that the returns would justify the cost, patent medicine manufacturers knew their existence depended on aggressive advertising. Patent medicine's existence preceded the maturation of the print-media audience attention market, but they already advertised extravagantly through multiple means, including medicine shows put on by traveling performance troupes doubling as sales teams. There are all sorts of things people might independently think to want and then seek out in the market, but patent medicines are not among them. Even having stumbled across a patent medicine for sale, there was no earthly way potential buyers could identify its purported use or conceive of a demand for it just by examining the contents of the bottle.[3] Other sellers eventually adopted the patent medicine manufacturer's practices of using advertising to attach meanings to goods – and as patent medicines became just one type of advertiser among many, the aura of ill repute that advertising had earlier acquired through its dominant association with patent medicines faded (Laird 1998, pp. 48–50). A number of advertising agents, in an effort to establish the notion that advertising was a profession and to establish their own professional reputations, actively distanced themselves from patent medicines as the field of medicine itself professionalized (Ohmann 1996, pp. 92–99; Scott 1910 [1908]). Still, as late as 1898, one-sixth of the manufacturers who advertised were manufacturers of patent medicines (Goodrum and Dalrymple 1990, p. 31). They remained enough of a source of demand in the attention market in the beginning of the twentieth century that when an exposé published in *Collier's* in 1905 followed by the Pure Food and Drug Act of 1906 gutted the still-large, $75-million-per-year patent medicine industry, many advertising agencies felt the pinch (Cruikshank and Schultz 2010, pp. 98–99).

Patent medicine manufacturers were at the leading edge of demand for audience attention; this triggered a response from suppliers of magazine advertising space, establishing a whole new sector of the print-media attention market. Magazine publishers experimented with content and lowered subscription and newsstand pricing to raise circulations; larger circulations increased the value of their advertising space to advertisers; the rapid expansion of the supply of audience attention, in turn, drew in more buyers. From 1870 to 1890 the number of distinct magazines and their circulations both grew. (The tally of defunct magazines grew, too. On average, new publications starting during this period lasted less than four years. Publications had both a high birth rate and a high mortality rate, but the birth rate stayed ahead of the mortality rate and some publications endured past the treacherous early years to enjoy long runs (Laird 1998, p. 75).) According to data compiled in 1900, from 1880 to 1890 the number of distinct monthly magazines increased 93 percent to reach 2,247 while their average circulation increased 44 percent to 11,317 (Sherman 1900, p. 121). A mid-twentieth-century analysis of the historic data estimated that there were 700 titles in 1865, 1,200 in 1870, and 2,400 in 1880 (Laird 1998, p. 75).[4]

Kinsman was not the only patent medicine manufacturer nor the only publisher to piggyback on piety. In the 1870s, as magazines were just beginning to emerge, "religious periodicals carried more national advertising than any other medium" (Ohmann 1996, p. 107), and the N.W. Ayer agency rose to prominence in part with a specialization in placing clients' advertisements in the religious magazines (Goodrum and Dalrymple 1990, p. 31). Lifestyle magazines were a new and successful innovation of the 1880s. Advertisements in many of these were interspersed throughout the whole magazine, not just in an easily-skipped section at the back (Goodrum and Dalrymple 1990, p. 31). Publisher Cyrus Curtis was a leader in this genre; he built "two of the most important national advertising media [of the late nineteenth century], the *Ladies' Home Journal* and the *Saturday Evening Post*" (Laird 1998, p. 52). Curtis established the monthly *Ladies' Home Journal* in 1883, spinning it off from the women's pages of *Tribune and Farmer*. The *Journal's* circulation reached 200,000 in 1885, while selling for five cents; doubled to 400,000 in 1888, still selling for a nickel; and grew another 50 percent to 600,000 in 1891, now with a price of ten cents an issue or a dollar a year. Beginning in the early 1890s, the *Journal* varied the cover illustration with each issue, "thus signaling the contradictory fusion of novelty and sameness which has since been crucial to the ideological subtext of magazines, and of mass culture in general" (Ohmann 1996, p. 28). In 1893, S.S. McClure began publication of his same-named monthly and sold it for fifteen cents an issue. "John Brisbane Walker, editor of the old *Cosmopolitan*, quickly dropped his price to 12 ½ cents. And in October, with much hoopla, Frank Munsey cut the price of his faltering monthly [*Munsey's*] from a quarter to a dime. Its circulation went from 40,000 that month to 200,000 the following February to 500,000 in April, and to a circulation that Munsey called the largest in the world by 1898" (Ohmann 1996, p. 25).

Another circulation-boosting, attention-collecting genre was muckraking. Richard Hofstadter explains muckraking journalism as more commercially than ideologically motivated. A few, like Upton Sinclair, were committed critics of the capitalist order, but more "were simply writers or reporters working on commission and eager to do well what was asked of them." Even Ida Tarbell, who made her name reporting critically on the Standard Oil Trust was an accidental muckraker, in Hofstadter's estimation, and later "became a eulogist of business." They "were hired into muckraking or directed toward it on the initiative of sales-conscious editors or publishers" (Hofstadter 1972 [1955], pp. 190–193).

From 1890 to 1900 the growth in magazine titles ended; as in so many other industries in the 1890s, a wave of industry concentration produced a small number of big winners. But the growth in readership continued as the surviving titles had bigger circulations than ever before (Laird 1998, p. 222; Sherman 1900, p. 121). In contrast to the most-read of the staid, established magazines like *Harper's* or *Scribner's* that in 1890 still sold at 35 cents a copy to a readership of 130,000, the newer, now leading magazines at the turn of the century sold at 10 to 15 cents per copy and reached a readership of 400,000 to 1,000,000. The old style of magazine publishers viewed the magazine as "a book in periodical form." The new magazine genres were "newspapers in periodical form" (Hofstadter 1972 [1955], pp. 190–191). They achieved attention harvests on an unprecedented scale. In 1865, total monthly magazine circulation was no more than four million, about one copy per ten people. In 1890, total monthly magazine circulation was 18 million. In 1905, monthly circulation was

64 million – about three copies per four people or, stated differently, four copies per household (Ohmann 1996, p. 29).

Magazines' modernization was entwined with US industrial capitalism's maturation and the resulting growth in the demand for audience attention. During the last third of the nineteenth century, manufacturers of a growing array of products, not just patent medicines, established brand identities and undertook an effort to wrest control of their distribution channels away from the middlemen. In some cases, manufacturers integrated forward into distribution. Others could still accomplish their aims while selling through administratively independent distribution agents. Whether or not manufacturers took direct administrative control of distribution, in a range of concentrated industries featuring branded goods, manufacturers began intensively cultivating consumer demand. The use of advertising to stimulate brand-specific demand among consumers weakened the jobbers' power in the distribution channel. When consumers demanded specific brands, the intermediaries between manufacturer and consumer came under great pressure to accept the manufacturer's terms; they had less leeway to choose which products to push hard and which to sell more lackadaisically. Earlier, when jobbers were still functioning as salesmen, a jobber had "some leverage against producers [which] probably made it possible for him to exercise influence over the terms and service he received from manufacturers. Once the manufacturer went over the wholesaler's and retailer's heads direct to the consumer via advertising, however, jobbing became more and more a distributive mechanism which routinely supplied the goods demanded by the public as the result of that advertising" (Porter and Livesay 1971, p. 224). Whereas many of the greatest fortunes in the early and mid-nineteenth century were mercantile fortunes, the greatest fortunes and greatest concentrations of economic power at the end of the nineteenth century accrued to manufacturers in highly concentrated industries, both producers of producers' goods (steel, oil) and producers of consumer goods (packaged foods, soaps). (Not every industry was so transformed.) The Kellogg Toasted Corn Flake Company was one of those successful national brand-name manufacturers who was able to impose market discipline over the distribution channel without direct administrative control. Their sales manager explained why they used jobbers, saying, "We distribute 100 per cent of our stuff – our entire product – through the jobber and wholesaler; we do this because they work cheap," an explanation that predecessors could not have given (Porter and Livesay 1971, p. 215).

The national brand-name manufacturers became the most innovative advertisers and their interests drove much of the change in the advertising industry (Laird 1998, p. 7). Successful magazines, meanwhile, achieved both national distribution and socioeconomic sorting, which made them nearly indispensable to advertisers of national brands. Magazines effectively reached an audience of interest to advertisers, sold the magazine to readers for less than the cost of production, and sold their readers to advertisers to make their profit (Ohmann 1996, p. 25). For a nationally distributed brand, one placement in a magazine with national circulation – circulating disproportionately among the prosperous, no less – was more efficient than dozens or hundreds of placements in the array of local papers that it would take to add up to the same circulation. For local retail merchants, local newspapers were still indispensable, but by the mid 1880s magazines were serious competitors for national brands' advertising expenditures, challenging newspapers' share of the attention market (Laird 1998, pp. 75, 170). To accomplish this, magazines themselves used an advertising-intensive marketing strategy both to attract readers and to sell those readers to advertisers.

Magazine publisher Cyrus Curtis was a spectacular success at reaping profits in the changing magazine industry and an active driver of that change. Curtis "spent unprecedented amounts of money developing the *Ladies' Home Journal* as an attractive, well-written publication, successfully targeted to the prosperous classes. He raised circulations by advertising these merits extensively in other publications, both magazines and newspapers." The *Journal*, on the basis of this high readership, pulled in more advertising revenues than any previous publication had ever achieved (Laird 1998, p. 53). Curtis knew that his readers' attention was a highly coveted commodity and contemporary observer Truman DeWeese credits him with being more forthright than the other publishers in describing his readers as his product. In a 1908 advertising manual, DeWeese approvingly quoted Curtis: "It is not my primary purpose to edify, entertain and instruct a million or more women with poems, stories and fashion hints. Mr. Bok [the editor] may think it is. Indeed, it is Mr. Bok's business to think so. He is merely the innocent victim of a harmless delusion and he draws a salary for being deluded. To be frank and confidential with you, the *Ladies' Home Journal* is published expressly for the advertisers." Curtis goes on to note the feedback between attracting audiences to satisfy advertisers and using advertising revenue to invest in audience-attracting content. "The reason I can put something in the magazine that will catch the artistic eye and make glad the soul of the reader is because a good advertiser finds that it pays him to give me $4,000 a page or six dollars an agate line for advertising space" (DeWeese 1908 [1906], p. 26). Whether or not they were as blunt about naming what they were doing, other publishers pursued the same advertiser-oriented strategy (Laird 1998, p. 223).

Like newspaper publishers, magazine publishers used advertising agencies to mediate between themselves and the advertisers purchasing their readers' eyes. As the magazine transformation was just beginning in the 1870s and 1880s, newspapers often still sold ad space directly to local advertisers and used agents primarily for placements made from out of town. Magazines, whose readers and advertisers were geographically dispersed, were more likely to manage all advertising through an agent. In 1867, Carlton and Smith, an ad agency from New York, bought the right to all advertising placements in a selection of religious magazines. "Carlton and Smith became, in effect, advertising concessionaires. This represented a further increase in advertising agency risk-bearing and completed the transition of the advertising 'agent' to the status of independent principal." By 1870, Carlton and Smith dominated the religious magazine field, which contained about 400 weeklies with aggregate circulation in the neighborhood of five million readers. J. Walter Thompson, who first worked for them, took over the agency in 1878. Under Thompson's leadership and name, the agency retained a focus on the magazine sector of the publishing industry (Pope 1983, p. 118). Additionally, ambitious magazine publishers were regular purchasers of audience attention as they pursued new readers to add to their own circulations. Advertisers probably would not have had much trouble finding him, yet Curtis developed a relationship with the N.W. Ayer agency, whose business expanded beyond religious magazines. Beginning in 1885, Curtis used Ayer to place advertisements for Curtis's magazines in other publications. As Curtis was both a major buyer and a major seller of attention, this developed into a credit relationship: Ayer placed Curtis's advertisements in other publications without charge and Curtis repaid the credit by allowing Ayer to place his other clients' ads in the *Ladies' Home Journal* without charge. In 1888 they made a $400 credit swap. A year later they renewed the arrangement on a vastly expanded scale: $200,000 worth of advertising placements *for* the *Journal* paid with $200,000 worth of advertising placements *in* the *Journal*. And still Curtis took in enough cash payments for advertising placements that he and his publishing company prospered (Laird 1998, p. 53).

Pricing audiences and dividing the spoils

Before circulation audits and advertising agencies and other elements of the advertising industry's modernization, the publishing industry had already been in two businesses at once: selling reading material to readers and selling readers to advertisers. Until the late nineteenth century, however, selling content to readers was the main business, perhaps subsidized by political patronage in the case of publications affiliated with a political party (Laird 1998, p. 72), while selling advertising space was an important secondary source of income for many publishers.[5] As sellers, in particular national brand-name manufacturers, increased the role of advertising in their sales strategies, the share of advertising in publishers' revenues grew. Advertising was 44 percent of newspaper publisher revenue in 1880. Around 1890, the two revenue sources equalized. By 1900 the balance had tipped and advertising made up more than half of the publishers' revenues, reaching 66 percent in 1919 (Waldron 1903, pp. 156–158; Pope 1983, p. 30; Kielbowicz 1990, p. 458.)

The change in the relative contributions of subscriptions and advertising to overall publisher revenues came in a context of overall explosive growth in print media. Even though most available data are imprecise, the trends are marked enough to show through the fog of the intervening years, incomplete record-keeping, and even deliberately false statements. The Post Office (whose records are the most reliable of the era) was a critical component of the newspaper and magazine distribution system; from 1880 to 1920, the volume of this class of mailings grew twenty times faster than the population. The Post Office measured volume by weight, so this represents both more individual issues and larger issues. The issues were larger mostly because they contained more pages of advertising (Kielbowicz 1990, p. 458). Some papers filled three-fourths of their printed area with advertising (Laird 1998, p. 73). By 1909, the Post Office was carrying 723 million pounds of publications, and the magazines averaged a trip of over a thousand miles. (Even newspapers sent through the mail traveled an average of almost 300 miles. Local distribution needn't use the Post Office.) A few years later, in 1913, the volume of newspapers and magazines sent through the mail passed a billion pounds, estimated to be about five billion individual copies from 28,707 different publishers, or about fifty per year per US resident, including children (Kielbowicz 1990, pp. 467, 471). This means the average individual received about one newspaper or magazine through the mail per week and the average household received several. This estimate is compatible with Ohmann's estimate that the average early twentieth-century household received four monthly magazines alone (Ohmann 1996, p. 29). Post Office data excludes street sales, newsstand sales, and home delivery. The city dailies, for example, were a major part of the newspaper industry but bypassed the Post Office by selling many copies on the street. A contemporary estimate by George Waldron that also included newspapers and magazines *not* sent through the mail put the number of individual newspaper and magazine copies per person per year at 41.2 in 1880 and 107.5 by 1900 (Waldron 1903).

Publishers printed and distributed rapidly increasing volumes of advertising-festooned paper because advertisers were paying for it. The dollar figures are uncertain as contemporary accounts are inconsistent and the historical record gets no less fuzzy over time. Pope relies on the useful, if necessarily only approximate, figures collected by the US Census Bureau's *Census of Manufactures* from 1905. These show aggregate spending for advertising placements in newspapers and magazines of $39.1 million in 1880, $71.2 million in 1890, and $95.9 million in 1900. The growth rate in print-media advertising spending then picked up, more than doubling each of the first three decades of the twentieth century to reach $202.5 million in 1909, $528.3 million in 1919, and $1.12 *billion* in 1929.[6] (This growth rate was not sustained into the 1940s and 1950s when a large share of advertising budgets shifted to radio and then television.) We can discern that print media was the largest single category of advertising spending, probably remaining in the range of 35 to 40 percent of total advertising spending throughout the period from the 1880s to the 1920s, with the other 60 to 65 percent divided amongst an assortment of other media (Pope 1983, pp. 26–27). These aggregate estimates are consistent with estimates of the number of national advertisers (four to five thousand) and anecdotes of the sizes of the largest advertisers' budgets (around 1900, advertising campaigns costing several hundred thousand dollars were not unheard of, but only the largest national advertisers would have been spending on that scale) (*Printers' Ink* 1913, p. 153; Pope 1983, p. 113; Cruikshank and Schultz 2010, pp. 100–120). A few dozen national advertisers with annual outlays in the hundreds of thousands (a few even reaching a million or more) plus a few thousand national advertisers with annual outlays in the thousands or tens of thousands, plus local and regional advertising – even a single large department store could be a significant local retail advertising spender – could yield the estimated totals we are working with.

Given that advertisers were ever more convinced by their experience and by advertising agents' persuasive efforts that spending vast sums of money on consistent, intensive print media advertising was worthwhile, there was an ever-growing pile of money to be divided amongst the various actors along the supply chain that provided advertisers access to readers. How much of the aggregate advertising expenditure of the nation would go to publishers as a whole and how much to the advertising agents positioned between the publishers and the advertisers? Within the publishing industry, how much advertising spending would go to newspapers? To magazines? To any specific, individual newspaper or magazine publisher? What costs would they have to incur to reach that market share? Amongst the advertising agents, how much would go to any individual agency? What costs would *they* have to incur to achieve that market share?

Despite their ongoing confrontations over the sizes of their shares, the basic system of agency compensation, developed during the first few decades of advertising agencies' existence when agents' coordinating role was still indispensable, had reached the status of (reasonably) settled precedent by the last decade of the nineteenth century. Advertising agencies were paid on a commission system. In principle, it worked this way: advertisers would pay a given price for advertising space in a publication; publishers reduced their own take by an agreed-upon percentage of the price and paid that amount to the advertising agent who made the placement. That is, advertising agencies' revenues took the form of a sales commission. For example, if the price of an advertising placement were \$100 and the agency's commission were 15 percent, the advertiser would pay \$100, the publisher would get \$85, and the agency would get \$15. In theory, the publisher was the first claimant on the advertiser's outlays. In practice, depending on the credit relationships among all the parties, the payments could be received in any order. Most commonly, an advertiser would pay the full placement price (e.g. \$100) to the advertising agency, who retained their commission (e.g. \$15) and passed on the publisher's share (e.g. \$85). An agency could still act as a wholesaler, like the earliest agents did, buying advertising space in bulk on their own account (with cash or credit) and reselling it in smaller lots to advertisers, but did so less often as the advertising industry developed. Regardless of the order in which credit was extended or cash was received, the language of the commission system became nearly universal by the 1890s (Laird 1998, pp. 232–234; Pope 1983, pp. 152–154).

Francis Wayland Ayer had been the first advertising agent to experiment with the commission system, establishing the "open contract" with advertisers in the 1870s. The open contract was open in two senses, both of which were novel at the time. First, advertisers were given full information about the price publishers charged for advertising space and the agency was paid a fixed commission. Other agents hid the price negotiations they conducted with publishers from the view of their clients, making the agents' share of the total a mystery. Second, the advertisers could purchase advertising space in a set of newspapers of their own choosing, rather than a package assembled by the agency (Laird 1998, p. 167; Ohmann 1996, p. 96). Although the open contract eventually became the industry's stated standard, even Ayer didn't use the open contract arrangement exclusively for a number of years and many agents resisted. Nathaniel Fowler, in most ways an antagonist of publishers and promoter of advertisers' interests, was still insisting at the close of the nineteenth century that advertisers don't need to know what the publisher charges the agent, only whether the price quoted by the agent to the advertiser makes the ad space purchase worthwhile. "It is none of the advertiser's business what the agent pays for space. It is decidedly his business what he has to pay for it" (Fowler 1900 [1897], p. 355). (But then, Fowler had been out of the space brokering business and focusing on copywriting for almost a decade by then, so perhaps he was behind the times.)

Despite the odd holdout, the open contract's language of commissions as the basis for agency compensation gained dominance; nevertheless, true transparency about pricing was less widely practiced. Publishers and agents had publicly announced list prices and might make a public show of commitment to their stated prices, but in reality would negotiate case by case. An agency that handled a large proportion of a publisher's placements might successfully pressure the publisher to accept a smaller payment without informing clients of the discount or sharing the savings with them. On the other side of their business, agencies might try to attract a client, or retain a client they feared losing, by offering to make a placement below the publisher's listed placement price. If an advertising agency reached an agreement with an advertising client that they would pay the publishers their expected share of the listed placement price (e.g. $85), but that the agency would accept a lower fee (maybe $10) yielding a lower total price for the client (in this example, $95 instead of $100), this was generally referred to as "commission sharing" or "commission rebating" not as a "retail discount," though the two are really functionally equivalent (Laird 1998, pp. 226–234; Pope 1983, pp. 152–154).

When considering their interests in vertical competition with advertising agents, publishers wanted advertisers to pay high prices for ad space with agents taking only a small cut. Agents, meanwhile, also wanted advertisers to pay high prices for ad space but they wanted to take a large cut for themselves and leave less for the publishers. Each group organized industry associations to serve their interests in vertical competition. In 1870, it was not unusual for agents to claim a 25 percent commission on advertising space sold. The American Newspaper Publishers Association, formed in 1887, supported newspaper publishers in their efforts to sell advertising space through agents on terms more favorable to themselves. They recommended a standard commission of 15 percent in 1889 and by 1894 dropped their standard commission recommendation to 10 percent. In an effort to limit the agents' opportunities to seize on negotiating advantages to newspaper publishers' detriment, they printed a list of approved agents who complied with recommended commissions and dealt honestly with publishers – and a blacklist of those whom they considered particularly predatory toward publishers (Laird 1998, p. 221; Pope 1983, pp. 132, 157). The association's policing of agents could not have been entirely successful; after a quarter century of the American Newspaper Publishers Association's work to subordinate advertising agents to publishers' needs, *Printers' Ink* determined in 1913 that only 280 advertising agents were approved by the association, yet another 438 (out of a total 718) were in business without such approval (*Printers' Ink* 1913, p. 153). The advertising agents, too, tried to organize for their collective interests and to constrain the publishers. For example, agents wanted publishers to charge the same final price to advertisers who bought directly as they charged to advertisers who purchased through agents. Publishers would not choose such a practice out of their own self-interest as they might have an opportunity to reduce the final price to advertisers and still increase their own take on transactions that cut out agency intermediation. Pope considers the American Association of Advertising Agencies ("the Four A's"), formed in 1917, to be the first effective trade association for advertising agencies (Pope 1983, p. 158).[7]

For both groups, publishers and agents, pursuit of their interests in vertical competition was undermined by the conditions of horizontal competition. Advertising agents in competition with other agents for advertiser spending often offered rebates (that is, lowered their own commission without reducing the publisher's share) in a bid to grow their volume of business. Similarly, publishers in competition with other publishers often offered to lower prices (that is, raise commission rates) for agents who would direct more advertisers their way. If we switch from the attention market participants' own language of commissions to the language of manufacturers and merchants – casting publishers as attention "manufacturers," agents as merchants, and advertisers as attention customers – we can see that battles over pricing discretion and profit shares in the attention market paralleled similar battles taking place in consumer goods. Manufacturers of national brand-name goods wanted to be able to control retail pricing, while retailers wanted the discretion to set prices in keeping with their own priorities. (Sometimes retailers wanted to charge higher prices than the manufacturers preferred, so as to maintain their own profit margins; other times they wanted to charge lower prices and use the heavily advertised goods as loss leaders.) This vertical struggle in consumer goods supply chains was played out in the business press, in the courts and legislatures, among trade associations, and in countless sale negotiations; if a retailer refused to comply with a manufacturer's preferred pricing, would the manufacturer refuse to supply to that retailer in the future? What could they gain and what could they lose? The same kinds of vertical struggles played out in attention supply chains. As the final buyers of attention, advertisers, like the buyers of consumer goods, wanted to get a good price while still having some assurance of product quality. They stood to benefit from price competition among publishers and agents if price dropped for quality service, but since much of the price negotiation was opaque, they had legitimate worries about whether their agent recommended the placements that were best for the advertiser's sales strategy, or just the ones that offered the agent the highest profit margin. The early agency days were characterized by a bargaining advantage for agencies, who were fewer in number and richer in information, over newspaper publishers. Commissions of 25 percent were common in 1870. When agencies proliferated, agent's commissions narrowed. Newspapers were pulled two ways by the proliferation of advertising agencies. To publishers' benefit, they could more easily refuse to sell advertising space through an agency that tried to drive hard bargains with publishers since they could easily supply their readers' attention to advertisers through a different agency, instead. However, agencies were also competing for advertisers' spending and often enough competed on the basis of price. When agencies competed for advertisers by offering cut rates on placements, they threatened to erode the overall price level on advertising space, to publishers' long run detriment. Despite all the conflicts of interest and contradictions, the commission system staggered on (Laird 1998, p. 233; Pope 1983, pp. 87–106, 132).

In addition to or instead of competing on price, agencies could compete on service. Rather than trying to retain a client by rebating a portion of their commission, an agency could try to retain a client on the basis of a reputation for reliably honest dealing in a business where justifiable mistrust increased risks and raised transaction costs. In a very limited way in the 1890s, and then in a big way after 1900, agencies also began offering creative services, developing the strategy and producing the content of advertising campaigns rather than just brokering placements (Laird 1998, pp. 221–222, 235–243). Early in the 1900s, as responsibility for advertising content was in the midst of transitioning from advertiser to agent, the Lord & Thomas agency of Chicago offered two tiers of service: placement only for a 10 percent commission, or placement and creative work for 15 percent. To provide the service that earned the higher commissions, the agency increased their staffing to six full-time copywriters (Cruikshank and Schultz 2010, p. 52).

The publishers of the largest magazines – Richard Ohmann puts the number of modern mass-circulation magazines in 1900 at around twenty – amassed enough market power to attempt to displace the functions of the independent advertising agent. There were few enough of them that advertisers did not have such a daunting information problem in finding them; conversely, as national brand-name manufacturers grew their shares of the markets in which they operated, the publishers faced a more readily solvable information problem in locating advertisers. In 1893, Frank Munsey embarked on a price-cutting, circulation-expanding strategy and claimed the largest circulation in the world by 1898, a plausible if uncertain claim (Ohmann 1996, p. 25). Having established such a large inventory of reader eyes, Munsey tried to break the commission system for agency compensation in 1898. In a move to bypass agents, Munsey promised to sell ad space to anyone for the same rate; that is, when bypassing the agencies, he would enable advertisers, rather than himself, to keep the commission usually collected by the agencies. But he also refused independent verification of his circulation, which agents used against him in public attacks on his credibility. When he began his attack on the agencies, many of Munsey's ad placements were still made through agents and when agents withdrew their orders in retaliation, Munsey was not able to fill the shortfall with orders placed direct from advertisers. Facing the loss of so much ad revenue, he backed down and reinstituted commissions on the usual basis (Pope 1983, p. 155). Cyrus Curtis, publisher of *Saturday Evening Post* and *Ladies' Home Journal*, also tried to bypass agents and often worked directly with advertisers, including providing advertisers with extensive creative services. But for a national advertising campaign, even Curtis' enormous audiences were an insufficient share of the national attention market to suffice on their own. For advertisers, working with a whole gaggle of publishers, as a major national campaign must, increased transactions costs enough that Curtis's goal of bypassing agents could not be sustained (Laird 1998, pp. 224–226).

Just as the pressure to standardize information about circulations grew until the epoch-making treaty negotiation by advertisers, agents, and publishers established the Audit Bureau of Circulations in 1914, the pressure to establish reliably reported, consistent pricing grew. Laird explains, "The individualism, constant negotiation, and lack of standardization that characterized nineteenth-century business practices in general had functioned reasonably well in advertising, if not smoothly, as long as the parties involved remained small and localized. As more and more advertising operations approached national scale between 1890 and 1910, however, the system by which those advertisers interacted with publishers approached such magnitude that the traditional mechanisms added increasingly unacceptable costs and uncertainties to each transaction" (Laird 1998, pp. 225–226). Also in 1914, the same year as the launch of the Audit Bureau of Circulations, the Associated Advertising Clubs of America (AAC of A) endorsed an industry standard of open access to price information. The benefit publishers and agents had derived from their earlier secrecy and lost with the new agreement was compensated for by the provisions of the resolution that forbade price competition. Prices for advertising placements and advertising agents' fees were thereafter publicly known, but they were not allowed to emerge from a market equilibrating process of competitive bidding. Rather, they were set by agreement at a standard rate that preserved profitability for publishers and agents (Myers 1960, p. 312). Just as many of the agencies' biggest clients used advertising (and monopoly power and collusion and any other means at their disposal) to avoid price competition in their own markets, advertising agents and publishers used negotiated pricing agreements to avoid price competition in *their* markets and instead wrangled over market share through reputation, service quality, and advertising of their own.

Increasing efficiency and intensifying resource use

As advertising agents gained the trust of advertisers, the price per presumed impression per eyeball fell. At the same time, the advertisers' confidence that they had in fact crossed the field of vision of the eyes they paid for rose. Advertisers might, then, have declared themselves satisfied. On the face of it, it seems they could have maintained a given level of advertising intensity while reducing advertising expenditures year to year. And yet they did not.

According to Waldron's turn-of-the-century calculation, from 1880 to 1900 the number of copies of newspapers and magazines per capita increased by a factor of greater than two and a half, while advertising expenditures per capita increased by a factor of less than two. (See Table 2.2.) Furthermore, we know that each newspaper and magazine copy contained more advertising in 1900 than in 1880. In other words, the growth rate of audiences' exposure to advertising was faster than the growth rate of advertisers' expenditures on advertising placements. As inadequate as the circulation data were, and as inconsistent as the pricing was, it is clear in the aggregate that the price per impression fell. Of course, not all impressions are created equal. A full-page, full-color, pictorial advertisement cost a whole lot more than a single-column, fourteen-line text advertisement. In 1883, the inaugural year of the *Ladies' Home Journal*, a full-page advertisement cost $200 and reached 25,000 readers, at a cost of $8 per thousand (Cruikshank and Schultz 2010, pp. 42–43). In the late 1880s, *Youth's Companion*, with a circulation of 400,000, sold a full-page, full-color ad placement for $14,000, a first for both format and price (Ohmann 1996, p. 26). That works out to $35 per thousand. By 1893 *Ladies' Home Journal*'s readership reached 700,000 and Curtis charged advertisers $4,000 for a full-page ad: in the aggregate, this was twenty times what they had paid for a full page a decade before but, at about $5.70 per thousand, this actually meant a drop of 30 percent in the unit price advertisers paid for readers. In the first decade of the twentieth century, Curtis said he still charged $4,000 for a full-page ad or $6 an agate line for advertisers to reach his circulation of "a million or more" readers of the *Ladies' Home Journal* (Cruikshank and Schultz 2010, pp. 42–43; DeWeese 1908 [1906], p. 26). (An agate line is a measure of column space based on the size of the type.) This means the price per thousand impressions was only $4 for a full-page ad, and just pennies per thousand readers if all an advertiser wanted to put in front of them was an inch or two of column space. By 1915, Charles MacFarlane, in order to calculate a cost comparison between print-media advertising and direct mail, claimed that a typical placement in a general circulation magazine would cost about $1 per thousand. Because of their more precisely sorted readership, placements in specialized trade publications could cost more: $2 in a business journal, $5 in the leading advertising journals, up to

Table 2.2 Newspaper and magazine subscription spending and advertising expenditure

Year	Copies per capita	Subscription and sales spending per capita	Advertising expenditure per capita
1880	41.2	$0.99	$0.78
1890	74.7	$1.16	$1.14
1900	107.5	$1.05	$1.26

Source: Waldron 1903, pp. 156–158

$10 per thousand to advertise to printers in the printing trade journals. Mac-Farlane's purpose was to promote direct mail, so he was unlikely to understate print-media advertising costs (MacFarlane 1915, pp. 13–14). Clearly the mass-circulation magazines and the grouping of newspapers into bundles were leading to economies of scale and dropping the unit cost of audience eyes.

Meanwhile, the number of impressions purchased by advertisers was increasing faster than unit cost was falling. As we have seen, aggregate print advertising expenditures kept rising. In the 1860s, W. Stanley Jevons noted an irony in resource use, in particular the use of coal. As production methods develop to use a particular resource more efficiently, we might reasonably expect to use less of that resource. Efficiency, after all, allows us to conserve on inputs while still producing the same amount of output. Improved steam engine design, for example, enabled the same amount of work to be done with a small fraction of the coal consumed by earlier coal-powered steam engines. However, Jevons noted that increased efficiency in use of coal was followed by *greater* consumption. Improved efficiency "renders the employment of coal more profitable, and thus the present demand for coal is increased" (Jevons 1866 [1865], p. 8). Something comparable happened with audience attention. As print media delivered eyeballs more efficiently, advertisers clamored for ever more attention. Products that it would not have paid to advertise before came to seem plausible subjects of advertising. Audiences that it would not have paid to target before came to seem reachable. Audiences were first more extensively and then more intensively mined.

Extensive mining of attention

The rise of the penny press and the subsequent multiplication of daily newspapers and advertising-oriented magazines constitute an extension of attention gathering. More advertisements crossed through more people's field of vision. Extensive strategies in the attention market were facilitated by the business model experimentation of publishers and the coordinating role of advertising agencies, as discussed previously, but also by developments in paper manufacture and printing technology, transportation methods, public infrastructure, and public institutions.

Information and attention may be immaterial in the abstract, but in practice they take on concrete, material forms. Printed-upon paper was the physical vessel in which information was conveyed to readers and, as a corollary, readers' attention was delivered to publishers. (Some of this attention was met with editorial content supplied by the publisher; some was met with advertising, for which privilege the advertiser paid.) The penny press was launched about as early as it became economically feasible thanks to technological advances in paper manufacture. The 1830s discovery of chlorine and its application to paper bleaching increased the volume of paper produced and dropped the price. Much of this increased volume of paper production went into an increased volume of newspapers. Before the Civil War, Richard Hoe invented a rotary press capable of 18,000 impressions per hour, a sixfold increase over the printing speeds of the flat-bed presses then in use, lowering unit costs for those publishers producing in high enough volume to make the new equipment worthwhile (Goodrum and Dalrymple 1990, pp. 17, 20).

Once printed, paper-and-ink information vessels had to cross physical distance to deliver their wares. Therefore, transportation technologies, among their many economic effects, were harnessed to the delivery of attention. Developments in transportation allowed producers of physical wares to gather inputs from and distribute their outputs to a wider geographic area; the same was true for attention supply chains and distribution networks.

The urban dailies each had a large, geographically concentrated readership, so they had the least distance to travel. They delivered newspapers into the hands of readers via a network of street sellers, often young boys, whose cries of, "Extra! Extra! Read all about it!" echo in our cultural imagination even though it has been generations since the last call was voiced (Ohmann 1996, p. 20). Otherwise, street crying declined as a form of advertising in the nineteenth century (Laird 1998, pp. 13–14). (In fact, by the end of the century, street crying had become so rare that anti-billboard activists complained that the visual intrusion of posters was like having someone yelling in your ear, which, they said, was obviously intolerable and unthinkable. If shopkeepers may not follow you down the street shouting at you, why should they permitted to assault your eyes with signs (Warner 1900, p. 282)?) Late in the nineteenth century, the sellers of clothing and cleansers and pots and pans and even patent medicines no longer shouted for audiences much themselves, but they printed their ads in the newspapers, and, one step removed, the newsboys still aimed at audiences' ears to sell the print. Deliveries done by foot and voice did not directly depend on any particularly new transportation technologies. Indirectly, the development of urban infrastructure made it a little easier to move the newsprint around the cities and also channeled the target audiences toward particular places where newspapers sellers could find them. Trolleys, once they were introduced for intra-urban transit, usefully gathered likely newspaper buyers at trolley stops, where they could be sold newspapers.

For newspaper subscribers taking home delivery, the publisher could run their own distribution operation (as plenty of newspapers still do today), but many publishers, especially publishers of rural weekly newspapers or of national magazines, relied on the US Post Office to cover the distance between printing press and readers' hands (as magazines still do today). The US Post Office, by design, subsidized newspaper and magazine distribution significantly, so the cost to publishers started low and remained low. But as the volume of print publications multiplied, the Post Office was pressed to adopt new technologies and new institutional policies to manage the deluge. Before the emergence of the twentieth-century regulatory state, the Post Office was the most labor-intensive function of the federal government, and the most routine point of contact between the citizenry and the federal government. Given the extent of federal resources at stake and the expanding role of regular mail service in the daily fabric of Americans' lives, postal policy was politically contested (Henkin 2006; Gallagher 2016). The regularly updated outcomes of the contest had significant bearing on the advertising industry.

Under Benjamin Franklin's leadership, the Post Office prioritized newspapers at its start. Franklin's perspective as a publisher surely shaped his argument that it was a public good for newspapers to gather and distribute news, and thus an appropriate use of government resources to subsidize the transit costs involved. Publishers were permitted to send newspapers to one another anywhere free of charge and send them to readers at far below cost. Letter postage, by contrast, was priced higher than the Post Office's cost of providing the service. In effect, letter writers subsidized newspaper distribution. Letters, being expensive, were not an expected part of most people's routines (Henkin 2006, pp. 17, 21; Kielbowicz 1989, p. 3).

Around mid-century, a highly mobile and increasingly literate population began demanding affordable and reliable means of exchanging letters. A flurry of rate changes and service policy reforms from 1845 to 1856 lowered the postage on personal mail. Also, new policies shifted the burden of payment from recipient to sender. Postage prepaid by the sender was first discounted, then required for most types of mail. Before the mid-century postage rate cuts, private mail services had been making a bid to meet the demand for long-distance communication, but the rate cuts secured the Post Office's position as the main conduit of correspondence (Henkin 2006, pp. 21–30). While rate cuts expanded postal access to eager letter writers and receivers, requiring prepayment helped reduce waste in operating costs. Since the sender had already paid, handling undeliverable, unwanted mail, or unexpected mail that the recipient never picked up was less of a drain on the Post Office (Kielbowicz 1989, p. 91). Publishers, however, were a powerful political lobbying group. They directed the only mass communications medium of the day, so politicians were wary of crossing them. In 1852, newspapers and magazines were for the first time charged according to the same rate structure and both secured an exemption from the 1856 prepayment rules (Fuller 1991, pp. 2–3; Kielbowicz 1989, p. 131).

In the next stages of its development, the Post Office increased the density of its presence, spreading its reach from every American's hometown to every American's home. One of the many anxieties of urbanization was the promiscuous mixing of postal patrons in the post office lobby. Men and women of all classes had at least occasional reason to appear at the post office, sometimes for the mail, other times for pickpocketing or other purposes requiring access to postal patrons. Some of the larger post offices established separate ladies' windows, but a more thorough solution to worrisome sex-and-class mixing was to obviate the need to visit the post office at all for routine correspondence. In the middle of the Civil War, the prospect of thousands of people learning of a loved one's death by reading the feared letter while standing in a post office lobby added a dash of extra motivation to experiment with home delivery (Henkin 2006, pp. 84–90). (The military did not yet have a standard practice of promptly informing fallen soldiers' families. Instead, the news of a soldier's death was most often passed along to his family by surviving peers whenever they happened to have the resources, wherewithal, and addressing information available to write (Faust 2008).)

Prior to 1863, home delivery was subject to an extra two-cent charge per letter. Private enterprises challenged the Post Office as providers of last-mile delivery service and in fact these private services handled more home deliveries than the Post Office itself. The Post Office's new policy of free home delivery, where it was adopted, made home delivery the default option and eliminated the extra charge. (And put private services out of business.) After a trial in a few cities in 1863, free home delivery reached 66 northern cities in 1864 (Henkin 2006, pp. 86–90; Post Office Department 1956, p. 5). By 1890, free delivery brought mail to the homes of those dwelling in cities and towns with a population of 10,000 or more, including in the South (Fuller 1991, p. 2). John Wannamaker, the department store magnate, became postmaster in 1889. During his time in the role, he championed the expansion of free home delivery to rural districts. He saw the post as a business stimulus that could integrate farmers into commerce and consumption. Although Wannamaker did not achieve his goal during his term as postmaster, rural free delivery was permanently established in 1902 and phased in over the following years. Many of the lowest-volume post offices were closed, and instead mail was carried from a post office farther away directly to the front door of some of the most geographically remote households (Gallagher 2016, pp. 187–191). For newspaper and magazine publishers, this meant reliable, low-cost access to the eyes of readers wherever they lived and worked.

Meanwhile, Congress tinkered with classifications and rates. The year of the first experiments with free home delivery, 1863, also introduced a three-category mail classification scheme (Post Office Department 1956, p. 2): First class was for individual correspondence and cost three cents for up to half an ounce regardless of distance. Second class was for all regular periodical publications and rates were still subsidized; weekly publications weighing no more than four ounces paid postage of five cents per quarter – since a quarter is 13 weeks, this rate is equivalent to five-thirteenths of a cent per individual copy mailed – and those publishing more than once a week paid the same per-issue rate, again charged quarterly: five cents times the number of weekly issues per quarter, up to thirty-five cents per quarter for a daily publication. Third class was for everything else, which included occasional publications, books, seeds, cuttings, and engravings, and rates were higher. Magazines won the right to insert loose advertising sheets into their regular publications and still mail the whole package at heavily subsidized second-class rates, but free-standing advertising circulars with no editorial content were included in the more expensive third class and had to pay two cents per three pieces or less, and then an additional two cents per each additional three pieces (Gallagher 2016, p. 152; Kielbowicz 1989, pp. 92, 132; Post Office Department 1956, pp. 21–33).

Publishers remained exempt from prepayment rules until a series of Congressional acts passed between 1874 and 1885. These acts finally required publishers to prepay their postage but won publisher's cooperation by lowering their postage rates and charging by the pound – first two cents per pound, later lowered to one cent per pound – rather than by the individual piece. To qualify for the publishers' discounted bulk postage rate, however, a publication had to be deemed legitimate second-class mail. Qualifying publications had to feature news, educational, or cultural content; identify the publisher; publish at least four issues a year; have a subscription list; and have no cloth or board bindings. The third assistant postmaster general was responsible for reviewing eligibility for second-class mailing privileges (Fuller 1991, pp. 2–3).

The 1874–1885 round of reforms enabled an upsurge in publications delivered by mail. Indeed, the publisher-friendly Post Office was one of the factors contributing to the emergence of the modern magazine. The post-1880 modern magazine was far more oriented toward advertising revenues than the subscription-dependent pre-1880 magazines had been. As Truman DeWeese said of modern magazines, "The reader must be flim-flammed with the idea that the publisher is really printing the magazine or newspaper for him" when in fact the publisher is printing the magazine for the advertisers (DeWeese 1908 [1906], p. 25). From 1880 to 1920, as publishers scrambled to meet advertisers' demand for audiences' eyes, many businesses adapted to the incentives embedded in the postal rate structure by publishing "house organs," magazines that did little more than tout the business sponsoring them but included just enough articles to persuade the Post Office to apply the subsidized second-class rate. With house organs added into the mix, second-class mailings grew twenty times faster than the population. The share of publishers' revenues derived from advertising tipped ever more heavily toward advertising (Kielbowicz 1990, p. 458). Audiences paid less to read more because they were no longer the customers; they were the product.

The falling postage charged to publishers was only sustainable with cost-saving innovations in postal operations. The postal rate reforms of the 1870s and 1880s came in combination with the cost-saving technological advance of the Railway Mail Service. Trains were a more efficient means of transportation than the means of transit they replaced – often boats or horse-drawn carriages, depending on the route. A car or two devoted to the mail could be hitched to the same engine as other cars carrying other cargo or passengers and share costs. In addition, moving mail cars were mobile worksites where postal workers sorted and routed the mail while in motion, which reduced the origin-to-destination transit time. The Railway Mail Service was one component of a rapid increase in the scale of postal operations. In 1880, there were 100,000 federal employees in total; a majority of them worked for the Post Office. At the beginning of the 1890s postal employment had grown. There were 62,401 distinct post offices, and though the smallest rural post offices would have employed just a single postmaster, urban post offices employed teams of clerks and mail carriers. About 6,000 workers worked for the Railway Mail Service (Gallagher 2016, pp. 182, 192; Fuller 1991, pp. 2–3). New transportation technologies and infrastructure coupled with reorganization of the use of existing technologies to reap economies of scale lowered the unit cost of delivering a piece of mail. Postal policy further lowered the cost to publishers through subsidies. These developments made postal patrons increasingly accessible to advertisers through the mediation of print media publishers.

Publishers could not take this state of affairs for granted, however. Mass circulation magazines and big city newspapers were written from and for an urban and suburban perspective and had the business goal of packaging a national audience for sale to national advertisers (Kielbowicz 1990, p. 452). The political wrangling around postal reform in 1879 had united "legitimate" publishers from both rural and urban areas against those mailing advertising sans editorial content. But publishers from rural districts, both conservative and populist, came to question their alliance with urban publishers, and postal officials began to regret the earlier deal struck with publishers. In the first two decades of the twentieth century, an alliance of rural interests, including many rural publishers, struggled to pull the postal privilege out from under urban publishers (Kielbowicz 1990; Fuller 1991).

Too many different interests pulled in too many different directions, and the twentieth century got underway without any new postal reforms passed in Congress. Postal officials hoping to reduce the operating deficits produced by the second-class mail subsidies tested the boundaries of their administrative authority. Without change in the statutes handed down from Congress, the third assistant postmaster general, the official responsible for handling second-class mailing permit applications, tightened interpretation of existing classification rules to exclude more material from second-class privileges. Although challenged in court by Houghton, Mifflin, and Co., the Post Office's sterner stance was supported by the US Supreme Court in a 1904 ruling. The court held that the Post Office did in fact have broad authority to make administrative decisions about the interpretation of the rules, though not to rewrite the underlying rate structure. Even without Congressional action, the stricter implementation did withdraw second-class privileges from many mail-order journals, which put some of them out of business (Kielbowicz 1990, pp. 463–465). The Post Office also tried to keep down operating deficits by suppressing labor organizing among postal employees and holding down wages. In 1902 President Theodore Roosevelt issued a gag order forbidding postal workers from lobbying Congress for improved pay and working conditions. By 1907 the poor pay and working conditions generated a staffing crisis that forced the government to give clerks and carriers a raise. The raise was not the end of the story, however. Unionization efforts continued and in 1913 sixty black workers in the Railway Mail Service division established the National Alliance of Postal Employees, a precursor to the interracial National Alliance of Postal and Federal Employees, formed decades later in the public-sector unionization surge of the 1960s (Gallagher 2016, p. 193).

Congress continued to study the problems of the Post Office, with particular attention to the matter of second-class mail. The distinction between so-called legitimate publications with information of a public character and advertising rags was fuzzy at best and getting ever fuzzier. A congressional commission in 1907 observed, "every periodical is designed for advertising purposes or no periodical is so designed" (Kielbowicz 1990, p. 458). Letter postage offset a large portion, though not all, of the postal budget shortfall generated by transporting magazines. Heavy users of first- and third-class mail resented the transfer from their pockets to the publishers' and favored rate reform (Kielbowicz 1990, pp. 466–472). In 1917, some adept legislative maneuvering folded postal rate changes into the War Revenue Act. The new policy raised rates on reading matter slightly and in stages (from one cent per pound eventually up to one and half cents per pound flat rate) but raised rates on advertising considerably (from at least two cents a pound for short distances to as high as ten cents a pound for advertising content transported 1,800 miles or more). The precise targeting of the rate increase managed to win it enough support – and sufficiently weaken opposition. Muckraking journalism was in decline, and therefore so, too, was Progressives' earlier support for subsidizing publishers' postage. Publishing interest subgroups were splintered. The rate policy protected rural and small-town publishers who did not sell as much advertising space and did not send their publications such long distances. Rural, especially Southern legislators represented small-town publishers' interests in support of the bill. The bill also offered some protection for local retailers from national distributors and constrained what many perceived as a cultural invasion from national magazines centered in the urban Northeast and industrial Midwest, and these interests reinforced rural legislators' support. The rural-urban and geographic region splits also mapped onto the split over World War I. Interventionist positions were most common in the urban Northeast where munitions manufacturers and financiers stood to profit. Isolationist positions were most common in the rural Midwest and South; they called eastern newspapers advocating entry into the war the "parasite press." The national magazine publishers opposed the rate change but, despite their continuing cultural influence and importance, could not gather enough allies and ultimately had to absorb higher postage costs, especially on the advertising content that had become the core of their business (Kielbowicz 1990).

Still, the attention industry was still a profitable line of business, especially for the largest firms. Publishers – making use of falling paper and printing costs to print more and longer issues; devoting an increasing proportion of total pages to advertising; with the able assistance of the Post Office, who in turn relied on road and railroad infrastructure – intercepted more eyes more times with each passing year. Pages of advertising per typical magazine issue multiplied from a few in 1880, to a few dozen in 1890, to almost 100 in 1900, then sometimes more than 100 in the 1900s (Ohmann 1996, p. 84). As the years went on, Americans saw more advertisements, a clear result of extensive attention-mining strategies.

Intensive mining of attention

Even before the matter of measuring the raw number of perception interceptions an ad placement could achieve was completely resolved, ambitious advertisers and advertising agents began to explore ways to intensify their use of the attention they accessed. Extensive strategies were perceived to be facing diminishing marginal returns; everyone in the attention market realized that as the volume of advertising each person was exposed to multiplied, their attention to any one advertisement could not be assumed. Merely knowing that an advertisement was delivered into the field of vision of, say, 50,000 people, came to seem insufficient. So many questions remained: *which* 50,000 people? How many of those were persuadable buyers of the advertised product? For that matter, how many potentially persuadable buyers were *not* part of the batch included in the media buy? Did those whose eyes passed over the advertisement even notice it? If they didn't notice it the first time, did they notice it the second or tenth or twentieth time? If they noticed it, were they persuaded? Were they even a little bit intrigued? More precise selection of the audiences to be advertised to and more effectively persuasive content constitute a more intensive use of audience attention.

In the 1890s, advertising agents worked with advertisers on choosing sensible-seeming placements for their advertisements. Even without sophisticated data analysis, which was unavailable, agents made at least some gestures toward answering the first few of the previous questions for their clients. (Though there were still unresolved conflicts of interest in the matter of choosing media. If the publications that were best for the advertiser's sales strategy were not the best for the agent's profit margin, whose interest would win out? The answer varied case by case.) Well into that decade, though, advertising agents remained aloof from preparation of advertising content and usually did little systematic preparatory research or continuing assessment. The rest of the previously mentioned questions remained for the time being unanswerable. Then, after 1900, agents very quickly added a whole range of activities to their operations, including conducting preparatory market research, writing copy, designing images and layout, and testing audience response to advertisements. Daniel Pope explains the sudden shift as a survival strategy for advertising agencies whose space-brokering *raison d'être* was eroding. With information about publications, circulations, and advertising rates ever more accessible to interested advertisers, agents no longer had any special knowledge, which means that even if they still offered a convenience, they were no longer indispensable intermediaries. The persistence of the commission system allowed them to stay in business, but to justify their commissions they began to offer more services to advertisers (Pope 1983, pp. 138–154). As a complement to Pope's explanation, we can characterize agencies' new activities as a shift toward intensification of attention use.

One way to use audience attention more intensively (or at least attempt to do so) is to be more selective about the attention intercepted. The first known instance of an advertising agency conducting market research to identify the audiences most likely to be fruitful advertising targets and the media through which they could be reached came in 1879. The N.W. Ayer and Son agency, working on behalf of a thresher manufacturer, researched where threshers were sold in greatest volume and identified the media serving those geographic regions. Ayer provided such services sporadically, though not rarely, in the following decades. In 1900, the agency identified clients they would like to attract, then produced market research and developed advertising strategies based on those findings on spec, as part of a pitch to try to win their business. But Ayer was an outlier in this practice. Most agencies didn't offer comparable services and many advertising agents scolded those who did market research work on spec for devaluing their work by doing it for free. Then suddenly in the 1910s market research became a common advertising agency practice and all the leading agencies added statistics departments. At J. Walter Thompson, Stanley Resor instituted market research, first as employee for a few years, then as part-owner when he and a few associates bought out the elderly Thompson in 1916 (Pope 1983, pp. 141–142).

The standards developed for the Audit Bureau of Circulations' reports obviously improved the certainty with which advertisers could measure the extent of their ad placements' reach. Their standards also contained information relevant to advertisers' attempts to increase the intensity of their attention access. In 1913, months before the agreement creating the ABC was reached, George Glavis, a former US Post Office classification department executive, published an article in *Printers' Ink* instructing advertisers in how to analyze publishers' subscription lists and warning advertisers against the underhanded ways publishers attempted to create a false impression of a larger circulation. Some circulation questions have ambiguous answers, and these ambiguities highlight the distinction between extensive and intensive strategies. For example, one copy of a publication may be shared among several people in a household or business. Should all of those who share access to the same copy be counted equivalently in the circulation totals? Publishers often continued to send issues to former subscribers who had not in fact paid for their subscriptions in the current period, or they boosted their circulation by offering discounted subscriptions or extra incentives. Should those who received a publication for which they paid less than the full subscription rate, or even paid nothing at all, be counted as the equivalents of full-price subscribers in the circulation totals? Glavis argued that they should not. "It is indefensible," he wrote, "to add to a subscription list the names of persons who, while it is thought they may be readers, have not displayed sufficient interest to send in subscription orders" (Glavis 1913, p. 86). The ABC helped create some standards for how the relevant information was reported and verified, but the relative valuations of various categories of possible readers remained debatable. In 1923, the Curtis Publishing Company, still dominant in the world of magazine publishing, produced a promotional pamphlet about circulation claiming that they held their circulation reporting to a higher standard than the ABC, offering no extra incentives or discounts to lure in readers and counting only full-price subscribers (Curtis Publishing Company 1923). A reader's subscription payment thus played a dual role for publishers. It was, of course, revenue in its own right. But it was also leveraged as a signal of the strength of reader interest. A reader with enough interest in the magazine to pay for it was presumed to be more attentive than a reader who came into contact with the magazine second-hand or underpriced. The greater presumed intensity of their attention could command a higher price in the attention market.

As advertisers became more selective about the audiences they purchased (a trend that was magnified in the use of individualized direct mail; see Chapter 4: Home Invasion), they also became more anxious about what content they put in front of those audiences. Early advertisers were most often firms dominated by the personality of an individual founder or owner, and the content of the advertisements was a projection of this dominating personality. The owner was the "I" behind the advertising speech (Laird 1998, p. 5). As the "visible hand" of managerial control took over the biggest national manufacturers (Chandler 2002 [1977]), who were also the biggest national advertisers, there was no longer a single person to speak for the firm. The managers responsible for advertising strategy were not in a position, as the earlier owners had been, to project and promote *themselves*, but they had to project and promote their product and felt pressure to show the effectiveness of their communications.

Writing advertising copy became a specialized occupation, the work of someone known for communications expertise, not necessarily someone with a strong personal identification with the product whose sales pitches they composed. The earliest known full-time copywriting employment arrangement (and hence first opportunity to pursue copywriting as a salaried job) came when John Wannamaker of department store fame hired John E. Powers to write his advertising copy in 1880, an arrangement that lasted until 1886. When advertisers of the 1880s and 1890s wanted specialized assistance with copy, though, they most often relied on the short-term services of freelance copywriters (Fox 1997, pp. 25–27; Laird 1998, pp. 173–179). Nathaniel Fowler became a freelance copywriter in 1891 when he sold his advertising agency and got out of the space brokering business so he could focus just on content (Laird 1998, p. 179); in his book on *Publicity* he (self-interestedly) urged advertisers to rely on specialized assistance in preparing ads, pointing out that the advertising space is wasted if the content does not engage readers and asserting that writing engaging copy is a specialized skill best left to the professionals. "It does not take a great writer to produce the words the people want to read. To make people read what they think they do not want to read requires a mind born in intelligence, educated in experience, and fitted to do all things well" (Fowler 1900 [1897], pp. 34, 344–345). Advertising agencies, with some foot dragging, began experimenting with offering copywriting services in the 1890s, passed a tipping point around 1900, and early in the twentieth century most copywriting moved into advertising agencies' arena of action (Laird 1998, pp. 172–183, 210–211). The right placement could *intercept* the right audiences' attention. To the extent that improved advertising copy could better *hold* the attention of those whose eyes the advertisement intercepted, the work of specialists in copywriting could be seen as an intensification of attention mining.

Even as copywriting was becoming the domain of specialists and more advertising agencies hired more men (and a few women) to do this work, copy was losing its dominance in the overall communication strategy. Those crafting advertising content came to emphasize visual formatting and image as much as the verbal information. In the 1890s, advertisements got bigger and the word count got smaller; images and un-inked space took up a greater proportion of the total area (Ohmann 1996, pp. 21, 176–180). Richard Ohmann writes, "Older advertising assumed a reader wanting a product and willing to search through dense columns of type to find news about it. The newer visual advertising set out to ambush the reader's attention, produce affect quickly, and lodge in the memory" (Ohmann 1996, p. 180). Advertising was indeed an ambush, or a seduction, or a mixture of both. Advertising professionals generally assumed resistance on the part of audiences. As Truman DeWeese put it, advertising is a "butter-in." Readers don't usually open a magazine for the purpose of being advertised to; they open a magazine to read the stories. But, "This mercenary intruder begins shouting 'corsets, premium hams, Ivory Soap, Fairbanks Gold Dust and Automobiles' the moment a reader settles down to a quiet hour with Thomas Nelson Page, Edith Wharton or William E. Curtis." The advertising content therefore has to be the most skillfully constructed item in the magazine (DeWeese 1908 [1906], p. 25). Similarly, Fowler argued, "Folks assume that they do not read advertisements, and this is the reason for the engagement of the best artists and the best writers, that the advertisement, by its excellence and attractiveness, may force itself before the public and into the public" (Fowler 1900 [1897], p. 264).

Technological changes in printing facilitated the visually-oriented techniques of intensification of attention use just as they facilitated the unit-cost-lowering extension of attention access. In the 1850s, the invention of stereotyping allowed a full-page layout to be printed from a cylindrical press. Publishers using this new technology could offer advertisers wider spaces, no longer limiting advertising layouts to a single column in width. Due to the high fixed costs of acquiring the new equipment, however, adoption was slow; only forty-five were in use in 1880; adoption accelerated after. In the 1880s, electrotyping enabled better illustration quality. In the 1890s, half-tone photograph reproductions supplanted many uses of line illustrations. Dailies regularly printed photos by 1900 (Pope 1983, p. 136).

The shift toward the visual and changes in verbal style required new kinds of literacy from audiences. Visual messages relied on familiarity with a set of visual abstractions – icons and references. Even as they were in competition with one another for consumers' dollars, advertisers were also riding along in one another's audience-acculturating slipstream, inadvertently aiding one another in cultivating audiences' interpretive capacities. Every advertiser relied on audiences' familiarity with the "bewildering matrix of signs" employed in advertising communications, a familiarity built up from repeated exposure to such advertisements, including those of competitors. "As they constructed the language of advertising over time, so could regular readers gradually take in its principles and join in the production of its meanings" (Ohmann 1996, p. 193). Concise codes for connecting meanings to commodities take many repetitions to establish, but the repetition then makes each individual advertisement more effectively communicative, another way in which we can see an intensification of attention mining.

As advertising content preparation and media placement selection specialized and advertising agencies, with their multiple departments devoted to these various tasks, worked hard to claim the mantle of professionalism, they also attempted to test results. Selecting media for placements on the basis of known reader characteristics and pointing to the excellence of the content on its literary or artistic merits is all well and good, but advertising professionals wanted to be able to demonstrate their effects on audiences. "In theory," writes Pamela Laird, "good copy has always been defined as copy that sold the advertised product or service. Yet measuring selling efficacy has never been as easy as comparing copy with conventions and other fabricated criteria. And determining whether a product or service sold or not because of its advertisements has never been as easy as correlating promotional practices with sales figures and assuming causal links" (Laird 1998, p. 275). But advertising professionals worked hard to make a persuasive case that advertising's effects were measurable and real.

The nascent academic field of psychology was linked with the pursuit of advertising effectiveness through the work of men like Harlow Gale and Walter Dill Scott. Gale's experiments began in 1895 when he was hired at the University of Minnesota's experimental psychology lab (Eighmey and Sar 2007). An intense "courtship" between the advertising industry and the psychology profession was clearly underway in 1901 with Scott's speaking appearance at a business convention. The "relationship was in full bloom" by around 1910 (Olney 1991, p. 174). Scott's 1903 book *The Psychology of Advertising* synthesized the state of knowledge in this new field and was reprinted a number of times in the following years. Gale seems to have been first, but then Scott and others, too, tested readers' attention and retention in their laboratories; they showed magazine pages (taken from publications as-is or mock-ups varying one element at a time) to participants and tested their reactions to assess how advertisement size, placement, visual and verbal content, and surrounding context affected associations with or recall of the advertised products (Eighmey and Sar 2007; Scott 1910 [1908]). Such experiments offered a veneer of scientific certainty to advertising professionals' expert recommendations. Advertising professionals also adopted the language of scientific management. They asserted that audiences, like the workers in a Taylorized workplace, need not be persuaded through reason, but could be trained through repetition to adopt the new consumption habits desired by the sellers. They offered scientific-sounding explanations of how their techniques could produce those desired changes in consumers' mental states, without the consumers even becoming aware of how or why they held such positive views of the advertised products and companies (Casson 1911; Hopkins 1966 [1923]). As advertising professionals' gained confidence in their ability to consciously shape audiences' unconscious habits of mind, they and the advertisers who hired them gained confidence that advertising could generate new demand. That is, ambitious advertisers need not limit themselves to informing the people who already wanted their products about where to find them. They could make people want their products (Laird 1998, pp. 277–279). "When folks want to buy any fool can sell them. When folks don't want to buy advertising must help to make them buy" (Fowler 1900 [1897], p. 39).

Advertising professionals not only sought to apply the lessons of the laboratory to the real-world business environment; they sought to turn the real world of business into a laboratory. Early in the twentieth century, avid experimenters like Claude Hopkins and Albert Lasker adopted techniques for assessing and revising advertising campaign strategies (Fox 1997, pp. 50–54; Hopkins 1966 [1927]). In 1904, for example, Lasker, working at the Lord & Thomas advertising agency with John E. Kennedy (the copywriter who had worked full time for Wannamaker in the 1880s), ran a test on the advertisements a client was running. By keying the ads, they could determine which placements generated inquiries. (The "key" could be varying the format of the address to which readers were instructed to send inquiries, and then making note of how inquiries were addressed as they came in, in order to correlate them with the publication. Or the advertisement could include an inquiry form for readers to fill out and send in and the form could include a code.) They were able to calculate that the clients' existing ads were spectacularly ineffective, costing them $20 per inquiry. Kennedy wrote the copy for a new advertisement, tested it in $715 worth of placements across a few publications, and generated 1,547 inquiries, for a per-inquiry cost of only 47¢. On the basis of such experience, in 1904 and 1905 advertising agency Lord & Thomas's house organ *Judicious Advertising* published a series of articles by Kennedy on keying and testing ads. The articles were then gathered into a pamphlet called *The Book of Advertising Tests*; their printing department was overwhelmed with requests for the book (Cruikshank and Schultz 2010, pp. 59–61). The more mail-dependent and/or credit-dependent a business was in their communications with consumers, the more possible it was to track every stage of the seller-consumer relationship. If an advertisement prompted a consumer to walk into a store and buy an item in cash without giving their name or referencing the ad they'd seen, the seller might never know who made the purchase or what contributed to making the sale. But if a mail order company ran a keyed ad, received an inquiry, followed up by sending a catalog, and then made a sale, they could track the pathway from advertising expenditure to sales revenue through the responses of individual consumers.

Advertising professionalism boosters like Claude Hopkins paid close attention to feedback: sales figures, audience response data, claiming that this took advertising away from intuition toward science (Laird 1998, pp. 276–277). Despite this gesture toward data and objective market research, for the most part "it was specialists' intuitions and biases that began to replace advertisers' intuitions and biases" rather than science replacing hunches. The specialists had to convince clients that their specialist intuition was superior (Laird 1998,

p. 255). They leaned on the language of science to make their case. Charles McGovern writes, "They became professionals, cultivating their expertise and selling it as a specialized, exclusive commodity. . . . Like other professionals, advertisers organized to promote their expertise and to serve as gatekeepers to professional practice" (McGovern 2006, p. 25).

Intensive strategies for attention use rewarded large scale. Advertising agency compensation was still based on a more-or-less fixed commission of the print media placements, so their revenue growth was more-or-less linear with respect to the value of the placements they brokered. The costs of providing creative services were large and mostly invariant with respect to the value of the placements brokered. It only paid for agencies to employ specialized creative workers if they applied their skills to advertising campaigns with large print-media buys. Large-scale national brand-name advertisers with large advertising budgets could hire a large agency to make a large number of placements, and the high fixed cost of art and copy could be spread over a large enough number of eyes to make sense. This expense devoted to creative work was feasible for agencies at large scale, and also plausibly useful to advertisers. Suppose effective art and copy could inspire just a one percentage point increase in the response rate among viewers of an advertisement. If that advertisement was seen by ten million viewers, a one percentage point increase in audience response could mean a hundred thousand additional sales, and more than that if those inspired to be first-time buyers became habitual buyers. Even for promotion of a ten-cent product, the salary of a superstar copywriter could make some sense in these circumstances.[8] Agencies could not, however, offer comparable creative services to small-scale clients.

Advertising professionals advocate changed business practices for advertisers and publishers

Advertising aimed not only to inform customers of how to fulfill existing demand, but to stimulate new demands for hitherto unfamiliar goods. Similarly, advertising agents aimed not only to inform advertisers of how to fulfill their existing demand for audience attention, but to stimulate new demands for audience attention. As agents positioned themselves on the side of advertisers in negotiations with publishers, they also worked hard to persuade advertisers to adopt advertising-intensive modes of marketing – which would necessitate purchasing more audience attention, leading to greater commissions for agents. Persuading advertisers to use advertising agents' services was central to the agents' business – Francis Ayer, head of one of the largest advertising agencies of the late nineteenth century, said that selling his own services occupied the majority of his work time; filling orders was secondary to soliciting them (Laird 1998, p. 160). Client by client, advertising agents before 1900 promoted sales strategies that relied on print media advertising by giving free, ad-hoc advice to advertisers. Some also engaged in larger communications campaigns. Rowell started the advertising industry journal *Printers' Ink* in 1888; the primary target audience was not advertising industry professionals, but advertisers. Rowell told them, "Advertising is not simply to tell people who want hats where to find them, but to make them want hats, or think they do." (Laird 1998, p. 163) If advertising agents could persuade advertisers to persuade people that they want hats, the result could (perhaps) be increased sales of hats and would (definitely) be increased sales of advertising space.

Convincing businesses to advertise was a tough sell at first. Nineteenth-century banks considered advertising a sign of weakness, which meant that advertising could make the business appear risky to the banks and thus constrain their access to credit (Fox 1997, p. 15). But advertising agents kept at it. "Space brokering's rewards were directly proportional to the space sold," writes Pamela Laird, "and the records of the early advertising agents are full of prideful tales of successful forays into the business world to solicit and encourage clients" (Laird 1998, p. 160). And within a few decades, the business style changed and advertising became an assumed matter of course. Advertising agents' cultivation of clients cannot be the only explanation; advertisers had to determine through experience that advertising served their business interests, and many interlocking aspects of the business environment contributed to making advertising-intensive sales strategies a new norm in many industries (Chandler 2002 [1977]; Laird 1998; Pope 1983; Porter and Livesay 1971; Strasser 1989; Also see Chapter 1).

An important component of the shift in sales strategies was manufacturers' move to use branding to gain bargaining power over retailers. This strategy relied on manufacturers communicating directly to consumers through advertising and relied on consumers to accept no substitutes from their retailer (McGovern 2006, p. 81). Advertising agents were cheerleaders for brand-name manufacturers' efforts. Artemas Ward was among the most voluble agents on this topic. He encouraged brand-name manufacturers to use available legal means to combat substitutions and encouraged newspapers to editorialize on this topic. Since publishers' revenues depended on advertising, he pointed out, it would be in editors' self-interest to side with the big advertisers on this issue. If a manufacturer's advertisements only succeeded in stimulating demand for a product type rather than a specific branded product, the manufacturer's rivals stood to gain from the advertising. He claimed that when undermined by substitutions, advertisers spent more (gross) on advertising than they retained (net) in profits, but that with appropriate protection against the perfidy of substituting retailers, advertising could generate net gains in profitability (Laird 1998, p. 162). Publisher Cyrus Curtis, too, encouraged national advertisers to build a brand reputation rather than a short-term sales-boosting strategy. "By dissuading advertisers from withdrawing programs that did not achieve fast results, Curtis prompted advertisers to study feedback patterns and to attempt to find unique ways to present their wares for forming strong and productive associations in the readers' memories" (Laird 1998, p. 224). He also gained predictable, long-term, high-volume advertising space sales for his publications.

Not only did advertising agents want to persuade sellers to advertise, they wanted to persuade them to use professional advertising services. In *Fowler's Publicity*, first published 1897 and reissued several times, Nathaniel Fowler worked on this persuasive effort. The book was an encyclopedic guide to advertising media, strategies, and content design, with detailed information about the nitty-gritty of the tasks involved in advertising, down to the matter of selecting font styles and sizes. Yet it was *not* a do-it-yourself guide. Instead, it was meant to make sellers more confident and extensive purchasers of the services of experts. Fowler insisted that the creation of advertising content should be left to the communications professionals. "Don't write your own advertisements if you can find somebody else to write them for you," he warned. (He was, after all, a freelance copywriter!) All the expense of putting your advertisement before the eyes of the public is wasted if the advertisement is not attractive enough to catch and hold the public's attention and to convey your message (Fowler 1900 [1897], pp. 40, 261, 344–345, 694–696). Fowler wished to convince his readers not only that column space was an item of merchandise, but that content, too, was better bought than self-produced. This was typical of the extensive "how to advertise" business literature genre.

Sometimes advertising professionals' influence on advertisers became more granular, not just advocating for greater advertising intensity in selling their current products, but shifting manufacturers' product mix, product design, and production volumes. In the first decade of the 1900s, for example, Quaker had some successful product lines and some that lagged. They were willing to spend up to $50,000 to promote one of their underperforming products and left it to superstar copywriter Claude Hopkins at their advertising agency Lord & Thomas to decide which one; whichever Hopkins thought he could sell, Quaker would invest in. Hopkins decided he thought he could sell the Puffed Wheat and Puffed Rice cereals and Quaker followed his advice, investing in the production and marketing of that product rather than others. (After the initial misstep of investing in newspaper advertising, placements that reached too many people with insufficient income to be interested in a 10- or 15-cent box of cereal, Hopkins' copy was placed in magazines with more affluent readers and the cereals became highly profitable) (Cruikshank and Schultz 2010, pp. 102–104; Hopkins 1966 [1927], pp. 146–149). Production decisions could thus be influenced not only by existing demand and existing supply conditions, but by advertising professionals' judgments about the products for which they could stimulate demand. Furthermore, advertising professionals' judgments could influence not only the production volume and promotional budgets, but the design of the products and their packaging.

The needs and desires of advertisers, needs and desires which were shaped in part by the expert advice of advertising professionals, influenced publishers. As publishers became more financially dependent on advertising revenue than subscriptions, their financial success became more dependent on packaging the readers that advertisers wanted to buy and compiling a publication that offered a congenial setting for advertising content.

Urban newspapers shifted from simply reporting news to "creating a mental world for the uprooted farmers and villagers who were coming to live in the city. City residents experience "a much larger number of more superficial human relationships" than do rural and small-town folks. The newspapers used gossipy, human interest stories to both interpret and supply some sense of human intimacy in urban settings. Additionally, as dailies needed enough content every day to serve as attention bait around the increasing volume of advertising, publishers and editors became more active news makers. "The papers made news in a double sense; they *created* reportable events, whether by sending Nelly Bly around the world or by helping to stir up a war with Spain. They also *elevated* events, hitherto considered beneath reportorial attention, to the level of news occurrences by clever, emotionally colored reporting. They exploited human interest, in short" (Hofstadter 1972 [1955], pp. 187–188). Urbanization was a massive social change and created a necessity for new practices of meaning-making. Print was the likeliest medium available for the mass communication that large agglomerations of people would need. There were many conflicting interests at play and there was no necessity that the interests of advertisers should come to dominate. Yet they did.

The conflicts were visible even at the time. E.L. Godkin, writing in *The Atlantic* in January 1898 lamented advertisers' power over public opinion. "The advertiser, rather than the subscriber, is now the newspaper bogie. He is the person before whom the publisher cowers and whom he tries to please. . . . There are not many newspapers which can afford to defy a large advertiser" (quoted in Fox 1997, p. 66). Advertisers were often very deliberate about exploiting publishers' reliance on advertising revenue. In the first decade of the 1900s AT&T, for example, wanted positive press coverage to help legitimate its monopoly position. The first step in their strategy was to pay for a lot of advertising space. Once publications were used to those dollars of income, they tended to be very compliant about placing favorable articles provided to them by AT&T. A 1909 letter from the editor of *Moody's Magazine*, H.W. Pool, to AT&T's public relations manager James Ellsworth, made the relationship between positive press coverage and advertising dollars explicit. Pool wrote to Ellsworth to offer him the back page of the magazine as a prominent advertising placement, and pointed out that it would be even more effective since the magazine would be running a complimentary article about AT&T inside (Ewen 1996, pp. 87, 96).

The turn-of-the-twentieth-century genre of muckraking was a case study in the conflicts created by advertising dependence. Publishers pursued muckraking in part because of reader interest. They could assemble large audiences with their shocking exposés, then sell advertising space around the exposé articles, and this profit opportunity motivated many an investigation. But, as Hofstadter explains, "The large magazine built on muckraking was vulnerable as a business organization." The publishers could not survive without advertising revenues; the advertisers were their primary customers. This placed limits on acceptable subjects for investigations. "Advertisers did not hesitate to withdraw orders for space when their own interests or related interests were touched upon." Advertisers had allies in their application of pressure. Bankers were discriminatory in their lending policies and regularly denied loans to publishers suffering the sudden loss of a big advertiser. It is also probably the case that audiences reached saturation and sank into outrage fatigue. In the nineteenth century, patent medicine companies often had clauses in contracts with newspapers that said that the contract would lapse if the state legislature in that newspapers' state passed any legislation damaging to patent medicine manufacturers' interests and sometimes also put explicit limitations on editorial content concerning patent medicines rather than relying on publishers to calculate their interest in opposing limitations on patent medicine sales. *Collier's* did publish a damning investigation of the patent medicine industry in 1905, which could be read as an indication that advertisers' interests did not always keep the lid on critical journalism. But it could also be read as evidence of how long advertisers could buy exemptions from criticism; the industry already represented a much smaller share of publishers' advertising revenues when the *Collier's* article was published. Such exposés notwithstanding, the advertising-funded business model for journalism was clearly not compatible with sustained critique of the largest and most powerful economic forces in the nation (Hofstadter 1972 [1955], pp. 192–194; Fox 1997, p. 66; Cruikshank and Schultz 2010, p. 98; Ohmann 1996, p. 123).

Walter Dill Scott's attention experiments showed that audience response to an advertisement was influenced by its context. For advertisers to get the greatest attention value from the space they purchased, they had to be concerned not only with editorial content, but about other ads. He suggested that publishers should exert some editorial control over the advertising content, lest an unattractive ad placed by one unskilled advertiser diminish the value of the advertising space in the eyes of more savvy advertisers (Scott 1910 [1908], p. 50). Curtis agreed with Scott and had already begun introducing such practices before Scott's book was published. In 1892, he hired a copywriter, a typesetter, and an artist to improve on the designs submitted by advertisers (at a time when only two advertising agencies had full-time copywriters on staff) and he exerted control over content and style to maintain the magazine's "look"; he forbade overcrowded, heavy type, for example. Once he was powerful and prominent enough that he could afford to turn down a space buyer, Curtis censored items that could advertise in the *Ladies' Home Journal*, which gave an implicit seal of approval to those whose ads were included. In 1910 Curtis published *The Curtis Advertising Code*, which stipulated such rules as no fraudulent ads, no "extravagantly worded" ads, no disparagement of competitors, no alcohol, no patent medicines, no mail-order, nor any other business that Curtis objected to either because of the product or because of the conduct of the company (Laird 1998, pp. 223–225). In this instance, Curtis' (not necessarily monetary) value judgments could override the plans of an individual advertiser, but even a publisher who could not afford to be so personally fastidious could make an estimate of how much more valuable their advertising space would be to those advertisers they did sell to if they refused to sell to advertisers whose placements degraded the value of neighbors. Even while trying to distinguish themselves, advertisers expected to be known in part by the company they kept.

Conclusion

Popular culture came to be steeped in print media at the same time that print media came to be saturated by advertising. The set of circumstances that allowed for media with wide geographic and socioeconomic reach, which in turn gave a growing share of the population access to a shared set of cultural referents to deploy in their own meaning-making, also gave advertisers a dominant influence in shaping the media. Publishers dependent on advertising as their main source of revenue, as some publishers were as early as the 1830s and as the average publisher was by 1900, had to attract readers. But needing to attract readers does not mean that publishers could give readers anything and everything readers might want; rather, publishers had to lure readers in ways that were consistent with the sales goals of the advertisers. Neither reader nor advertiser was entirely sovereign in shaping publishers' choices about the forms and content of print media, but on balance advertisers held the advantage.

Turn-of-the-twentieth-century advertisers liked to address consumers as though they were citizens "voting" with dollars or even as kings with sovereignty to choose freely. After all, no one could be forced to buy a particular consumer product and even those barred from voting in elections (all women in most elections, most or all black men in most elections, noncitizens – and this was the time when the foreign-born share of the population was at its historical high) could spend whatever money they had (McGovern 2006, pp. 75–77). For the most part, sellers had to persuade rather than coerce buyers. But in the attention market, whatever degree of consumer sovereignty there was belonged to the attention buyers: the advertisers. Whoever pays the piper calls the tune, and the publishers were paid primarily by the advertisers.

When advertising agents drifted away from their close affiliation with publishers to ally more closely with advertisers, the advertiser-agent alliance successfully pressured publishers to standardize the packages of reader attention they sold. By 1920, advertisers had gained far more precise and more reliable information about the quantity, qualities, and unit price of the audiences they bought (or considered but chose not to buy) than they had been able to access before 1900. Advertisers could, usually with the professional guidance of advertising agents, select and address audiences quite deliberately rather than riskily casting their sales pitches into the dimly perceived currents of print media circulation. The most pressing financial incentive for publishers, therefore, was to assemble readers into packages compatible with advertisers' sales strategies. "The closer the adaptation of the goods advertised to the readers, the more [a publication's] space is worth per copy," Fowler said (Fowler 1900 [1897], p. 358). And the reverse is also true: a publication that gathers readers adapted to the goods advertised raises its value to advertisers. There are other purposes for which a mass medium could be employed to foster a shared consciousness among readers. There were Populist papers rhetorically punching up against big business and down against new immigrants, muckraking journals exposing corruption, African American newspapers committed to racial uplift, and others that were more mission-driven than profit-driven. Those publishers treating readers as the raw material to deliver into advertisers' cultural and economic interventions, however, were the best-resourced and most financially sustainable, and they commanded the largest share of Americans' collective attention.

Notes

1 Francis Wayland Ayer was the founder and "son" of the N.W. Ayer and Son agency; the senior Ayer's name was meant to convey gravitas, but the son is the one who ran the business from the beginning.
2 The table combines multiple sources of information and the counts may not be exactly comparable – it seems unlikely that so much of the growth in the number of dailies happened precisely in the single year from 1899 to 1900, for example. Nevertheless, the sources are consistent in documenting a steep growth trend and are at least approximately consistent in documenting levels.
3 If bold enough to consume it, they might discover that they could get drunk on it – some but not all formulas were alcohol-heavy – but there were more clearly marked routes to acquire alcohol.
4 The two sources give different counts for 1880. The higher count probably uses a broader definition of "magazine" to include those published at various frequencies; Sherman's lower count is specifically restricted to monthly magazines only. There was, in any event, some blurring at the boundary between weekly newspaper and magazine.
5 Especially before 1850, the same content could serve both ends because many publishers did not make any distinction between commercial and noncommercial copy. They would gladly publish "puff pieces," that is, favorable articles paid for and usually supplied by the subject of the article. These were not distinguished from editorial content (Laird 1998, p. 59). Norms for how clearly the boundary between editorial and sponsored copy must be marked have shifted in both directions in the intervening years. At the end of the century, Fowler explained the benefits and risks of puff pieces disguised as editorial content: if the source remained undiscovered, it was read more credulously to the benefit of the puff piece's sponsor; if the source was discovered, the reader would be disgusted and the advertiser's reputation would be injured (Fowler 1900 [1897], pp. 456–457).
6 All figures are in current dollars, not adjusted for inflation.
7 The Advertising Clubs of America, founded in 1904 and later renamed the Associated Advertising Clubs of the World (American Advertising Federation 2019), was already actively promoting the professionalization of advertising, organizing conventions, serving as an umbrella organization for more specialized advertising industry groupings, and publishing a large volume of pro-advertising industry literature by then. The Associated Advertising Clubs of America, later renamed the Advertising Federation of America, was founded in 1905 and undertook similar activities (Myers 1960, p. 308). Both AAC of A and AAC of W were particularly active in promoting truth in advertising standards. These groups were not specifically devoted to agents' interests when they were in conflict with publishers or advertisers, however.
8 John E. Kennedy made $16,000 in 1904, a staggering sum at the time and more than ten times what his average copywriting colleagues were making (Cruikshank and Schultz 2010, p. 56).

Bibliography

American Advertising Federation. Accessed 2019. *Advertising Hall of Fame Website*. www.advertisinghall.org/members/member_bio.php?memid=596

Casson, Herbert. 1911. *Advertisements and Sales: A Study of Advertising and Selling from the Standpoint of the New Principles of Scientific Management*. Chicago, IL: A. C. McClurg.

Chandler, Alfred. 2002 [1977]. *The Visible Hand: The Managerial Revolution in American Business*. Cambridge, MA: Belknap Press.

Cruikshank, Jeffrey L., and Arthur W. Schultz. 2010. *The Man Who Sold America: The Amazing (but True!) Story of Albert D. Lasker and the Creation of the Advertising Century*. Boston: Harvard Business Review Press.

Curtis Publishing Company. 1923. *What Is Circulation?* Philadelphia: Curtis Publishing Company.

De Weese, Truman. 1908 [1906]. *The Principles of Practical Publicity*, 2nd Edition. Philadelphia: George W. Jacobs & Co.

Eighmey, John, and Sela Sar. 2007. "Harlow Gale and the Origins of Psychology in Advertising." *Journal of Advertising* Volume 36: 147–158.

Ewen, Stuart. 1996. *PR! A Social History of Spin*. New York: Basic Books.

Faust, Drew Gilpin. 2008. *This Republic of Suffering: Death and the American Civil War*. New York: Vintage Books.

Fowler, Nathaniel C. 1900 [1897]. *Fowler's Publicity: An Encyclopedia of Advertising and Printing, and All That Pertains to the Public-Seeing Side of Business*. Boston: Publicity Publishing Company.

Fox, Stephen. 1997. *The Mirror Makers: A History of American Advertising and Its Creators*. Urbana and Chicago, IL: University of Illinois Press.

Fuller, Wayne E. 1991. "The Populists and the Post Office." *Agricultural History* Volume 65: 1–16.

Gallagher, Winifred. 2016. *How the Post Office Created America*. New York: Penguin Press.

Glavis, George. 1913. "The Worth of a Subscription List to Advertisers." *Printers' Ink* Volume 84 Number 2: 86–91.

Goodrum, Charles, and Helen Dalrymple. 1990. *Advertising in America: The First 200 Years*. New York: Henry N. Abrams.

Henkin, David M. 2006. *The Postal Age: The Emergence of Modern Communications in Nineteenth-Century America*. Chicago, IL: University of Chicago Press.

Hofstadter, Richard. 1972 [1955]. *The Age of Reform: From Bryan to F.D.R.* New York: Alfred A. Knopf.

Hopkins, Claude. 1966 [1927 and 1923]. *My Life in Advertising and Scientific Advertising*. Chicago, IL: Advertising Publications, Inc.

Jevons, W. Stanley. 1866 [1865]. *The Coal Question: An Inquiry Concerning the Progress of the Nation, and the Probable Exhaustion of Our Coal-Mines*, 2nd Edition. London: Palgrave Macmillan and Company.

Kielbowicz, Richard B. 1989. *News in the Mail: The Press, Post Office, and Public Information, 1700–1860s*. New York: Greenwood Press.

Kielbowicz, Richard B. 1990. "Postal Subsidies for the Press and the Business of Mass Culture, 1880–1920." *The Business History Review* Volume 64: 451–488.

Laird, Pamela Walker. 1998. *Advertising Progress: American Business and the Rise of Consumer Marketing*. Baltimore: The Johns Hopkins University Press.

Lamoreaux, Naomi. 1985. *The Great Merger Movement in American Business, 1895–1904*. Cambridge and New York: Cambridge University Press.

MacFarlane, Charles Alexander. 1915. *The Principles and Practice of Direct Advertising*. Hamilton, OH: The Beckett Paper Company.

McGovern, Charles F. 2006. *Sold American: Consumption and Citizenship, 1890–1945*. Chapel Hill, NC: The University of North Carolina Press.

Myers, Kenneth. 1960. "ABC and SDRS: The Evolution of Two Specialized Advertising Services." *The Business History Review* Volume 34: 302–326.

Officer, Lawrence H., and Samuel H. Williamson. 2019. "The Annual Consumer Price Index for the United States, 1774-Present." *Measuring Worth*. www.measuringworth.com/uscpi/

Ohmann, Richard. 1996. *Selling Culture: Magazines, Markets, and Class at the Turn of the Century*. London and New York: Verso.

Olney, Martha. 1991. *Buy Now, Pay Later: Advertising, Credit, and Consumer Durables in the 1920s*. Chapel Hill, NC and London: The University of North Carolina Press.

Pope, Daniel. 1983. *The Making of Modern Advertising*. New York: Basic Books.

Porter, Glenn, and Harold C. Livesay. 1971. *Merchants and Manufacturers: Studies in the Changing Structure of Nineteenth-Century Marketing*. Baltimore: Johns Hopkins Press.

Post Office Department. 1956. *United States Domestic Postage Rates, 1789–1956*. Fishkill, NY: The Printer's Stone.

Printers' Ink. 1913. "How Many Advertisers?" Volume 84 Number 4: 153.

Rowell, George P. 1869. *Rowell's American Newspaper Directory*. New York: Rowell.

Rowell, George P. 1877. *Rowell's American Newspaper Directory*. New York: Rowell.

Rowell, George P. 1906. *Forty Years an Advertising Agent, 1865–1905*. New York: Printers' Ink Publishing Company.

Rowell, George P. 1909. *Rowell's American Newspaper Directory*. New York: Rowell.

Scott, Walter Dill. 1910 [1908]. *The Psychology of Advertising: A Simple Exposition of the Principles of Psychology in Their Relation to Successful Advertising*, 2nd Edition. Boston: Small, Maynard & Company.

Sherman, Sidney. 1900. "Advertising in the United States." *Publication of the American Statistical Association* Volume 7 Number 52: 119–162.

Strasser, Susan. 1989. *Satisfaction Guaranteed: The Making of the American Mass Market*. New York: Pantheon Books.

Waldron, George B. 1903. "What America Spends in Advertising." *Chautauquan* Volume 38: 155–159.

Warner, John DeWitt. 1900. "Advertising Run Mad." *Municipal Affairs* Volume 4: 267–293.

Wu, Tim. 2016. *The Attention Merchants: The Epic Scramble to Get Inside Our Heads*. New York: Alfred A. Knopf.

3 Pricing the eyes of passersby

Outdoor advertising

Introduction

In the closing decades of the nineteenth century, poster advertising proliferated, more advertisers took up the medium, and the business practices of billposters modernized. Unfortunately, thorough aggregate data for the medium of poster advertising are all but nonexistent. We know, however, that it grew from a medium used exclusively by traveling circuses, local theater, and patent medicines to a major advertising venue for large-scale respectable retailers and national manufacturers of branded goods. Billposting businesses detailed in the billposters' leading professional journal are a sampling, not an aggregate, but they are suggestive. In the summer of 1900, the northern California outdoor advertising firm of Owens, Varney, and Green was posting approximately 150,000 sheets per month. They had boards in San Francisco (population 340,000), where they charged 12¢ per sheet per month and also in Oakland and a handful of small nearby towns where they charged from 5¢ to 7¢ per sheet, which would yield yearly revenues on the order of $150,000 to $200,000. There were approximately 40 cities of at least 100,000 population in which a billposter belonging to the Associated Billposters was at work, most of them charging at least 12¢ per sheet. A second tier of more than a hundred mid-sized plants in smaller cities would have been doing business in the tens of thousands of dollars yearly and 500 smaller-scale members of the national association were doing business on the order of several hundred to several thousand dollars a year (Associated Billposters Association of the United States and Canada July 1900, pp. 17, 28). On the demand side, in 1900, the American Tobacco Company spent $600,000 on billboard advertising of cigars alone (Sherman 1900, p. 134). This indicates that circa 1900 the total revenues of the billposting industry were in the tens of millions of dollars a year, smaller than publishers' advertising revenues but a significant share of the advertising industry.

The outdoor advertising supply chain

To serve advertisers' pursuit of eyeballs in public spaces, the outdoor advertising industry professionalized in the late nineteenth century. What had been an arena of lawless, no-guarantees attempts to grab attention developed into a much more standardized, predictable mode of doing business. The earlier state of affairs had advertisers order broadsides from a printer and then hire a bill-poster to paste them up. The billposter was equipped with a bucket of paste and a brush but neither owned nor leased nor otherwise secured exclusive rights to any display space. Rather, he (billposters were so far as we know all men) pasted the broadsides on any convenient surface, at which point his obligation to the advertiser had been fulfilled. The owner of the fence or wall might tear the poster down, or another billposter might paste over it, but that was of no concern to the billposter. Alternatively, he could paste a few posters where the advertiser would be likely to see them, dump the rest in the river, and claim to have fulfilled his obligation. It would be hard for the advertiser to know the difference.

Beginning in a small way in the 1870s and in a large way in the 1890s, billposters took on responsibility not only for applying the advertisers' post-ers to vertical surfaces but for supplying the surfaces and maintaining the dis-play for an agreed-upon period of time. The billposter's obligation no longer began with the receipt of the broadsides and ended when the last sheet was affixed to fence, wall, or earlier poster. Instead, the billposter's work began with leasing space (land, walls, or rooftops) from landowners and erecting a bill-board on that space. Billposters referred to their collection of billboards as their "plant" and sought to entice advertisers by touting the size and quality of their plant. The advertiser could then contract with the billposter for the posters to be displayed in particular locations for a specified period of time. Following the long-familiar paste and brush portion of the process,[1] the billposter took responsibility for inspecting the displays regularly, repairing any that were dam-aged, and neither pasting over nor allowing others to paste over the poster until the length of display in the contract was fulfilled. This was known as listed and protected service – listed because the billposter supplied to the advertiser a list of locations where the posters had been hung which made verification far easier, and protected because the display was protected for the length of the contract (Associated Billposters Association of the United States and Canada Sept. 1897, pp. 10–11). The fee an advertiser paid to a billposter had in an earlier era been a payment for a task – the task of hanging posters. With listed and pro-tected service, it became a payment for access to audience attention. Audience attention had always been the aim and the hope, but now there was something far closer to a guarantee.

The content component of the poster advertising process changed with the rise of billboards and the dramatic development of lithography technique. The printing industry was split into two major sectors: lithographers producing color images usually with little text and traditional printers of usually minimally illustrated text; they used different tools and different techniques and special-ized in different products. Lithographers rather than job printers became the primary suppliers of posters. As they did for trade cards, in-store display materi-als, and all manner of advertising ephemera, lithographers had a large catalog of stock images for advertising posters so that advertisers without the budget to design or commission an original poster could select an already-extant image and customize it with their business's name and address. This was the largest component of the lithographers' business, although as early as the 1870s national brands began collaborating with lithographers to design custom-made, brand-specific posters (Laird 1998, p. 79).

The development of a market in outdoor advertising space-over-time operated in a reciprocal relationship with the development of the lithographers' art. Poster design shifted quickly to emphasize colorful images over black block text. Posters got larger and a standardized selection of sizes emerged from the interplay between poster production and board construction. Billboards were sized to fit the standard posters and posters were sized to fit the standard billboards (Poster Advertising Association January 1920, p. 53). A standard sheet of poster paper was 28 inches high by 42 inches wide, a poster's size was designated by the number of sheets, and billposting services were priced per sheet for a month's display (Associated Billposters Association of the United States and Canada Aug. 1900, p. 13).

Just as newspaper advertising agents like George Rowell integrated the national market for the attention of newspaper readers, agents specializing in mediating billboard space transactions – known as solicitors in this sector of the attention market – integrated the national market in the attention of pedestrians, streetcar riders, and (later) motorists. Some billposters, such as O.J. Gude of New York, developed their businesses to a regional scale, but national placements still required contracting with many billposters. Solicitors allowed national advertisers to purchase placements all over the nation in one transaction. (Gude was both a solicitor and a billposter.) For those who still wanted to deal directly with the billposters, the leading professional organization cut the information-gathering portion of the task to nearly nil by publishing a national list of member billposters. The published list started as just a list of names and towns but grew to include additional information such as town populations and prices.[2]

Monopoly

Monopoly was critical to the modernization of the outdoor advertising industry. For billposters, establishing and sustaining local monopoly, in the sense of being the sole seller of billboard space in a particular geographic range, was an indispensable component of converting access to attention into salable property, that is, achieving monopoly in Edward Chamberlin's sense of the word: owner of their individual output (Chamberlin 1962 [1933]). In fact, until it was successfully suppressed, competition among billposters slowed innovation. The development of the billposting industry provides a case study in Joseph Schumpeter's theory of monopoly as a facilitator of dynamic innovation (Schumpeter 1942). Although Schumpeter was thinking of the development of new manufactured products, monopoly facilitated the creation of this new fictitious commodity, as well.

Schumpeter vigorously dissented from the economic orthodoxy that gives highly competitive markets all the credit for fostering efficiency. That analysis, he charged, was a static analysis. At any given moment using existing technology, price competition will indeed force producers to adopt the lowest-cost methods of production. But in a dynamic analysis, intense price competition ceases to look so conducive to productivity gains. Producers facing intense price competition are compelled to cut all costs not associated with short-term survival. They do not have the luxury of investing in product or process innovation. New product development and efficiency gains resulting from new technology are best developed over time when price competition is muted either by monopoly power or by an oligopolistic accord amongst producers. Far from being an enemy of modernization and progress, monopoly can facilitate innovation. In Schumpeter's model, market competition disciplines producers not through competitors' incremental increases in productivity but through the ever-present threat of a product or process innovation that will shake the market to its foundations (Schumpeter 1942). Sclerotic monopolies can and do exist, but survive only as long as they retain sufficient power to suppress the threat of new entries or product substitutes. The market discipline driving outdoor advertising innovation came from the presence of print-media advertising space as a substitute for billposting rather than from competition among billposters.

Competition among billposters, when it was not suppressed, hampered the transformation of billposting from a service with uncertain outcomes to the sale of access to attention in two ways. Both of the obstacles resulting from competition had to do not as much with the rules of competition as they had to do with the ease of breaking the rules and the pressure to do so. Competing billposters had no reason to respect one another's postings. In the early stages of the business none of them had property rights in the surfaces on which they posted and they freely and frequently posted over one another's posters, if the property owners did not tear the posters down first. The lack of property rights in surfaces left postings unprotected while the lack of respect for postings did nothing to encourage investment in specially designated poster surfaces. Just as competition gave billposters little regard for one another, competitive pressures also strained trust and respect between billposter and advertiser. Billposting presents a classic principal-agent conflict. It was difficult for advertisers to know whether billposters really had pasted up all the posters and where they were hung. "It used to be that quite a large proportion of paper given to billposters to post found its way into sewers and furnaces," admitted *Display Advertising*. Since they had so little confidence in the service, advertisers' willingness to pay was low, and the lower the price the less willing and able billposters were to provide meticulous service consistent with the interests of the advertiser (Associated Billposters Association of the United States and Canada December 1897, pp. 20–21).[3]

Monopoly provided an opportunity to overcome both of these problems. A monopolist billposter could charge higher prices and use the higher revenues for investment in product and process improvements, as Schumpeter's model predicts. With a monopolist's financial wherewithal and absence of competitors, the sole billposter in town could invest in billposting surfaces without worrying too much about theft of space or vandalism by a competitor. Or, if investment in space came first, the quality-of-service-based competitive advantage of having a large plant helped to secure a larger share of local business, leading to monopoly. Monopoly clearly eliminated conflicts among billposters by eliminating all but one billposter in a given geographic area. Monopoly also made it possible to ease principle-agent conflicts. Property rights in display spaces enabled billposters to guarantee unobstructed display for a contracted period of time. Advertisers and billposters could agree in advance on locations of display and the billposter could then send confirmation to the advertiser when the posting was completed, making it easier for advertisers to inspect the work. Without competitors posting over the posters, billposters had to worry then only about defacement by weather and teenagers, and their more capacious operating budgets allowed them to regularly inspect and repair the posters they hung until the end of the display contract.

Billposting is intrinsically a very place-bound business, but billposters found regional and national organization to be a useful tool in sustaining local monopoly. This was the impetus behind the formation of the Associated Billposters' Association of the United States and Canada.[4] The Association was formed in 1891 in a reorganization of the earlier International Billposters' Association of North America, which had been in existence since 1872. In 1906, the Associated Billposters' Association merged with some affiliated organizations, including the publisher of the Association's journal, and with a national association of distributors, forming the Associated Billposters and Distributors of the United States and Canada. In 1912 the organization was renamed the Poster Advertising Association. Later, another name change made it the Outdoor Advertising Association of America, which is still in operation (Fisk undated).

Protecting the shared interests of Association members generally required the Association to police members' behavior strictly. The Association held members to nationally set pricing standards and quality of service standards – at least until a Federal Court ruled in 1916 that the price-fixing policy was illegal (*Printers' Ink* 1922). The pricing and service standards were inseparable: quality service could not be provided at cut rates and high rates could not be justified without quality service. Local monopoly was an ironclad principle. The Association would admit only one member per town. If two billposters from the same town sought membership, the Association would assess both their applications and accept only one – if, indeed, they accepted either. Complete coverage of the US by Association billposters was an unwavering goal. The journal periodically printed a list of towns without a billposter and encouraged members to establish plants there. Expanding the Association's reach also involved eliminating non-members from the field. The Association considered towns where a billposter who was not an Association member was at work to be open towns. The Association's appeals for members to establish billposting plants in those towns meant going into business in opposition to existing non-member bill-posters with the clear goal of driving them out of business. The Association was strict with members and ruthless toward competitors. An Association member typically put his membership at risk if he engaged in price-cutting. However, the national office was willing to grant special dispensation for temporary rate cuts to meet competitors' prices until the competitors were driven out of business (Associated Billposters and Distributors of the United States and Canada 1906, p. 19).

Manufacturers of nationally branded goods increased their advertising spending rapidly during the late nineteenth century, faster than did local retailers (Laird 1998, p. 221). For outdoor advertising to be a part of campaigns conducted at a national scale – and national campaigns were a rising share of total advertising expenditure – billposters needed a mechanism of geographic market integration. For print media, the integration was accomplished by nationally distributed magazines and by advertising agents mediating contact between national advertisers and a very large number of newspapers with local distribution. The Associated Billposters addressed the challenges of national integration for poster advertising. Their membership lists made it easier for advertisers who wished to deal directly with billposters while posting in many cities. For cases where the advertiser wished to use a single solicitor to manage the dozens of local contracts needed for a national advertising campaign, designation of official solicitors and an insistence on standard, fixed prices and commissions helped protect billposters' interests when in conflict with the interests of solicitors. The formation of the Associated Billposters' Protective Company in 1900 to handle national poster placement contracts strengthened the billposters' control and bargaining strength in negotiations with advertisers and intermediaries (Associated Billposters Association of the United States and Canada February 1900, p. 14, April 1900, p. 9).

In the Associated Billposters' drive to dominate outdoor advertising, their strategy of national integration was complemented by aggressive geographic expansion. Following US territorial conquests, billposters wrote to the association journal from Indian Territory, the Philippines, and Cuba, celebrating newfound business opportunities. According to an article in the May 1902 issue of the *Billposter-Display Advertising*, the opportunity presented by Indian Territory depended on the growing number of white settlers – "Do you know that there are more white people in the Indian Territory than in Oklahoma?" – and on the suppression of American Indian cultural difference – "Do you know that there *are good* Indians who are not *dead*? . . . Do you know that there are blue-eyed, blond-haired Indians who teach music and art?" (Associated Billposters Association of the United States and Canada May 1902, p. 16). The following month, the *Billposter-Display Advertising* reprinted an article from *Printers' Ink* describing billposting conditions in Havana and seeking to put to rest fears that Cubans were racially, linguistically, or otherwise unfit audiences for US commercial communications. Many of them could not read English or could not read at all, but they showed great interest in posters, the article insisted, and the posters' clear graphics and limited text made it easy for Spanish-speaking Cubans to receive the message across the language and literacy divide (Associated Billposters Association of the United States and Canada June 1902, p. 14). The next year, an article describing billposting in Manila opened, "Whether the constitution should follow the flag or not is a controversial subject for statesmen to determine, but what is more important for advertisers, perhaps, is the fact that the billposter, with his brush, nerve, bundle of bills and a bucket of paste, is bound to follow close in the wake of a conquering column of Uncle Sam's warriors" (Associated Billposters Association of the United States and Canada September 1903, p. 5).

The Associated Billposters' aggressive expansion encompassed areas within the existing borders of the US, too, as more and more small towns and country routes came within the reach of some billposter's plant, typically by a billposter in a larger nearby town expanding his plant rather than by a newly established plant. Associated Billposter Association members were exhorted to expand into any as-yet unclaimed towns. "Every city of 1,000 population should have a billposting plant," a 1900 article opined. The volume of work would not make it a full-time job, but the profit rate would make it "worth the attention of a share of the time of a good man." Part of what made small towns potentially profitable was the low cost of space: "Locations can be obtained for a song." (A song, to be precise, was estimated to be equal to $100 maximum (Associated Billposters Association of the United States and Canada September 1900, p. 13).) Just as George Rowell had been able to interest Boston merchants in newspaper placements in the hinterlands in the 1860s (Rowell 1906), F.E. Fitch of Albany found in the 1900s that centrally located retailers were interested in his country route billposting service (Associated Billposters Association of the United States and Canada May 1902, p. 8), a discovery also made by other billposters in other places (Associated Billposters Association of the United States and Canada January 1903, p. 75). National manufacturers could also be persuaded to buy space on country route billboards, although developing country route services required billposters to advertise themselves to both regional and national advertisers so that potential clients would know that the service they wanted could now in fact be had (Associated Billposters Association of the United States and Canada February 1902, p. 6, May 1902, p. 8). Billposters characterized country consumers to advertisers as curious and eager, their capacity to pay attention to advertising appeals not yet stretched so thin as that of city residents (Associated Billposters Association of the United States and Canada March 1900, p. 23). Country route expansions challenged the association's local monopoly policy: as town billposters expanded, the territory they claimed sometimes overlapped and in 1900 the national association called upon the state-level associations to establish firm geographic boundaries (Associated Billposters Association of the United States and Canada May 1900, p. 17). Four months later only Indiana's state association had taken up this disciplinary/regulatory task, triggering a chiding commentary in the journal (Associated Billposters Association of the United States and Canada September 1900, p. 13). But at the same time that two billposters were vying for some towns, other towns were still left uncovered, and the Association's exhortations to expand continued.

Through national integration and the pooling of resources the Association could promote billboards as an advertising medium. From the beginning, their publications were intended to function as promotional literature for potential clients. In 1909 the Association established a national promotions bureau, devoting even more resources and focused attention to attracting national business and providing technical assistance to billposters seeking to increase their volume of local business. They established a separate journal dedicated specifically to addressing advertisers, separating that function from the association governance function of the organization's official journal (which by that time had been renamed *The Poster*) (Poster Advertising Association "A Chat with the Billposter" October 1909).

The Association was so confident in the justification for monopoly that they made no effort to dissemble about their purposes. Until 1909, the same journal that functioned as the main avenue of national-level internal communications doubled as a piece of promotional literature designed to persuade advertisers to use billboards. "Nothing will encourage your local merchants to adopt billposting more than a good knowledge of the medium. Let him read THE BILLPOSTER; it will give him the necessary information," encouraged the association in the September 1900 issue of the journal (Associated Billposters Association of the United States and Canada September 1900, p. 13). There were as many articles concerned with touting the benefits of outdoor advertising as there were articles dealing with organization politics, technical issues of running a billposting business, and so on. This meant that the sales pitch to potential clients came bound between the same covers as diatribes against rate-cutters. In effect, Association members promised potential customers that they would charge them more. The promise also, of course, included the clause that the higher price was worth it because the quality of the product was higher.

Their shamelessness was notable as the Association's regulation of prices was clearly an instance of price-fixing in violation of the Sherman Anti-Trust Act. Yet for years they got away with it. Though membership in the Association grew, making it harder and harder to post bills without Association membership, an opposition did exist. Billposters opposed to the Association were sufficiently numerous and organized to publish their own journal, *Billboard*, and the Association considered this enough of a threat that members found to subscribe to the opposition journal would be disciplined and solicitors found advertising in *Billboard* would be barred from doing business with Association members (Associated Billposters Association of the United States and Canada November 1899, pp. 9–10). The Association was finally called to task in 1916 when Judge Landis of the United States District Court in Chicago decreed that their price agreements and limitations on the number of entrants into the industry were illegal and the Association was enjoined from persisting in such practices.

The (now renamed) Poster Advertising Association argued that the organization was necessary for the welfare of the industry, and even as he ruled against them, Landis admitted that this had been the case. The Association appealed the decision, but in 1922 when the Supreme Court had not yet taken up the case, they decided to withdraw the appeal to avoid potential bad publicity and Judge Landis's decree was allowed to stand (*Printers' Ink* 1922). Price regulation had been central to the Association's mission, so Landis's decree prompted some rethinking of the mission and justification of the Association. By this time their activities were sufficiently diverse that the organization survived the blow and continued to exist as a professional development, promotional, lobbying, and legal aid organization (Poster Advertising Association 1919; see p. 29 of the August 1910 issue of *The Poster* for evidence of intensified lobbying and legal aid work before the decision).

Attaining a monopoly on the provision of billposting services fostered the attainment of a monopoly on audience attention. Attention is rival (meaning when used by one person or purpose it is less available to other users or purposes) and advertisers perceived it to be increasingly scarce – as early as the 1890s advertisers and advertising professionals were expressing concern about the difficulty of getting their messages through the overwhelming clutter of commercial communications. By attaining a capitalist monopoly of the billposting business, billposters made attention sufficiently excludable that they were able to collect a monopoly rent from advertisers for access to the eyes of passersby.

The usefulness of outdoor advertising to the advertiser was entirely tied to the number of gazes. In the absence of price competition driving prices down to the cost of providing the service, Association billposting rates were based primarily on the number of intercepted gazes, not cost. (Similarly, the sale of streetcar riders' attention was dominated by a few large firms who charged rates calculated on the basis of the length of the contract and the number of passengers carried (Sherman 1900, p. 127).) In 1906, for example, Association rates started at 7¢ per sheet for four weeks' display in the smallest cities and towns and increased with population. (See Table 3.1.) In the more populous cities, more people would pass by a given display, and billposters could charge more for those additional eyes.[5] The minimum rate for a single week's initial display or for "chance may offer" postings, meaning the posters would be hung if billboard space were available with no guaranteed start date or length of display and no inspection or repairs, was 4¢ per sheet. Member billposters were allowed to charge more than the Association minimum for a town of their size, but not less. Members quoting or working for rates lower than the Association minimum could be fined, suspended, or expelled from the organization (Associated Billposters and Distributors of the United States and Canada 1906, pp. 15–17).

Some small-town billposters complained that the minimum rate was too low to meet their costs of operation (Associated Billposters Association of the United States and Canada October 1903, p. 21) while others argued that it was sufficient. W. C. Tirrill of Lima, Ohio wrote into the journal to chide other

Table 3.1 Associated Billposters and Distributors of the United States and Canada minimum
billposting rates, 1906

Population	Price per sheet for four weeks	Rates for less than four weeks: if the four-week rate is	The first week costs	Second week	Third week	Fourth week
< 50,000	7¢	7¢	4	2	1	0
		8¢	4	2	1	1
50,000–100,000	9¢	9¢	4	3	1	1
		10¢	4	3	2	1
100,000–500,000	12¢	12¢	4	4	3	1
500,000–2,000,000	14¢	14¢	4	4	4	2
> 2,000,000	16¢	16¢	5	4	4	3

Source: Associated Billposters and Distributors of the United States and Canada 1906, Constitution and
By-Laws.

country members for their whining and to explain how he operated a small-
town business profitably on Association minimum rates (Associated Billposters
Association of the United States and Canada April 1899, p. 10); his detailed
cost accounting and instructions for erecting billboards with salvaged lumber
are oddly reminiscent of Thoreau's account of building his cabin at Walden
Pond. The chance may offer minimum is a reasonable approximation of the
cost of the initial poster hanging. Small-town minimum rates, which appeared
ample to some and insufficient to others, would seem on average to make a fair
approximation of the billposters' cost per sheet for four weeks' display, including
the regular inspections and possible repairs required after the initial hanging.
Price increments in excess of minimum rates are monopoly rents charged for
access to a larger (or for some reason more desirable) audience. The billposters'
costs were highest at the beginning of the period of display when posters had to
be pasted to the boards. In smaller cities, the rates for display times of less than
four weeks were more than half the full four-week rate. In large cities, however,
the monopoly rent was such a large component of the total price that even the
second and third weeks of display, when the billposter incurred few additional
costs, cost the advertiser as much as the first week.

During the 1910s the billposters' product descriptions, that is, their charac-
terizations of the local population, became more focused on quality claims in
addition to basic population numbers. The advertisers' ultimate goal, of course,
was to sell more goods, so they cared not only about the number of eyes but
the disposable incomes of the bearers of those eyes and billposters learned to
address those concerns directly. Billposters' own advertisements began to look a
lot like local boosterism and featured economic data such as per capita income,

occupational distribution, and major employers. For a less-biased account than that offered by billposters, advertisers could consult the *Mahin Advertising Data Book*, published regularly in the 1900s and 1910s, which reported economic data on populations in cities and towns nationwide using a standard format for all towns (Mahin 1908).[6] Although not promoting a particular locality, Mahin, a Chicago-based advertising agent who was also an official solicitor for the Associated Billposters, was in agreement with the self-promoting billposters' basic premise. The advertisers are interested in spending power, not just eyes.

Efficiency gains: lowering the cost per gaze

Audience compulsion

Urbanization was a boon to outdoor advertising. A billboard in a city street was seen by many more people than the painted side of a barn on a rural road. City dwellers were more dependent on purchased goods sooner than were rural folk, so they were an audience that many manufacturers very much wanted to reach. And urban people traveled daily between home and workplace, home and store, home and location of leisure, so there were many more opportunities to intercept their gaze than there were opportunities to catch the eyes of a farm family whose workplace was their home and surrounding fields. Too, the overall trend throughout this period was for people to travel farther and farther in their daily rounds. The development of transportation facilitated the geographic expansion of the city beyond the earlier dimensions of the walking city (Chudacoff and Smith 1994, pp. 77–107).

Urbanization accelerated in the late nineteenth century and by 1920 the US had reached a tipping point: half the population now lived in cities. Billposters did not create the newly emerging spatial patterns of residence, work, and shopping, but they harnessed these new patterns to their own profitable ends. Billposters' pitch to advertisers rested heavily on the degree of compulsion they could exercise over audiences. An advertisement on a printed page could be easily flipped past, but a large poster on a high-traffic street is guaranteed to enter the field of vision of all passersby. Daily commuters would be compelled to see that poster every day as long as it was displayed (Associated Billposters Association of the United States and Canada March 1900, p. 11).

While addressing the problem of local transportation, streetcars effectively channeled the population on the move through concentrated routes (Chudacoff and Smith 1994, pp. 82–90). Billposters with placements along streetcar routes to offer trumpeted the predictably high concentration of eyes passing by. Shoppers traveling by trolley, they crowed, could be compelled to see the advertisers' poster *while on their way to the stores*, already in a shopping frame of mind! Viewers of a newspaper ad sitting in their living rooms at home, by contrast, might easily forget the ad by the time they head out to shop hours or days later. (Specialists in advertising placements on the streetcars themselves could make the additional claim that streetcar riders would be sitting with the advertisement in their field of vision with little competition for their attention with "ample time" to study it (Fowler 1900 [1897], pp. 190–192).)

Automobiles opened up new possibilities for compelled viewing. Although not restricted to preset streetcar routes, they expanded the geographic range of travel, making more billboard placements possible. All passengers were compelled by the design of the automobile to sit facing forward and the driver was required by the nature of his (or, less often, her) task to look forward. A 1916 article in the *Poster* (as the journal had been renamed when the association became the Poster Advertising Association) hailed the automobile as an ally of poster advertising because, they averred, recreational motoring was displacing reading at home as a leisure activity. An analysis done in 1918 figured that a billboard placed at a curve in the road would occupy car drivers' and riders' field of vision for a full four seconds apiece, a guarantee no newspaper or magazine could make, at a cost of one-fifteenth of one cent per day per automobile (Poster Advertising Association April 1918, p. 31).

Complementing the compelled viewing time achieved by effective placements was extended viewing time achieved by illumination. The outdoor advertising industry was an early and enthusiastic adopter of electricity. Electric illumination allowed billposters and sign painters to tap into previously inaccessible hours of audience attention. By 1914 the R.C. Maxwell Company, a large sign-painting enterprise in New Jersey with a large share of the responsibility for transforming the Atlantic City boardwalk into a site of commercial cacophony, considered electric illumination to be so central to their business that they purchased an interest in the C & B Electric Sign Company. In 1920, R.C. Maxwell purchased the entire capital stock and in 1924 dissolved C & B as a separate business (R.C. Maxwell Collection, Box 1, Hartman Center). There is an element of compelled viewing to the illumination, as well, as illumination made advertisements among the most easily visible features of the nighttime streetscape.

Material inputs

Management of audiences was a form of efficiency gain. Increased population density and the increase in frequency and length of travel over predictable routes allowed a well-placed poster to enter the field of vision of many more people much more often than had been possible in the more agrarian recent past.[7] The field of psychology and the language and attitudes of scientific management sought efficiency in the design of advertising content, too. (See Chapter 2.) But refinement of audience wrangling technique was not the only means of increasing efficiency.

Although the commodity in question, attention, is immaterial, the means of producing it still relied on material inputs, some acquired through private investment, others through access to public infrastructure. Billposters making private investments in their firms experimented with billboard construction and paste production, and made significant plant and equipment improvements. Starch paste displaced flour paste (Associated Billposters Association of the United States and Canada February 1899, p. 11). Billposters hailed the introduction of iron billboards, finding that posters hung on iron needed far less maintenance than those hung on wood, reducing the need for replacement paper and labor time devoted to repair. Mr. Simmons of Duluth, Minnesota wrote that the higher initial construction cost was easily recovered through lower mainte-nance costs (Associated Billposters Association of the United States and Canada June 1903, p. 15). At an earlier link in the poster advertising supply chain, technological improvements in paper production and lithography also offered increased quality and decreased cost. Advertisers rather than billposters paid for the posters directly, but both stood to gain.

The substitution of cars for wagons improved efficiency for billposters with geographically dispersed plants, but this private investment was only beneficial when complemented by public investment in infrastructure. At the turn of the twentieth century, rural roads were impassable for portions of the year, mean-ing that country route billposting was a seasonal business. Road improvements could therefore extend the country route billboard's useful season (Associated Billposters Association of the United States and Canada February 1902, p. 6, January 1903, p. 37). Meanwhile, illumination extended the poster's working day by several hours, especially in the winter. Lighting a billboard in a northern city from 4:30 until 10:30 p.m. adds six extra hours of visibility to the nine daylight hours an unlit billboard could offer. But, like the investment in a car, investment in illuminating a particular billboard was dependent on infrastruc-ture beyond the individual billposter's direct control – in this case an electrical power grid.

Cost savings could also be squeezed from the support activities surrounding and sustaining the core business of pasting posters on surfaces in people's line of sight. Standardized, streamlined business practices included improved book-keeping practices and pre-printed, clearly formatted blanks for documenting listed and protected service, for invoicing customers, and for paying property owners. The specialized business communications of a good solicitor lowered transactions costs enough to offset the solicitor's commission.

Under the Associated Billposters' regime of administered prices, cost savings for the billposter were not motivated by the need to keep up with price com-petition. Neither did efficiency gains follow the arms-race dynamic of a price war. Instead, efficiency improvements widened billposters' profit margins and enabled them to increase the scale of their business. Locations that had been marginal could now be brought under cultivation; cities already within the Associated Billposters' territory became ever-more-densely papered and ever more country routes came into the Associated Billposters' reach.

Sequential rents in outdoor advertising

Poster lithographers, billposters, and landowners all carved their incomes out of manufacturers' and retailers' outdoor advertising appropriations. Each needed the others to secure a share of that advertising appropriation, but all competed over the size of the slice each would receive. Their relationships were simultaneously complementary and conflictual.

In the early period, billposters acted outside the dictates and directives of property law. They paid no rent for posting surfaces; without the rights secured by rent payments, they could make no credible claims to advertisers regarding the number of gazes intercepted, and therefore they collected no rent on access to eyeballs. Paying rent to urban property owners and erecting billboards allowed billposters to establish a monopoly on a billboard-sized slice of the field of vision of passersby. Charging a monopoly rent to advertisers for the fictitious (and immaterial) commodity of audience attention allowed billposters to meet the rents charged by landowners for the fictitious (and material) commodity of land. Billposters lived in the margin between two fictitious commodity prices: the going rate for eyes and the going rate for land. The market value of urban land depended in part on its proximity to passersby, but it took the work of the billposters to fully realize that value. The billposters' ability to collect rents on access to attention required the payment of rents to landowners. Neither could realize their rents without the other; they were complementary. But the share retained by each necessarily came at the expense of the other; they were contradictory.

Similarly, neither poster lithographers nor billposters could get anything without the other getting something, but they had to share advertisers' expenditures between them. More for one meant less for the other. When iron billboards and starch paste lowered the need for replacement paper to maintain a display over the length of the contract, the saved expense enjoyed by billposters and advertisers was lost revenue for lithographers.

Everyone realizing revenues from any phase of advertising was taking a share of the selling cost away from jobbers and retailers. They might do so indirectly, as when manufacturers substituted consumer advertising spending for other distribution costs. Or they might do so directly, as when retailers funded their own advertising.

Urbanization and the governance of public space

As a newly urbanized population sought to solve the problem of city living, government at the state and municipal levels was drawn into regulation of urban spaces, including the use of urban spaces for outdoor advertising. Billboards were private property, but their utility was bound to their being publicly visible. This put them in the clash zone of several conflicting interests. By definition, the actions of the private property owners who leased space to billposters and the billposters who erected billboards and pasted posters affected neighboring property owners and passersby on public streets – affecting neighbors and passersby was the entire purpose of the exercise. The erection of billboards could lower the aesthetic and monetary value of neighboring property or, possibly, increase its value, as the billposters were fond of arguing with illustrations of derelict empty lots hidden from view by neatly maintained and artistically designed billboards (Poster Advertising Association 1922). Conversely, property owners' ability to realize rents from the lease of their space to billposters was affected by other people's uses of nearby property. If a streetcar route passed by or a nearby attraction drew crowds, the advertising value of the space increased and the well-placed property owner could cash in. If, on the other hand, the neighbors built a structure that obscured pedestrians' and passengers' view, the owner of the now-hidden property no longer had any useful advertising space to sell. The one point of agreement between billposting enthusiasts and billposting opponents was that some regulation was needed.

The Associated Billposters lobbied effectively to ensure that new regulations would secure the property rights that gave them a form of the audience-attention commodity to sell but would not bind so tightly as to restrict the reach of their market. The billposters were appreciative of regulation that protected the sanctity of their billboards or otherwise limited the ability of cut-rate competitors to operate. They did *not* want license fees to be too high, but they *did* appreciate license fees that were high enough to serve as an obstacle to entry by competitors who might try to undercut their prices – and they also appreciated the recognition conferred by licensing that theirs was a legitimate business. They did *not* want onerous restrictions on the placement or size of their billboards, but they *did* appreciate restrictions on affixing posters to walls and fences.

Although the billposters were quick to see the nefarious hand of the newspaper interests behind all efforts to limit the reach of the billposting industry, there were reasons other than periodical publisher's financial self-interest to object to the proliferation of poster advertising. Members of groups such as the American Civic Association opposed wonton billposting (and the more extreme members of the group opposed *all* billposting) because they wished to restrain the reach of the market, not just protect the newspapers' share of the market. As the look of the cities changed rapidly and disoriented long-term residents and social elites, they came to attach great importance to aesthetic considerations (*Municipal Affairs* 1899, p. 715). While waves of intra- and international migrants poured into the cities and weakened the traditional elites' hold on social authority and political power, newly vulnerable elites desperately sought to maintain the social geography of the city and the visible imprint of their power and influence. The impetus behind the anti-billboard movement was the same as the impetus behind the historic preservation movement, which also originated in the late nineteenth century (Holleran 1998). Outdoor advertising was attractive to advertisers in part because of its effectiveness at addressing the masses, some of whom were precisely the people traditional elites wanted to make invisible.

Billboard opponents considered billboards a sort of pollution. A broad swath of the upper-middle class gained an appreciation of natural landscapes – they were self-conscious about it being a new taste – and took up the habit of going on tourist excursions to wildish places. With only a very short lag, billposters followed them there bearing messages from eager advertisers. Hoping to bring a touch of the rural into the cities, believers in the power of a wholesome environment to achieve social uplift were able to direct a share of public spending to the construction of parks. The parks attracted visitors . . . with billposters following hot on their heels. The public land of the park itself could be and usually was declared off-limits to advertising, but the private property along the approaches and perimeter could be papered over. Making money on the sale of advertising space at a natural wonder or a city park was, in the reformers' view, an antisocial act. It was a combination of nature and public expenditure that created the attractions that drew visitors, not any action on the part of the billposter or property owner. Accordingly, any income the billposter or property owner derived from proximity to natural beauty was an "unearned increment." Reformers resented the something-for-nothing rents the billposters raked in. Were they not "exacting a franchise from the public"? Was not offending the eyes as much of a public nuisance as offending the ears and thus equally subject to legal restriction?[8] And reformers resented billposters even more since the very act that secured the unearned increment despoiled the attraction that made the unearned increment possible in the first place, an attraction that the reformers appreciated for its non-market values (Kimball 1901, pp. 101–105; *Scribner's* October 1903, pp. 507–508; Warner 1900; Wight 1903, p. 493; Woodruff 1907, pp. 345–347). The billposter following in the wake of Uncle Sam's soldiers was to those high-minded citizens a nightmarish vision (Kimball 1901, p. 102).

Billposters could not help but be aware that they were not universally loved and so, complementing their court appearances and lobbying efforts, they aggressively courted public opinion. The Associated Billposters countered objections based on the morally questionable content of billboards by self-policing – refusing to carry advertising for the treatment of venereal disease, for example, or declining to hang posters containing images in violation of current norms of sexual propriety (Associated Billposters Association of the United States and Canada June 1903, pp. 12–13). During World War I they demonstrated their good citizenship by donating space for the display of military draft announcements and food conservation messages. (At least some prominent outdoor advertising firms expected payback for their good citizenship and called in favors from government officials to quickly regain nighttime lighting privileges for their illuminated billboards. Wartime blackout orders had cut many hours of display time. In the aftermath of the war, they also debated the possible public relations impact of turning the space that had been used for wartime public service announcements over to their own self-interested anti-Prohibition appeals (R.C. Maxwell Collection, Box 2, Hartman Center).) They countered aesthetic objections by arguing that their business in fact beautified the city. They were fond of before-and-after photos of derelict empty lots obscured by neatly maintained billboards displaying artistic posters. They argued their case in the language of their upper-class reformist opponents; in 1922 the Poster Advertising Association published a booklet entitled "Posters and the City Beautiful" (Poster Advertising Association 1922).

Billposters were keenly aware of the social class dimensions of the battle. The Association's journal occasionally ran satirical pieces about the reformers seeking to constrain their business and the reformers were caricatured in class terms. Although reform activists were often women, the caricatures were of upper-class men who were implicitly feminized by the descriptions of their hyper-refinement and delicacy. Resentment of Progressive reformers' wealth, understandable coming from those with a chance at becoming wealthy if only the reformers would stay out of their way, was apparent in a satire mockingly sympathizing with a reformer made uncomfortable by the hunger pangs inspired by the view of a poster advertising food seen through his window ... and then relieved of his discomfort by sitting down to his ample breakfast (Associated Billposters Association of the United States and Canada May 1900, p. 16, November 1903, p. 26).[9] This satire also makes visible a conflict in the valuation of urban real estate. For those leasing space to billposters, the development of the market in the eyes of passersby increased the income-generating value of their land. For many of those in view of the new billboards, the altered surroundings lowered the aesthetic value of their homes and may well have lowered the resale value. As billposters secured implicit property rights in the eyes of passersby, exemption from advertising appeals became a kind of luxury good. Purchasing exemptions from advertising appeals became a class-differentiating pattern of consumption, particularly consumption of housing and of vacation travel.

As outdoor advertising gained in popularity among prosperous local businesses and powerful national brand-name manufacturers, billposters acquired influential allies in their struggle to keep outdoor advertising legally prolific. F.E. Fitch, a sharp strategic thinker with a billposting plant in Albany, New York, reacted effectively to a new ordinance introduced in the Albany Common Council in February of 1903 that would have all but eliminated billboards from the city. The bill had the backing of a politically powerful newspaper owner, but Fitch persuaded four of Albany's leading businessmen (who were also clients of his billposting services) to send a letter to all the local businesses alerting them to the proposed new law and providing them with a form letter to send to the Aldermen expressing their opposition. Three hundred businessmen signed and mailed these letters, enough that the council decided to drop the measure (Associated Billposters Association of the United States and Canada April 1903, pp. 15–16). Inspired by Fitch's success, Ed. Fournier of North Yakima, Washington averted a proposed fifteen-fold increase in the billposting license fee (along with a more-than-doubled theater license fee that had his most important client threatening to close) with a petition delivered to the mayor (Associated Billposters Association of the United States and Canada June 1903, p. 17). When newspaper interests, fiscally strapped city officials, or Progressive reformers tried to establish limits or increase taxes and fees on outdoor advertising, the billposters' political organizing was usually at least as successful as the reformers', as the reformers themselves ruefully acknowledged (Woodruff 1907, p. 347). Frequently the billposters blocked the

Progressives' model bills from even making the legislative agenda (Schultze 1984; Bailey 1987).

Municipalities under pressure from multiple angles experimented with the use of a selection of regulatory tools, varying with the relative degrees of influence wielded by billposting fans and foes in their town. Many sought some direct authority over billposters' persons by requiring billposters to be licensed. Despite the new expense, Association billposters quickly came to appreciate licensing as it limited competition and the nuisance of small-scale snipers. Many municipalities, often the same ones, sought direct authority over the billposting business's effect on city space by writing rules setting placement and construction specifications for billboards. The need for such rules was often justified as a measure to protect health and safety. Every once in a while, a billboard would indeed fall over, occasionally injuring or killing an unfortunate pedestrian. Some cities required that billposters obtain a permit for each individual billboard in their plant. Some imposed setback and size standards on billboard construction, sometimes even applying such rules retroactively to existing structures. Billposters protested that the safety justification for placement and construction standards was a ruse, that the rules were more onerous than those for non-advertising construction such as buildings and fences, and that the real purpose was to interfere with their ability to carry on a legitimate (and often licensed) business. They cried foul when rules were applied retroactively to already-existing structures, imposing a huge expense if a preexisting plant were to be brought up to new code. They howled especially loudly when the size limitations imposed by municipal regulation were incompatible with standard poster sizes, making the largest billboards allowed by local law all but useless as business assets. Many municipalities also experimented with indirect power over billposters' business activities by wielding the tool of taxation. Imposing taxes specifically on billposters' business activities and assets, usually the billboards themselves, increased the cost of doing business and so could be expected to decrease the scale of the business. In some cases, the primary intent was probably to curb the volume of outdoor advertising and any benefit to local government budgets was a very attractive side effect. In other cases, fiscal exigencies may have been the primary driver of billboard taxation.

Billposters constantly tested the reach and rigor of the new regulations' enforcement and frequently wound up in court. The intent of their testing was often to probe a layer deeper and test the basic legitimacy of the regulations. Flouting regulations and then arguing the case in court was a way to challenge the laws. New restrictions were also challenged in court directly by billposters seeking injunctions against enforcement before acting in defiance of the law. Though billposters may have at times been less than entirely satisfied by one or another of the courts' rulings, the cumulative effect of the hundreds of decisions handed down over more than two decades, at times appealed through several levels of the judiciary up to and including the Supreme Court, was that the rights of private property owners to lease space to billposters, the exclusive property rights of billposters in the billboard surfaces they built and maintained, and the rights of advertisers to place almost any content they pleased on those surfaces received explicit government sanction.

When outdoor advertising was taken up by legislative bodies or by the courts, the outcomes nearly always recognized and helped standardize the business of selling access to the eyes of passersby. Widespread licensing of billposters clearly legitimated their activities in the eyes of the state. With a combination of arguments for free speech and the impossibility of legislating aesthetic values, billposters and their clients successfully evaded any significant limitations on the content of billboard ads (Schultze 1984; Bailey 1987). Despite a reasonably extensive and organized resistance, the state collaborated with industry to achieve this expansion of the market realm. Public space was now a site for the appropriation of attention as a form of private, salable property.

The anti-billboard reformers were caught in a contradictory position. They objected to the extensions of the market realm that intruded on their attention, offended their aesthetics, and excited their resentment. But there was a limit to how much change they could really bring themselves to advocate for. As Richard Hofstadter put it, the middle-class citizen "was too substantial a fellow to want to make any basic changes in a society in which he was so typically a prosperous and respectable figure" (Hofstadter 1972 [1955], p. 210). Yet the billposter also thrived in this world.

Conclusion

The audience attention market required property rights in attention. Property rights in attention, in turn, require a degree of excludability, monopoly in the Chamberlinian sense. In order to have something to sell, the seller must be the exclusive owner of his output before the sale. The billposting sector of the advertising industry achieved excludability through the Associated Billposters' aggressive pursuit of monopoly in the narrower, more commonly used sense of the word. They went to great lengths to suppress competition and secure a high degree of price-setting power. When they were able to exclude others' posters from their billboards and offer advertisers credible guarantees of display at agreed-upon locations for an agreed-upon period of time, the nature of the transaction between advertiser and billposter changed; rather than an exchange of money for the service of gluing posters to visible surfaces, it became an exchange of money for access to the eyes of passersby. The price was proportional to the number of intercepted gazes, not to the cost of providing the service. Under this monopoly pricing regime, billposters, especially in large cities, were positioned to secure large rents. They were monopolists in the Schumpeterian mold, however. The constant threat posed by the advertisers' ability to substitute other advertising methods compelled billposters to keep innovating if they were to keep claiming a share of the surplus.

The audience attention market also required mechanisms for the exchange of attention. The Associated Billposters and billposting solicitors acted to generate a more streamlined, centralized, but highly skewed flow of information about available billboard advertising. The "Big List" of member billposters, official solicitors' intermediation, and the Promotion Bureau's pamphlets increased advertisers' ease of communication with billposters – at least, with billposters belonging to the Association. By standardizing the range of services offered and price scales, the Association limited the scope of negotiations with advertising clients. This was, of course, to their own benefit, though, ultimately, advertisers had to be satisfied enough with the service to keep buying.

The realization of the value of audience attention was only achieved in the context of an interlocked set of simultaneously complementary and conflictual relationships. Advertising was a weapon in the battles among manufacturers, wholesalers, and retailers, so the demand for advertising emerged from the conflicts within consumer goods distribution chains (Porter and Livesay 1971). For example, manufacturers' advertising expenditures were in large part an effort to lower the selling costs absorbed by jobbers and retailers, yet they still relied on jobbers and retailers to get the goods to the final consumers. Claude Hopkins' memoir illustrates the paradox. He was explicit about his role as an advertising agent in lowering merchant's fees. He advocated the use of advertising campaigns featuring coupons to be redeemed at a retail store, thus pressuring retailers to have the item in stock. Hopkins warned manufacturers not to double their selling costs by spending on consumer advertising and also spending on jobbers' distribution costs (Hopkins 1966 [1927], pp. 132–141). Advertisers therefore earned the share of their income that came from manufacturers at the expense of jobbers and retailers, even as the advertising industry still earned a large share of its total revenue from retail advertising. One portion of advertising professionals' business was devoted to helping manufacturers squeeze retailers; the other portion of their business depended on retailers thriving.

Billposters went farther in suppressing horizontal competition among themselves than did advertising professionals in other sectors of the industry. Instead, their horizontal competitors were often those who sold audience attention through other media, especially print. Meanwhile, like those in other sectors of the advertising industry, billposters were embroiled in vertical competition along the attention market's supply and distribution chains, which was comparable to the vertical competition their clients faced in their own industries. Purveyors of outdoor advertising space established monopoly rents on the eyes of passersby but then had to pass on a portion of that as rent paid to landowners; without paying rents to landowners, they could not have charged rents on the eyes of passersby. Similarly, they were compelled to pay commissions to solicitors; without solicitors, they would have a hard time generating a large volume of out-of-town business. Still, the billposters paying would prefer a lower commission to a higher one. One of the benefits of local monopoly and national association was the ability to hold down commissions paid to solicitors.

While staking claims to shares of the attention market, billposters were also pushing the boundaries of the attention market. The apparatus of government did not give billposters everything they wanted at every moment, but the state was more often billposters' ally than their foe. The state recognized the property rights necessary to the billposters' business, invested in infrastructure improvements that billposters took advantage of to increase the density of their geographic coverage within the existing boundaries of the US, and engaged in imperial conquests of new territory that American billposters treated as new attention harvesting grounds (despite their misgivings about the racial fitness of the people inhabiting the conquered territory). Whatever checks there were on the expansion of the attention market came primarily from Progressive reformers who raised aesthetic objections to the proliferation of poster advertising. Their arguments did not carry the day and their elitism still has the power to offend, but the questions they asked still echo: is attention fair game for commercial appropriation anywhere and everywhere it may be found? Or should there be protected spaces where non-pecuniary interests determine the uses of our attention?

Notes

1 As billposting businesses grew, billposters no longer actually posted bills – their employees did. As proprietors of billposting plants absented themselves from the physical work of posting bills, a handful of women, most often the widows of the previous proprietors, entered the field. See, for example, the death notice in the February 1902 issue of the *Billposter-Display Advertising*: Mr. Lodwick of Portsmouth, Ohio died, but "Mrs. Lodwick has announced her determination to continue the business" (p. 7).

2 I read the complete run of *Display Advertising* from 1897–1898 and the *Billposter-Display Advertising* from 1899–1903. I also read the *Billposter and Distributor* 1905–1906 and sampled extensively from the *Poster* 1910–1920. This description and broad syntheses later in the chapter that are not otherwise referenced are drawn from those sources.

3 Although I do not adopt exactly the language and methodology developed by Douglass North, portions of this case study in the coevolution of institutions (e.g. the property rights regime) and organizations (e.g. billposting firms) could be translated into the framework developed in *Institutions, Institutional Change and Economic Performance* (North 1990). Note in particular his disavowal of the claim in his earlier work with Robert Thomas that institutions would tend to evolve toward greater efficiency (p. 7).

4 As the scale of billposting enterprises increased from a sole operator with a paste bucket and brush to an entrepreneur employing dozens of men with paste buckets and brushes, intra-industry conflict became class conflict rather than market competition. Members of the Billposters' Association looked very favorably on their own organization to defend their interests, but far less favorably on their employees' organization. The Association's journal occasionally carried accounts of strikes or other labor unrest, and the actions of organized workers were always reported in a mocking, dismissive tone. (See, for example, May 1899, p. 12, January 1900, p. 26, December 1902, p. 6)

5 Outdoor advertisers talked about the circulation value of specific locations within a city, but reliable independent audits at that fine-grained level of detail were not consistently performed until the Traffic Audit Bureau was established in 1933.

6 The *Data Book* was printed and bound cheaply on the expectation of frequent replacements with newer editions, so very few copies survive. I was able to locate only one copy of only one volume.

7 What was efficient for the attention-selling billposter was a new cost for the advertisers whose increasingly far-flung potential customers had to be reached through advertising rather than through costless proximity, though the larger volume of business made it worth the advertisers' while.

8 The examples of obviously intolerable and illegal noise nuisances reformers used as analogies to rhetorically establish the nuisance character of billboards were, in fact, the normal practice of street crying which had been a common selling practice until around the time of the Civil War (Laird 1998, pp. 13–14).

9 As the billposting business grew, the most successful billposters grew to be quite wealthy. The class animus felt by billposters toward reformers was replicated within the ranks of billposters as the proprietors of more marginal plants watched the most prosperous billposters engage in the conspicuous consumption rituals of social ladder-climbers. These prosperous billposters also tended to be the most influential within the Association, and other members began to express doubts as to whether the Association could really be trusted to represent their interests.

Bibliography

Associated Billposters Association of the United States and Canada. 1897–1898 monthly. *Display Advertising.*

Associated Billposters Association of the United States and Canada. 1899–1904 monthly. *The Billposter-Display Advertising.*

Associated Billposters and Distributors of the United States and Canada. 1905–1908 monthly. *The Billposter and Distributor.*

Associated Billposters and Distributors of the United States and Canada. 1906. *Constitution and By-Laws.* OAAA collection box CB1, Hartman Center for Sales, Advertising, and Marketing History.

Bailey, Kristin Szylvian. 1987. "Fighting 'Civic Smallpox': The Civic Club of Allegheny County's Campaign for Billboard Regulation, 1896–1917." *Western Pennsylvania Historical Magazine* Volume 70 January: 3–28.

Chamberlin, Edward. 1962 [1933]. *The Theory of Monopolistic Competition,* 8th Edition. Cambridge, MA: Harvard University Press.

Chudacoff, Howard, and Judith Smith. 1994. *The Evolution of American Urban Society,* 4th Edition. Englewood Cliffs, NJ: Prentice Hall.

Fisk, H. E. undated. *Organization in the Outdoor Medium – Industry.* OAAA collection box HI1, Hartman Center for Sales, Advertising, and Marketing History.

Fowler, Nathaniel C. 1900 [1897]. *Fowler's Publicity: An Encyclopedia of Advertising and Printing, and All That Pertains to the Public-Seeing Side of Business.* Boston: Publicity Publishing Company.

Hofstadter, Richard. 1972 [1955]. *The Age of Reform: From Bryan to F.D.R.* New York: Alfred A. Knopf.

Holleran, Michael. 1998. *Boston's "Changeful Times": Origins of Preservation and Planning in America.* Baltimore: The Johns Hopkins University Press.

Hopkins, Claude. 1966 [1927 and 1923]. *My Life in Advertising and Scientific Advertising.* Chicago, IL: Advertising Publications, Inc.

Kimball, Arthur Reid. 1901. "The Fight Against Advertising Disfigurement." *Scribner's* Volume 29: 101–105.

Laird, Pamela Walker. 1998. *Advertising Progress: American Business and the Rise of Consumer Marketing.* Baltimore: The Johns Hopkins University Press.

Mahin, John Lee. 1908. *The Mahin Advertising Data Book* Volume 8. Chicago, IL: Mahin Advertising Company.

Municipal Affairs. 1899. "Municipal Aesthetics from a Legal Standpoint." Volume 3: 715–723.

North, Douglass. 1990. *Institutions, Institutional Change and Economic Performance.* Cambridge: Cambridge University Press.

Porter, Glenn, and Harold C. Livesay. 1971. *Merchants and Manufacturers: Studies in the Changing Structure of Nineteenth-Century Marketing*. Baltimore: Johns Hopkins Press.

Poster Advertising Association. 1909–1911 monthly. "A Chat with the Billposter." OAAA collection box HI1, Hartman Center for Sales, Advertising, and Marketing History.

Poster Advertising Association. 1919. *Why the Association*. OAAA collection box HI2, Hartman Center for Sales, Advertising, and Marketing History.

Poster Advertising Association. 1909–1920 Monthly. *The Poster*.

Poster Advertising Association. 1922. *Posters and the City Beautiful*. OAAA collection box HI2, Hartman Center for Sales, Advertising, and Marketing History.

Printers' Ink. 1922. "Anti-Trust Case, Against Poster Advertising Assn., Dismissed." Volume 119 Number 1: 28.

R. C. Maxwell Collection, Boxes 1 and 2, Hartman Center for Sales, Advertising, and Marketing History.

Rowell, George P. 1906. *Forty Years an Advertising Agent, 1865–1905*. New York: Printers' Ink Publishing Company.

Schultze, Quentin. 1984. "Legislating Morality: The Progressive Response to American Outdoor Advertising, 1900–1917." *Journal of Popular Culture* Volume 17: 37–44.

Schumpeter, Joseph. 1942. *Capitalism, Socialism, and Democracy*. New York: Harper and Brothers.

Scribner's. 1903. "The Right to Keep the World Beautiful." Volume 34: 507–508.

Sherman, Sidney. 1900. "Advertising in the United States." *Publication of the American Statistical Association* Volume 7 Number 52: 119–162.

Warner, John DeWitt. 1900. "Advertising Run Mad." *Municipal Affairs* Volume 4: 267–293.

Wight, Peter B. 1903. "The Real Billboard Question." *Chautauquan* Volume 37: 491–494.

Woodruff, Clinton Rogers. 1907. "The Crusade Against Billboards." *The American Review of Reviews* Volume 36: 345–347.

4   Home invasion

Advertising delivered door to door

Introduction

The modernization of advertising and the modernization of the United States Post Office are woven together. First, the Post Office was an indispensable intermediary for the relationship between publishers, audiences, and advertisers. From its inception, the Post Office was structured to subsidize the distribution of newspapers – there is a historical reason that so many newspapers have the words "post" or "mail" in their names. Changes in postal policy, infrastructure, and technology all shaped the advertising-saturated magazine explosion at the end of the nineteenth century (Henkin 2006; Gallagher 2016; Fuller 1991). The virtual spaces of the nineteenth and twentieth century print media depended fundamentally on the material means of their production and transmission, and many audiences engaged with those media through publications delivered by mail (Kielbowicz 1989).

In addition, advertisers and some advertising professionals sought ways to garner attention directly through the mails, without the intermediation of a newspaper or magazine publisher. Under different names, the practices of direct-mail advertising existed in their premodern state earlier in the nineteenth century, as did any of the other forms of advertising. (Before the term direct-by-mail advertising was coined in the 1910s, sending advertising through the mails was referred to most often by referring to the materials sent: "circularizing" by sending circulars or, if the materials sent did not fit the expected format of a circular, mailing "form letters" or "announcements." There was not yet an umbrella term linking the varied uses of the mail as an advertising medium and the word "advertising" was not often applied (Harder 1958, p. 4).) Advertising circulars swelled the mails before the Civil War. David Henkin writes, "Already by [the mid-nineteenth century], many Americans (principally those in cities) inhabited a world full of paper detritus" (2006, p. 155). Like a dandelion casting thousands of seeds to the wind in the hopes that one or two would find fertile ground, or like the early billposters, who scattered broadsides across the landscape with little sense of where they went or whom they reached, the early circularizers cast their advertising materials into the mails with little information about their fate.

Before the Civil War, all mail had to be picked up by the addressee at the post office, so all that was required to mail a letter was the name of a person and the name of a post office. A name and post office became, as David Henkin writes, "a legitimate site – an operational address – in the new communications network," though it was one subject to error and confusion as there could be multiple people with the same or similar names receiving mail at the same post office (2006, p. 11). Postage could be collected at either end of the delivery, by the sender or by the recipient. Some circularizers saved on cost by dropping their materials into the mail without payment. But of course, many address-ees were uninterested in paying the postage for advertising materials they did not request and thousands of pounds of paper passed from print shop to post office to garbage heap without ever once crossing the field of vision of the target audience (Henkin 2006, pp. 154–155). This was a pure waste not only for the advertiser, but also for the Post Office; in 1856 a new policy enacted by Congress began requiring prepayment on all advertising materials. Florida Senator David Yulee explained the reasoning for the new law, saying about the unsolicited circulars, "very few of them are taken out at the offices, but they are transported at great expense to the government" (Kielbowicz 1989, p. 91).

Beginning with a few northern cities in 1863, the Post Office experimented with free home delivery. ("Free" here does not mean that the postage was free, but that there was no *additional* charge for delivering mail to the home rather than requiring the recipient to pick it up from the post office. Before the Post Office began sending letter carriers door to door as a matter of course, the Post Office charged an extra fee for home delivery and there were also some private delivery services available which would collect mail from the post office and bring it to a customer's door for a fee.) Free home delivery expanded first throughout the larger cities, and then spread out to areas of lower popula-tion density until rural free delivery reached the last, most geographically iso-lated households in the country in 1902 (Gallagher 2016, p. 190; Henkin 2006, pp. 86–90). This transformation of Post Office operations required a means of uniquely identifying each residence and spurred the creation of the addressing system we still use today (now with the twentieth century addition of the ZIP code):

- Name
- Number and street
- City and state

As a result, Henkin writes, "the home served as a constitutive address and a primary site of exchange for a majority of users" (Henkin 2006, p. 90).

The street address system increased the reliable specificity with which mail could be directed to a particular recipient. The sender needed more infor-mation to initiate a delivery. Simultaneously, as cities expanded beyond their earlier walkable dimensions and the urban dwellers and urban purposes were sorted into distinct zones of the city, the address *provided* more information.

For advertising purposes, the addressing requirements of home delivery made mail-addressing information more demanding to acquire, but once acquired it was more informative. If an advertiser, or an advertising professional working on his behalf, had a mailing address, that address carried with it information about neighborhood of residence within a city (which signaled income) and also carried a near guarantee that properly addressed mail would *enter the home* of the addressee. Someone in the house would have to look at it, however briefly. (Before 1923, when a new policy required homes to have mailboxes or mail slots, mail carriers were forbidden to leave mail unattended; they had to deliver the mail into the hands of someone in the receiving household or business. Many carried a small wooden implement to use as a doorknocker to save their knuckles from the effects of rapping on doors hundreds of times a day (Gallagher 2016, p. 151).)

Because addressing information led so reliably to eyeballs, it was deeply attractive to advertisers. The information processing challenges of the direct-mail medium were more daunting than those of billposting or periodical publication advertising, so modernization in this sector was a more drawn-out process than in the others and the practices did not become as standardized. With all of its messy improvisation and fitful evolution, the modernization of direct-mail advertising practices nonetheless did the most to transform the informational relationship between advertiser and audience. Direct mail allowed advertisers to select a target audience individual by individual, disaggregating the batches purposefully compiled by publishers or opportunistically captured by billposters from the shared use of public streets. The individualized nature of the medium also allowed for more precise assessment of the advertising's *effects*. Direct-mail advertising appeals could often make a precise link between the individuals addressed by the advertising and their later purchasing behavior.

The distributing business, in which advertising distributors carried advertising ephemera around the city and handed it off to target audiences, often by going door-to-door, was considerable. This business was often pursued in conjunction with billposting. In Newark, New Jersey the distribution arm of the Newark Bill Posting Co. moved an average of a half a million pieces per month in 1902 and, in November of that year, A. Van Beuren distributed 1.1 million pieces in New York City. In total, distributors moved billions of fliers, product samples, and advertising ephemera into people's hands or homes every year at prices that typically ranged from $1.50 to $3.00 per thousand (Associated Billposters Association of the United States and Canada February 1902, p. 9, March 1902, p. 9, January 1903, p. 18). But as advertisers raised their expectation of assurance that their messages did in fact strike the retinas they aimed for, distribution of unaddressed material was something of a dead end. Laird writes, "By 1900, the periodical press dominated advertising media in both volume and the creative attention advertisers were willing to pay to it and for it. The complexities and unreliability of getting ephemera into consumers' homes and workplaces became more serious obstacles at the same time that magazines and newspapers improved their successes at meeting this challenge." (Laird 1998,

p. 219) In the following couple of decades, direct-by-mail advertising professionals also improved their successes at meeting the challenge of delivering advertising to audiences – or, equivalently, delivering audiences to advertisers.

Mining data to compile the mailing list

As direct mail modernized, practitioners became fixated on eliminating waste, no longer accepting the high degree of chance associated with the dandelion-seed-like dispersal of earlier efforts. "[H]owever excellent the caliber of the appeal," wrote H.C. Burdick in a 1916 how-to guide on direct mail, "it hasn't a chance in the world to succeed if the list is poor – if the message falls on unfertile ground." He advocated severe culling of the list, writing, "let only those [names] which show latent business opportunities be included" (Burdick 1916a, pp. 4–5). That same year, Robert Ramsay made the same point, writing, "The advertising has yet to be written that will sell sausage to a Hebrew, stuff in non-refillable bottles to members of the W. C. T. U.,[1] or baby-food to bachelors. It can't be done" (Ramsay 1916a, p. 21). Using the botanical metaphor again, Burdick wrote in *Postage*'s second issue, "Direct mail advertising must reach the right kind of soil to blossom" (Burdick 1916b, p. 17). The "right kind of soil" must be well-fertilized with purchasing power, not only consumer desires. An illustrated promotion for direct mail as an advertising medium shows a giant mail carrier stepping over "the temporary homes of the workers" to deliver mail to "the home of the established man" (Paper Makers Advertising Club 1915e).

Data could be compiled from the direct data-collection efforts of the advertiser. For retailers in particular, direct-mail giant Homer Buckley wrote, "The first source for the list is charge customers. These names can be taken off the ledger." Cash customers can also be added to the list "by asking customers to kindly give you their names and addresses so that they may be insured of receiving literature which might be of interest to them as it is issued. It is seldom that customers are not willing to give you their names" (Buckley 1916a, p. 55). For local retail, Leonard Wolf advocated augmenting the list with those who are not existing customers but are known personally to live nearby. Then, "Arrange the names by streets and in numerical order. Check each street list, to see that no household is omitted" (Wolf 1916, p. 61). Existing customers can also be asked for their friends' contact information (Farrington 1910, pp. 262–263).

Mailing lists could also be constructed by piggybacking on the audience commodity constructed through the use of print media. Indeed, the first businesses to commercialize mailing list data were businesses that sold through mail order. They flooded the mails with catalogs, taking advantage of loopholes in postal policy to travel at the subsidized rates applied to newspapers and magazines. Those who responded by mailing in an inquiry were by definition likely prospective customers and well worth paying the postage to reach with additional sales material. Mail order pioneer Samuel Sawyer wrote, "The most valuable addresses are those of people who have replied to your advertisement" (Sawyer 1900, p. 36).

During the Gilded Age, Sawyer and other mail-order pioneers, notably E.C. Allen, however, were not just interested in selling goods. Instead, their mail-order catalogs served as lures to draw in potential door-to-door salesmen who would pay fees to be outfitted as agents. "[R]ather than encouraging readers to prefer Ivory to soap – thereby cutting out the middlemen who had formerly done so much to shape buying habits – Allen urged his audiences to see themselves as middlemen," explains Richard Popp. But while encouraging audiences to see themselves as middlemen, Allen and Sawyer themselves viewed their audiences as products and carried on an active trade in the inquiry letters they received. The most common kind of arrangement was for one business to rent out batches of letters to another, who would sift through them for prospects and make copies, then return them, though outright purchases could also be negotiated. Rentals cost less than purchases. Older letters cost less than newer ones. The mail-order industry in the 1870s and 1880s had a "dual nature." They were retailers selling goods to customers via the mail. They were simultaneously "information brokers who sold data to other marketers" (Popp Forthcoming).

A generation or two later, even those advertisers whose main goal really was to sell goods, rather than sell people on being salesmen, and even those who expected to complete final sales in person learned to adapt the practices of the mail order houses. They, too, could make use of newspaper and magazine advertisements to generate mailing lists by including instructions to write for further details or, to better standardize the format of the inquiries, pre-printed mail-in reply coupons. Begin, advised Mahin, with "dragnet advertisements in mediums of general circulation" (Mahin 1916 [1914], p. 237). Charles MacFarlane wrote in 1915, "The General [print media] Advertising provides an outlet for the Direct Advertising; the Direct Advertising sells the goods" (MacFarlane 1915, p. 8).

Mailing list construction took place in the context of an expanding information economy. Personal information collected for a variety of purposes, not just advertising audience assembly, became available, often in commodity form, and then became an input into mailing list construction. For business-to-business advertising, credit rating bureaus were a common and information-rich source of data for direct-mail targeting. Dun and Bradstreet was a leader in commodifying commercial credit data and was the most frequently cited as a source of names and addresses for direct mail (Cited by, e.g. Maurice Elgutter 1916, p. 31). Dun and Bradstreet grew out of the first credit reporting agency in the US, the Mercantile Agency, formed in 1841. By the 1870s under R.G. Dun's leadership, they employed 10,000 investigators in 69 branch offices and handled 5,000 queries daily (Beniger 1986, p. 257; Lauer 2017, p. 6).[2] Credit reports could also sometimes be used for consumer good marketing; Elgutter referred to "credit rating books, if there are such in your city," as a source of names of wealthy men who are prospective buyers of luxury consumer goods (Elgutter 1916, p. 33). The construction of institutions for consumer credit surveillance were well underway, but consumer credit bureaus "long refrained from selling promotional lists" out of fear that doing so "would tarnish their reputation for impartiality and stir resentment among subscribers (on whom they also depended to furnish consumer information)" (Lauer 2017, p. 19).

The personal data of the well-to-do could also be harvested from social registers such as Blue Book or Who's Who, and from professional association membership lists. (Some lists dipped farther down the socioeconomic status ladder than others.) Telephones were adopted by the more prosperous first, so telephone directories served at first as filtered lists of the well off, but became more comprehensive and less informative about income as telephone service quickly became more commonplace.[3] Commercial directories offered a fairly comprehensive list of the names and addresses of businesses in a city. Engaging the services of news clipping bureaus could yield updates on businesses opening, closing, expanding, or moving, and could also yield more extensive personal information about the socially prominent to supplement the simple name-and-address entries of a social register (Burdick 1916a). The first clipping bureau, a new type of information economy business whose purpose was to make the reams of information contained in newspapers searchable by topic, opened in 1884 (Beniger 1986, p. 283). They proliferated in the following decades. John Lee Mahin wrote in the 1910s, "At clipping bureaus, one can buy lists of names of persons who are accustomed to travel, those who are reported ill of certain diseases, those who contemplate building, and other information which is gathered from the newspapers" (Mahin 1916, p. 238). At least for select audiences, advertisers a hundred years ago were already sometimes granting the experience of receiving an eerily timely advertisement.

Social barriers to data collection

When manufacturers and large-scale wholesalers worked to amass a mailing list, they were threatening the existing distribution of control over information and the existing distribution of decision-making authority. A centralized database of customer information was of a piece with a broad shift toward increasingly centralized managerial control. It was also related to the shift from push marketing to pull marketing.

When communications were slow and data management systems minimal, operating over a wide geographic area required widely distributed decision-making authority. People served as, in James Beniger's description, "portable and programmable information processors." But as communications technologies improved, distribution of control became less important. Instead, control could be centralized and orders given from afar (Beniger 1986, p. 167). The jobbers had carved out a secure niche earlier in the nineteenth century under the push marketing model of distribution. In the 1840s and 1850s they had consolidated their position and were the main link between manufacturers and retailers. Even as vertical integration threatened jobbers' status in the 1870s and beyond, those who held on remained repositories of knowledge about supply chains, and also about existing and potential customers. (Beniger 1986, pp. 156–160; Chandler 2002 [1977]; Porter and Livesay 1971). They were also often loath to share that knowledge. Even as vertically integrated firms expanded their direct involvement in distribution by directly employing traveling sales agents, those agents were not always keen to make their knowledge fully accessible to managers. Back at the central office, sales managers encouraged jobbers and directly employed traveling salesmen to see direct-mail campaigns as a complement to their labor, a means of improving the productivity of their sales pitches. The advertising professionals angling for a cut of the marketing action encouraged this view. Their argument was that a direct-mail campaign can pave the way for an in-person sales visit. A jobber or salesman who has been preceded by promotional literature delivered through the mail does not arrive a stranger. The customer has a little prior information, some familiarity that can ease the salesman's entry. (And if the potential customer's reaction to the promotional literature is, "no way no how," the salesman can find that out much faster and save a lot of wasted effort.) Any reasonable jobber or salesman, they said, would comply with requests for data about prospects in their territory, how those existing and potential customers could be contacted through the mail, and anything else they knew about them – personal information that could be used to cultivate goodwill, business information about the scale of their operations, how promptly they pay their bills, and so on (Harder 1958; Buckley 1916b, p. 36; Buckley 1916c, p. 15).

And yet many salesmen did not leap at this opportunity. When they were supplied with data cards to fill out and remit to the central office, few did it with any thoroughness. In an article in the inaugural issue of the direct-mail journal *Postage*, Robert Ramsay recounted an anecdote of a company attempting to compile a mailing list by mailing each agent "a multigraphed letter in which was 'filled in' the exact number of names wanted from that agent" and a thorough explanation of how much benefit the agents would receive from their data sharing. The response was underwhelming. "A week passed. Instead of the dealers making passionate efforts to comply with the request of the company – three or four replies were received." Follow-up letters only slowly and partially succeeded in wresting more names out of the agents (Ramsay 1916a, p. 20). Part of the resistance could just be resistance to adding another new task to their day. But another part of the resistance was a substantive concern about what transferring control over data would mean for their status. Many saw their own individual knowledge of their territory as the source of their claim on a share of the pie: they connected their commissions to their knowledge monopoly. If they gave up their informational monopoly, they became more easily replaceable. First of all, if their knowledge of the territory were in a central repository, another individual could replace them. Secondly, the mail could displace, rather than complement, the traveling salesman's role in distribution (Harder 1958).

The expanding administrative state also became a source of commercially useful data. In 1910 Frank Farrington told retailers that "lists of names can be bought from town and county clerks and assessors" (Farrington 1910, p. 262). H.C. Burdick advised in 1916 that, "Governmental and State records are available . . . for lists maintained on a nation-wide instead of local scale"

(Burdick 1916a, p. 10). The administrative state, however, was an ambivalent partner in the commodification of personal data. For example, as cars proliferated, states quickly began to keep records of car ownership. By 1916, only South Carolina and Texas had no centralized records of car ownership; a handful of states required registration only once when the car was first purchased; most required car owners to register with the state annually. For the thousands of businesses providing automobile services and accessories, these state registries were a goldmine (Tuttle 1916, p. 48). Seeing the commercial value of the names and the chance to augment state revenues, some states would duplicate car registration information for a fee ranging from as little as $2 per thousand to as much as $25 per thousand. Other states refused to sell the data – although car licensing was a matter of public record, so with some additional effort data miners could request access to the information and duplicate it for themselves. Making a trip to the state registry and copying the data was a costly enough undertaking that direct-mail giant Homer Buckley recommended buying these names from a list house (Buckley 1916d, p. 58).

The Post Office itself was an ambivalent partner in the commodification of personal data. The Post Office was the medium through which mailing list data was made operational, but a 1902 policy forbade postmasters from providing a list of people receiving mail through their office, with or without payment (Burdick 1916a, p. 54). Some postal employees, no doubt, could be bribed; Burdick commented, "names can probably be secured direct from the carriers – approaching them, of course, while off duty." (Anthony Comstock, in his crusade against indecent mail, accused pornographers of bribing postal clerks to get names and addresses.) But it is hard to say how large a black market in personal data postal employees enabled (Burdick 1916a, p. 8; Henkin 2006, p. 157). Postmasters were permitted to check a mailing list for accuracy and eliminate the names of those who had moved away or correct inaccurate addresses, but they could add no new entries.

Existing customers could be tapped for data about themselves and also their social networks. Although direct mail promoters suggested that collecting existing customer's data should be easy, Maurice Elgutter let slip the possibility of some resistance. He wrote an imagined scenario in which a customer, when asked for his name, growled, "What do you want my name for?" But Elgutter insisted that a polite explanation from the clerk and the promise of receiving special promotions and sale information will gain "meek" compliance with the request. (This is exactly the same exchange now offered by loyalty programs: your data in exchange for discounts.) And what if the clerks themselves resist acting as data collectors? "They will [collect data] if you insist on it, and show them that you mean business" (Elgutter 1916, p. 32). Both clerks and customers, he suggested, may need to be disciplined. Frank Farrington encouraged retailers to cultivate their existing customers as data sources. When anyone writes for a catalog, the retailer's response should include a blank form to submit the names of friends who may also want one. "The sending of such names is of course entirely gratuitous," he wrote, "but women are pretty apt to send them" (Farrington 1910, pp. 262–263). His phrasing certainly suggests he had encountered resistance to data sharing from men. Junk mail was already widely perceived as a nuisance, so customers had reasons to hold back information that would generate more unwanted mail for people they liked.

The mailing list as asset and as commodity

Once constructed, the mailing list was of great value to the advertiser. It allowed precisely targeted sales messages. However, without a continuing investment in upkeep, a mailing list's value depreciated rapidly. Americans were a mobile bunch and so the accuracy of a mailing list fell off quickly. "[C]ircularizing Tom, Dick, and Harry, by the end of the year one begins to believe that the whole world has turned vagabond and taken to wandering," observed Robert Ramsay in 1916 (Ramsay 1916a, p. 21). The postmaster of the Chicago Post Office said that in 1913, 40 percent of the mail handled in Chicago was incorrectly addressed (Paper Makers Advertising Club 1915b, pp. 20–21). Ramsay's 1916 estimate suggested that list turnover could be 20–30 percent a year (Ramsay 1916a, p. 21); a more optimistic writer estimate in the same publication suggested that an accurate retail store list would be 10–20 percent inaccurate a year later (Buckley 1916a, p. 55).

Many businesses with goods to sell – whether or not they sold through the mail – found direct mail to be a worthwhile advertising medium. If they produced and maintained their mailing list for themselves, they treated the list as a business asset. If they followed best practices in the field, they made a large initial investment in the list, then ongoing investments in maintaining the list. They also incurred the operating costs of *using* the list. A self-produced list was jealously guarded. The competitive advantage of having the best list would be lost if competitors gained access to it. Some list owners could be persuaded to generate some extra return on their investment in list construction by selling the data to other advertisers in non-competing lines. Others, fearing loss of exclusive control over the data would not even do that (Harder 1958, p. 47). "We know concerns that guard their mailing lists so carefully that they will not permit them to be used for obviously beneficial cooperative efforts," Carl Greer observed ambivalently:

> They seem to think that their competitors cannot possibly find their customers. This, we think, is a vain and unjustified belief. Yet it is a satisfaction to know that there are businesses that appreciate the value of their lists as one of their principal assets
>
> (Greer 1925, p. 24).

There were, however, firms whose core business *was* sharing mailing list data. These were businesses that filled a gap: More advertisers could be made interested in advertising their goods by mail than could execute the direct-mail advertising campaign themselves. This gap was a business opportunity for those who could operate the advertising campaign on the advertiser's behalf. In 1876, the Addressing, Mailing, and Duplicating Company took out an ad in the New York City business directory. They must have had competitors, as they identified themselves as the "largest and best equipped establishment in the United States for the purposes specified"; those purposes included "Envelopes, Newspapers, Wrappers, etc., addressed to all Trades, Professions, and Private Families from lists kept continually revised" (Harder 1958, p. 50). For the Addressing, Mailing, and Duplicating Company, therefore, a mailing list was a different sort of asset than it was for those advertisers who executed their own campaigns. The mailing list was an essential input into the service they sold to others: the service of addressing and mailing others' printed materials.

Although the Addressing, Mailing, and Duplicating Company was seemingly not entirely alone in its line of business, it did not appear to have many competitors. A 1926 article in the direct-mail advertising journal the *Mailbag* identified Arthur Williams as the "patriarch" of direct mail and said that when he started the Trade Circular Addressing Company in 1880 he had only two competitors, one in Chicago and one in New York (quoted in Harder 1958, p. 51). And competition did not build quickly. In 1885, the Chicago business directory listings for "addressing" included only two companies; some failed, a few more joined, and the total for the rest of the decade never exceeded seven; in 1891 there were six (Harder 1958, pp. 51–52). By 1916, Chicago was recognized by those in the profession as having an especially high concentration of direct-mail activity; articles in the trade journal *Postage* and other contemporary writing about direct mail advertising made casual reference to the "list houses" in Chicago and New York. If Chicago had only a handful of addressing business in the 1880s, it is unlikely anyplace else had many more.

Beginning in the 1890s, however, specialized direct-mail advertising businesses expanded rapidly. The categorization in the Chicago business directory changed from "addressing" to "circular letters" and the number of business listed doubled to twelve over the course of the 1890s, more than doubled again by 1910, and reached 70 in 1920. The rapid growth continued through the 1920s; there were 170 direct-mail advertising businesses in Chicago alone in 1930 (Harder 1958, p. 54). In addition to businesses focused specifically on direct mail, some multi-service advertising agencies offered direct-mail services alongside their core business of placing advertisements in print publications. Charles Austin Bates boasted of such a department, capable of supplying mailing lists, as early as 1896 (Bates 1896).

A number of agencies began offering direct mail as a complement to print media, focused on responding by mail to inquiries generated by print-media advertisements. Lord & Thomas promoted their use of direct mail follow ups as a means of testing print-media advertising with a series of articles in their house organ *Judicious Advertising* in 1904 to 1905 (Cruikshank and Schultz 2010, p. 61). The Mahin Advertising Company of Chicago – the agency headed by John Lee Mahin, oft-published and oft-covered in the advertising industry trade papers – offered follow-up service as a complement to designing and placing media advertisements. *Mahin's Magazine*, the agency's house organ, covered the topic of the "follow-up system" several times in 1902 and 1903 and advertised a pamphlet on the "follow-up system" as one in a series of six pamphlets detailing Mahin's services to clients. The newness, in the new century, of systematically following up inquiries by mail is suggested by the fact that *Mahin's Magazine* frequently set the term "follow-up system" in quotation marks (*Mahin's Magazine* Volume 1). Before beginning his own house organ, Mahin published on the "follow-up system" in *System Monthly* following the same typographical practice (Mahin 1900). Other articles in the same publication also set "follow-up system" and related terms in quotation marks (e.g. Zenner 1900) and a brief piece in *Mahin's Magazine* described the "follow-up system" as having only recently overcome the skepticism that greeted its first introduction (Volume 1 Number 2 May 1902, p. 21).

While agencies such as Mahin or Lord & Thomas were certainly managing mailing list data derived from print-media ads placed on their clients' behalf, it is not clear from their promotional materials whether they made this data available to *other* clients or ever used it to begin a pure direct-by-mail advertising campaign. An oblique hint comes from Samuel Sawyer's *Secrets of the Mail Order Trade*, in which he writes that the next best names and addresses, after those drawn from inquiries received in response to one's own print-media advertising, are names and addresses gleaned from inquiries responding to *similar* advertisements. He did not, however, explain where one would get ahold of responses to other businesses' advertisements (Sawyer 1900, p. 36). There is little reason to think that competitors shared their customer data since to do so would risk losing sales. An advertising agency without too rigorous a standard regarding conflicts of interest might, however, have shared one client's customer data with another for sufficient remuneration. (Another hint comes from Bates' assurance that his agency would *not* share mailing data supplied by one client with any of their other clients (Bates 1896). Perhaps his competitors did.)

Having a specialized business collecting, managing, and sharing audience data carries a clear potential for aggregate efficiency gain. If competing businesses managed their own lists and hid their data from one another, there would necessarily be an enormous amount of duplicated effort. If they followed similar data collection practices, drawing names from the same sources and filtering on the same criteria, they would reach similar results, making the duplication of effort a pure loss. If those businesses all outsourced their mailing list management to the same list house, they would reach the same results without the duplicated effort. The list house could charge each client less for the data than any one of them would spend to mine the data themselves and still turn a profit – the more clients willing to buy the same data, the higher the profit. In 1916, Robert Ramsay reported that names could be purchased for as little as $3.00 per thousand, though a more typical price was $10.00 per thousand. (One W. Clement Moore took out a small box advertisement in *Postage* promising a few specific classes of names – "lady mail order buyers," "teachers" – for even less: $0.25 per hundred or $2.25 per thousand.) The cut-rate lists were likely to be less accurate and/or contain only the easiest-to-identify names, so whatever was saved on name purchases would just as likely be wasted on mis-directed mail pieces. Burdick wrote that purchased names could run as high as $0.10 per name for the most difficult lists to compile. Ramsay estimated that it would cost about $0.10 per name (or $100 per thousand) and perhaps more for a business to self-produce a list with sufficient care to avoid waste circulation, so the cost to self-produce outstripped the typical cost to buy an average list by about a factor of ten (Ramsay 1916a, p. 21; Moore advertisement in *Postage* Volume 1 Number 2, p. 62; Burdick 1916a, p. 11). This helps to account for the growth of the market for list houses. However, countervailing forces prevented reliance on specialized list houses from becoming a universal standard practice.

One countervailing force was a sticky principal-agent problem. Beginning in the 1890s, billposters learned to moderate the principal-agent problem by offering listed and protected service. Advertising agents making print-media placements could, like billposters, demonstrate that the contracted advertisement placements were in fact made; the publishers that ran the ads were pressured into submitting to reliable circulation audits my the mid-1910s. But there was no equivalent mechanism for testing the quality of the mailing list data provided by a list house. In 1900 Samuel Sawyer warned that commercially available name lists were "dear at any price" and would be a waste of postage costs even if acquired for free (Sawyer 1900, p. 36). In 1916, with the market for lists expanding, Ramsay told advertisers to expect that a list at the usual price of $10 per thousand names would be approximately 20 percent inaccurate, and cheaper lists even more so. Incorrectly addressed third-class mail would disappear into the post office never to be seen again. The letters could be sent first class so that undeliverable pieces would be returned, which served both to test list accuracy and to allow reuse of undelivered mail pieces, but that doubled postage costs from one cent to two cents per piece (Ramsay 1916a, p. 21). Inappropriately selected recipients who failed to respond to a potentially effective sales letter were indistinguishable from ideally selected recipients who failed to respond because the sales letter was flawed. Given the difficult-to-ascertain quality of the list houses' lists – and, as list houses proliferated, the relative quality of one list house's data over another's – there remained a possibility that a business could self-produce a list superior in address accuracy and targeting precision to what could be bought, and therefore superior to what competitors might buy. If competitors, too, decided to self-produce out of mistrust in the list houses, there still remained the chance to outcompete rivals in the realm of list construction.

Mailing list data businesses could themselves be more or less specialized in the type of audience data they collected. In 1916, John Lee Mahin (who himself published an annual report of aggregate regional marketing data in the 1900s) wrote, "Several houses make a specialty of listing dealers according to sections, ratings, and the kind of merchandise handled, and guarantee the names to be live and that the addresses are correct." Such a business would serve manufacturers seeking to push their products through the next links in the supply chain.

For those looking to be put in direct contact with final consumers, "there is also a business in selling names that are taken from answers to mail-order advertisements" (Mahin 1916, pp. 237–238). The Motor List Company of America, founded in Des Moines in 1912, specialized in trawling for names, addresses, and car and motorcycle ownership data in state motor vehicle registries. By 1916 they had a database of a million names. They supplied selections from that data, for a fee, to anyone for whom car owners made a likely market, which need not be limited to directly car-related items (Tuttle 1916, pp. 46–48). Ross-Gould Mailing Lists of St. Louis, by contrast, advertised 7,000 classes of prospective customers. A few of the classes, by way of illustrating their range, were: Apron Manufacturers, Wealthy Men, Fish Hook Manufacturers, Shoe Retailers, Farmers, Feather Duster Manufacturers, Auto Owners, Druggists, Doctors (advertisement in *Postage*, Direct Mail Advertising Association 1916b, p. 62).

None of the articles or books were explicit about the exact format in which a list purchaser would gain access to the data. Direct-mail advocates emphasized the importance of multiple mailings and the cost would become prohibitive if the advertiser had to pay for each individual use of the names on a list each time a new piece was mailed as part of the same campaign. Therefore, it seems most likely that when advertisers purchased a list, they would receive a copy of the data that they could keep, perhaps in a ledger or as a set of cards for a card file. The list houses could be reasonably confident the advertisers who paid for their lists would not share the data for free with competitors and would have to hope that the depreciation of any mailing list's accuracy would motivate advertisers to re-purchase updated lists regularly.

Mailing list operating costs

Making use of a mailing list involved many complementary and potentially costly tasks, regardless of whether it was the advertiser or an advertising business – addressing company or list house or multiservice advertising agency – that owned the list. A direct mail advertising campaign involved designing materials (which can be broken down further into writing copy, illustrating, and designing layout), producing multiple copies of materials (which includes producing paper and applying the words and images to paper with one of the available printing techniques), acquiring mailing list data and selecting appropriate recipients from that list, and addressing and posting the material. Presuming that the first mailing succeeded in generating some response, replies had to be received and processed. The response data generated from a first mailing (or print media advertisement) informed subsequent rounds of mailings. As Truman DeWeese wrote in 1908:

> Time was when the direct orders from a piece of advertising constituted the net results of the investment and the advertiser was doubtless satisfied. Through model follow-up systems, however, the person who evinces the slightest bit of postal card curiosity is certain to be bombarded with

epistolary literature until he throws up his hands and capitulates with an order for the goods.

Or, he admits, until the advertiser concludes that further nagging will be of no use (DeWeese 1908, pp. 126–130).

Every sector of the advertising field involved some number of firm types and some larger number of component tasks in the advertising process. The bundling of those tasks within the purview of one business type or another was frequently revised and the distribution of tasks for direct mail retained more variation than for other advertising media. By 1915 when direct-mail advertising professionals formed their association, most print-media advertising was handled through advertising agencies that did the copywriting and graphic design work as well as making placements. The publishers then printed and distributed the advertising materials as part of the larger package, including editorial content, that was sent to readers. The distribution of tasks across the firms involved in direct mail was less standardized. Regardless of which type of firm employed them, the people who executed these tasks had to be paid and supplied with materials.

Creative content

Writers and commercial artists designed the materials; they might be employed directly by the advertiser, or they might be employed by a multiservice advertising agency or a direct mail operation, or by a job printer, and any of these employers might engage the writers and artists on a permanent or freelance basis. Copywriting worked on the superstar model: a small number of the best-known practitioners raked in incomes far in excess of the mass of people working in the field. The same W. Clement Moore who advertised names at a quarter the typical price also offered cut rates on content creation; in 1916 he advertised his copywriting services at the very low price of $0.50 for a small advertisement, $1.00 for a "6x9 circular" (Direct Mail Advertising Association 1916b, p. 62). The far more prominent Louis Victor Eytinge, author of advertising books and articles and a regular contributor to *Postage*, took out a half-page advertisement in the May 1916 issue of *Postage* in which he claimed that he charged an advertiser $165 for five letters – a charge easily justified by the $25,000 in sales generated as a result (Direct Mail Advertising Association 1916f unnumbered page). Even supposing that Eytinge's letters were somewhat longer than the 6 × 9 circular Moore offered to write for $1.00, his charge of $33.00 per letter was clearly an order of magnitude higher.

The superstar system for copywriting had emerged around the turn of the century in connection with print-media advertising, just as advertising agencies took over content creation from the advertisers themselves. During the transitional period some superstar freelances contracted directly with the advertisers, but soon even the superstars began working within agencies (Laird 1998, p. 227). In 1904 one of the early copywriting superstars, John E. Kennedy, made more than ten times as much as his run-of-the-mill copywriting colleagues at the Chicago agency Lord & Thomas: $16,000 a year for Kennedy compared to $1,400 a year for a less-celebrated copywriter. Kennedy's work often employed the model of a print-media advertisement to generate inquiries and a sequence of follow-up letters to those who responded to the print-media ad. A couple of years later, the competition for copywriting talent had intensified and competitors lured away even lesser known copywriters from Lord & Thomas with salary offers up to five times what Lord & Thomas was paying (Cruikshank and Schultz 2010, pp. 56, 61–64). But the superstars' incomes grew as fast or faster. Half a decade after paying Kennedy $16,000 for the year, Lord & Thomas paid Claude Hopkins the staggering sum of $1,000 *per week*. Hopkins's reputation was built on both copywriting and media strategizing; he regularly combined judiciously selected media placements with well-targeted letter campaigns. One of his big successes combined a consumer-oriented print-media campaign promoting Palmolive soap by offering manufacturer's coupons to customers and a letter campaign to retailers warning them to make sure they had Palmolive in stock to meet the consumer demand (Cruikshank and Schultz 2010, pp. 101–106).

Paper

Paper was the material that carried copywriters' words to audiences. Paper mills remained distinct and didn't tend to bundle their papermaking operations with other advertising services supplied directly to advertisers. Although they didn't often directly supply the advertising services that complemented their own, paper companies did produce promotional materials encouraging advertisers to adopt paper-intensive advertising practices. The Beckett paper company published a widely-consulted direct-mail guide, and issued a revised, expanded edition ten years later (MacFarlane 1915; Greer 1925). The Chicago Paper Company designed retail letterheads "to help printers secure business stationery orders" (Fay 1916, p. 16). Advertising, after all, was an important source of demand for their products. By 1900 advertising contributed more than subscriptions did to newspaper and magazine revenues, underwriting demand for the cheaper grades of paper. The expansion of direct-mail advertising promised to build the market for higher grades of paper and open up opportunities for papermakers to differentiate their higher priced product lines with distinctive and attractive colors and textures. Advertisers could, perhaps, be persuaded to buy a variety of specialized papers to make their sales letters more attractive – not just pretty, but attention grabbing. However, at the same time that papermakers were looking to increase demand, they faced some supply constraints. A short notice in the May 1916 edition of *Postage* called readers' attention "to the fact that there is a serious shortage of raw material for the manufacture of paper, including old papers and rags. The collecting and saving of Rags and Old Papers would greatly better existing conditions for the American Paper Manufacturers." The notice claimed, "something like 15,000 tons of different kinds of paper board are manufactured every day in the United States" and much of it could be reused if it weren't, as it usually was, burned or otherwise wasted (Direct Mail Advertising Association 1916g, p. 16)

Papermakers directly encouraged advertisers to use direct-mail advertising, but also encouraged printers to be their allies in promoting direct mail. In 1915, the Paper Makers' Advertising Club issued a pamphlet series targeted at printers, encouraging printers to become promoters of direct-mail advertising, and to become proficient in providing direct-mail services (Paper Makers Advertising Club 1915a, 1915b, 1915c, 1915d, 1915e). The Paper Makers estimated that the printers' aggregate annual paper bill was $75 million, and that this $75 million in sales to printers made up 88 percent of paper producers' total business. They saw direct mail as a promising growth opportunity for printers that could in turn substantially increase demand for paper (Paper Makers Advertising Club 1915a). Since printers bought most of the papermakers' output, most final users of paper purchased it through printers as part of the printing service.

Printing

Printers had good reason to heed papermakers' encouragement. After the Depression of the 1890s and the merger wave of the early 1900s, many industries were highly concentrated. Players in the oligopolistic industries competed on the basis of non-price components of the marketing mix, including product differentiation through advertising and branding, and enjoyed comfortable profit margins. Joseph Schumpeter called such avoidance of price competition "corespective" behavior (Schumpeter 1942). Ironically, given the importance of printing to the advertising-intensive regimes found in the many industries where branding and product differentiation muted price competition, the job printers themselves were still engaged in cutthroat price competition in a decentralized industry. Competition among job printers intensified late in the nineteenth century as the entire job printing sector gained in absolute terms but lost advertising market share relative to periodicals. Improved printing technologies for periodicals narrowed the gap in image quality between freestanding lithographs and images included in magazine advertisements, and periodicals leapt ahead in the reliability with which they could put the advertising they printed in front of audiences (Laird 1998, pp. 62–71). From 1880 to 1910, although the total revenues of the industry as a whole grew markedly, from $91 million to $251 million, the number of distinct printing establishments grew even faster, from 3,468 to 10,708. In other words, the industry grew but the average individual firm's revenues shrank (Paper Makers Advertising Club 1915d, p. 9).

Sellers in many other markets spent more on selling than on manufacturing, partly because of falling unit manufacturing costs achieved with new mass production technologies and partly because of increasingly elaborate marketing. Relative to this standard, printers advertised comparatively little. The selling costs for typewriters and for drugs were five times the manufacturing costs. Furniture-selling costs were twice the manufacturing costs. But printers, locked into cutthroat price competition, did not sustain a comparable marketing budget. Their selling costs were only 15 percent of their manufacturing costs (Paper Makers Advertising Club 1915d, p. 3). Direct-mail pioneer Homer Buckley critiqued what advertising printers did undertake for themselves, describing it as "too much concerned with the details of price," full of "mere figures and dry facts and technical details" (Buckley 1916a, p. 37). It may seem advantageous to produce something so self-evidently useful that it all but sells itself with only informative, not persuasive, advertising. In fact, however, the thousands of small printing firms crowding the market often had excess capacity and they did not enjoy the generous profit margins that manufacturers of nationally-promoted branded goods enjoyed even after they paid their advertising costs – which, of course, included printing costs. The Paper Makers suggested that printers could increase their profit margins by increasing their selling costs. In essence, the papermakers were urging the printers to join the corespective business climate of their most prosperous clients. They could compete on service and product differentiation rather than price. The Paper Makers' pamphlets instructed printers in how to offer direct-mail advertising services, advising clients on both content creation and mailing list creation, perhaps even getting into the practice of acquiring and managing list data themselves (Paper Makers Advertising Club 1915a, 1915b, 1915c, 1915d, 1915e). Homer Buckley agreed with the Paper Makers' assessment in an address he gave to the Ben Franklin Club in Philadelphia (Buckley 1916a2). If printers could loosen their own financial constraints with creative marketing, they could, perhaps, put less price pressure onto the papermakers who supplied them.

Despite the sunny assurances of the papermakers' pamphlets, printers faced daunting challenges. Not only were printers in competition with one another, but new innovations in office equipment made some of the tasks printers did more technologically accessible. Office equipment manufacturers responded to existing bottlenecks in office information processing by designing and manufacturing new machines. New office machinery expanded the range of techniques available for making multiple copies of printed materials and thereby also expanded the range of firm locations in which the production of multiple copies could be done. For high-end work, the printers still held the advantage in product quality. But for duplicating a straightforward sales letter, a variety of machines could do the trick, churning out hundreds or thousands of copies of text (Beach 1905). Office machine manufacturers, like papermakers, were enthusiastic publishers of advertising guides promoting direct-mail marketing. The Lanston Monotype Machine Company of Philadelphia was itself an active direct advertiser, with a monthly house organ to promote sales of the monotype equipment. One featured article, later reprinted in *Postage*, was "The Why of Direct Advertising." The "why" given was that it could increase sales for the advertiser. Not coincidentally, advertisers preparing direct mail campaigns might well make use of a monotype machine (Lanston Monotype Machine Company 1916, pp. 23–25).

Printers also faced competition from vertically integrated businesses that could substitute for their services using the same types of printing equipment the printers did. When the Bates advertising agency expanded their range from simply brokering advertising placements with publishers, one of the services added during the 1890s was printing done in-house (Bates 1896). Homer Buckley, who later spearheaded the formation of an association for direct-mail advertising professionals, started his first direct-mail business in 1905 with four departments: composing letters, typewriting, mailing list, and mailing. Within the first few years, the business also brought some printing in-house (Harder 1958, p. 56). Meanwhile, a printer who added advertising services could potentially differentiate from other printers, but their new service would instead enter competition with established advertising professionals, some of whom also did some of their own printing, and whose professional organizations worked in various ways to make their field unwelcoming to newcomers. One among the many motivations for direct-mail advertising specialists to organize was to raise barriers against printers who added advertising service departments (Direct Mail Advertising Association 1916a, p. 10).

Simple pieces of advertising matter, a postcard or a sales letter of no more than a page or two, could be produced for a few pennies a copy. Five cents a copy would be reasonable for a run of a few hundred or more (e.g. Ramsay 1916a, p. 21; Buckley 1916b, p. 37). For a few more cents per copy, an advertiser could indulge in higher quality paper (Cody 1916, p. 20). Among the advantages of direct mail, however, was the space to make the sales case at greater length than even a full-page newspaper advertisement allowed. Instead of short sales letters, an advertiser could produce multi-page brochures and catalogs. They could print in multiple colors with sharp borders on high-quality paper, expanding the design possibilities beyond the newspapers' low-resolution application of black ink to flimsy newsprint. Quality, of course, cost more. The Paper Makers' pamphlets included a sample direct-mail campaign that supplemented small pieces of sales material sent each month to 10,000 recipients for pennies a piece with a catalog sent to 5,000 recipients at a total printing cost of $850, or 17¢ each (Paper Makers Advertising Club 1915c, p. 21). (Postage, too, would cost more on the larger items.) Even with a carefully targeted list, only a small minority of recipients would end up purchasing the good and so a printing cost of 17¢ per catalog sent could easily average out to several dollars per final sale, even before figuring in the costs of acquiring the names of prospects, addressing the catalogs, and paying the postage. It made little sense to promote low-cost grocery items this way. But a costlier mailing was a reasonable sales strategy whenever there was a large enough field of prospective customers over which to distribute the fixed costs of producing fancy brochures, and the good being promoted sold at a high enough price to justify a selling cost of a few dollars per successfully concluded sale.

Addressing and mailing

Given a mailing list (which may have cost several cents a name), and a mailable piece of sales literature (which cost something and perhaps quite a lot to have written, plus a few more cents per copy to print), each of the hundreds or thousands of distinct names and addresses had to be applied to the hundreds or thousands of identical pieces of sales literature. The addressing could be done by the advertiser from the advertiser's own list. Or it could be done by an addressing company from the advertiser's own list. (Promotional materials from Charles Austin Bates' advertising agency, for example, described the addressing service they offered. The service promised that if a client provided a list to the addressing department, that list would be kept confidential (Bates 1896).) Or it could be done by an addressing company from the addressing company's list. Regardless of who owned the list and who did the addressing, there was a clerical labor bill to be paid. (These costs are discussed later in the section titled "Technologies and Labor Practices of the Information Economy.")

The Post Office took over from there. The postage rates and terms of service set by Congress and administered by the postmaster and postal bureaucracy powerfully shaped the context in which direct-mail advertising campaigns were waged. The Post Office had at all times distinguished different types of mail and charged differential rates that had a redistributive effect amongst different types of postal patrons. Newspaper rates were lower than the cost to the Post Office of transporting newspapers; personal letter rates were higher than the cost to the Post Office of transporting the letters. In effect, letter writers subsidized newspaper distribution costs. At the time of direct-mail advertising's professional organization in the 1910s, freestanding advertising material could be sent at a rate of one cent for up to an ounce with no forwarding or return service for incorrectly addressed material. Material sent at this rate had to be mechanically reproduced identical copies. First-class mail cost two cents for up to an ounce, did include forwarding or return service for incorrectly addressed material, and did not carry the requirement of mechanically reproduced identical copies (Post Office Department 1956). Postage was an unavoidable cost of doing business. The Post Office's classifications of mail matter were institutionally imposed limits of what it was possible for advertisers to mail to whom. The political power of publishers and their long history of defending their claims on postal subsidies left the smaller and newer direct-mail sector of the advertising industry more often adapting their activities to Post Office policies than forcing Post Office policies to adapt to direct mailers' needs.

Even when designed for other purposes, Post Office policies did provide a setting in which direct-mail advertising could operate. A round of postal reforms passed in the years 1845 to 1856 radically reduced the postage on individual correspondence. Newspapers and, after 1852, magazines still received generous subsidies, but new policies requiring prepayment on individual correspondence allowed the Post Office to lower stated rates for such mail while also more successfully collecting enough to cover their costs. Henkin writes, "[T]he 1845 postage reform radically diminished the proportion of newspapers in the mail and helped to transform the post from a broadcast medium to an interactive communications network" (Henkin 2006, p. 66). Mail became a routine part of more people's lives. Urban northerners were the most engaged, but people just about everywhere knew how to use the post and did so sometimes (Henkin 2006,

p. 31). People who regularly received individual letters were reachable through the mail, which benefitted advertisers along with other mail users.

In the middle of the next generation's wave of reforms, the 1879 Mail Classification Act attempted, not entirely successfully, to better differentiate advertising circulars from periodicals. At that time, despite differences across sectors of the publishing industry, newspaper and magazine interests came to an agreement amongst themselves and with postal authorities to impugn advertising circulars as illegitimate periodicals. The Act was intended to subsidize informative periodicals, as the Post Office had done since its inception, while charging advertising matter the much higher third-class rates. Advertisers making use of the mail as a direct advertising medium were not yet sufficiently numerous or organized to mount a successful opposition to the effective rate increase on their operations. Instead, advertisers like mail-order giants Sawyer or Allen, and many smaller but otherwise similar operations, adapted their advertising to be more magazine-like so it could still receive the second-class subsidy. In practice, the distinction between informative periodicals and advertising turned out to be an increasingly hard distinction to police, and a generation later the classification rules came under scrutiny again (Kielbowicz 1990, pp. 456–458; Popp Forthcoming).

Another important change in the mail recipients' experience came when the Post Office fostered a stronger connection between the mail and a recipient's specific place of residence. Beginning in 1863, the Post Office began its first experiments with delivering mail directly to recipients' homes, rather than requiring recipients to call for their mail at their local branch. Within thirty years, home delivery reached everyone in a city or town with a population over 10,000, and rural home delivery began in 1903 (Henkin 2006, pp. 86–90; Fuller 1991, p. 2; Gallagher 2016, pp. 187–191). With home delivery, receiving mail was no longer an errand to be done away from home, but a necessary consequence of postal operations. With no particular effort demanded of the recipients, mail *would* be placed in their hands. This was convenient for individual correspondence and critical for unasked-for mail like direct-mail advertising.

The newspaper and magazine publishers had long held an advantage in delivery of advertising through the mail. By packaging the advertising with news content, they had made use of the subsidized second-class mailing rate. But a postal rate change inserted into the 1917 War Revenue Act reduced publishers' advantage. The new policy differentiated the news and advertising content of publications sent through the mails and charged a dual postage rate: one cent per pound on reading matter (raised in stages over the next few years to one and a half cents per pound) and a higher, distance-dependent rate of between two and ten cents per pound on the advertising content. The specifics of the rate change divided the interests of various sectors of the publishing industry and they failed to block the change, while other mail users who had been more visibly and vocally advocating for a redistribution of the burden of financing postal operations prevailed. Advertising professionals specializing in direct mail were becoming more visible as they organized under the umbrella of the Associated Advertising Clubs of America and advertisers showed increasing interest in the direct-mail advertising medium. Direct mail advertising interests joined with a wide range of other mail-user interests in the National One-Cent Letter Postage Association, which had been pressuring Congress to reduce the subsidies to publishers and reduce the postage rates to one cent for any letter up to an ounce in weight for everyone else. Although the One-Cent advocates didn't get the low flat rate they wanted for everything else – first-class mail rates actually increased temporarily during the war – the new rates charged on advertising content contained in publications reduced the cost differential between delivering advertising via magazine and the third-class postage rates applied to advertising letters traveling solo (Kielbowicz 1990; Post Office Department 1956).

Technologies and labor processes in the information economy

Encoding information

Information may be immaterial in the abstract, but it requires a material medium. The overwhelmingly dominant material medium available for the duplication and transmission of information throughout the nineteenth century and into the beginning of the twentieth was paper and ink, physically transported. The technologies for applying ink to paper had developed tremendously over the course of the nineteenth century, especially for material that was to be duplicated without variation. The technologies and infrastructure needed to transport printed-upon paper – especially rail service – had also developed. By late in the century, thousands of identical copies of the highest circulation magazines and newspapers could be churned out and sent over great distances affordably. Thousands of identical posters could be posted on billboards in cities and alongside country roads across the country. Once encoded for use on some form of printing press, information, whether text or image, could be replicated a large number of times as ink on paper – the steam-powered cylindrical press generated a *very* large number of copies very quickly indeed: tens of thousands an hour. Ink on paper carried information effectively to a human reader but was more difficult to duplicate. (Copying machines that could duplicate an ink-on-paper original were available, but involved the cumbersome use of chemical baths and blotting papers and could make a limited number of copies (Beach 1905).)

Addressing mail pieces for one given direct mailing did not require thousands of exact duplicates, however. Instead, it required making one duplicate each of many distinct small bundles of information: the name and address. If the content of the mailer was to be personalized at all (e.g. a letter beginning Dear Mr. ___), the duplication problem was exacerbated. This was a serious technological challenge in information processing. It was a challenge shared by publications sent through the mail. The Addressing, Mailing, and

Duplicating Company's 1876 advertisement promised to solve the addressing problem for newspapers as well as for advertising circulars (Harder 1958, p. 50). Publishers at least had subscription and advertising revenues to cover the cost of addressing. The sender of an unsolicited advertising letter was under more cost pressure since many copies would get no response and so generate no revenue at all.

The most accessible and well-established technology for replicating addresses was pen, paper, and a literate human. The most fundamental application of pen-and-paper technology to direct-mail advertising was the card file. By the time direct-mail advertising professionalized enough to have a dedicated professional journal in 1916, every article or book chapter dealing with the physical medium of the mailing list insisted on the card file. The card file allowed each individual record to be on a separate physical unit – unlike, say, a list with multiple entries on a larger piece of paper. Because each record could be handled individually, the card file facilitated removing or editing inaccurate records, adding new records, reordering records, or selecting different subsets of the records for different mailings). The advantages are clear, but the innovation was scarcely a generation old. A January 1901 article on the history of the card ledger, published in *System Monthly*, reported that "ten years or more have elapsed since the first 'card index' was written up to supercede the book index to ledgers" – that is, the card file was used first as an indexing tool for records still kept in ledgers with multiple entries on a single sheet. Despite some resistance from "cranks," during the 1890s the demonstrable efficiency gains from switching record-keeping entirely to cards led to widespread adoption of card-filing systems "for one or more purposes wherever attention is paid to office economy" (Poesche 1901).

Every how-to explanation of the card file suggested variations on the theme. Experienced list compilers and users recommended cards preprinted with distinct labeled areas for information on each desired variable: always name and always address; other variables of interest differed with the practices and purposes of the list compiler. These would often include a summary of past communication between company and customer – what materials the company sent and when; what inquiries and purchases the customer made and when – along with personal information about the customer such as profession, age, sex, income, and family status (Slemin 1916; MacNichol 1916; Burdick 1916a, pp. 38–57). An article in the first issue of *Postage* suggested that keepers of mailing list data should model their practices on newspapers' files on those people whose obituaries will be published when they die. Kenneth MacNichol constructed his article as a fictional dialogue and had the "Advertising Man" say, "Have you ever wondered how newspapers gather the material that enables them to print a complete family history with photographs when Jones dies or Miss Pitt elopes with the chauffeur? It all rests on a filing system that they call the Morgue. Everyone who is worth a paragraph has an envelope filled with data, clippings, photographs, all ready for instant reference. . . . I have an idea that we could use a Morgue in this business" (MacNichol 1916, p. 30). When starting a new list, the size of the card and the layout of the preprinted data-entry boxes were decisions of considerable importance.

Information was encoded not only by entering data on the card, but also by the physical arrangement and appearance of the cards (Poesche 1901; Zenner 1900). With a database or spreadsheet on a computer, it is almost effortless to sort on variable A, then on variable B. If you change your mind later, you can sort on variable C, then on variable B, and lastly on variable A. With a card file, such sorting is logically simple, but effortful and time consuming to carry out. Should the cards be sorted first by geographic region, or by profession, or by date of last communication, or something else? And what variable should direct the second-order sorting? And third? Suppose the ordering of the cards in the file is arranged first by date of last communication, second by geographic region, and third by profession, but some particular campaign is focused on doctors, say, and so makes profession the most salient variable for selecting recipients. How can the doctors' records be quickly identified and pulled from the file? Which variables are worth marking by differently colored cardstock or by tabs or clips?

The data encoded in the card file is inert until put to use by clerical labor. A well-designed card file could reduce the amount of clerical labor needed as compared to more rudimentary record-keeping, and certainly an information-ally rich card-file system simplified the cognitive demands of the clerical labor. A 1916 how-to book, *Sales Promotion by Mail*, explicitly pointed out the rela-tion between the information built into the card-file system and the cognitive demands of the clerical labor: "When the intelligence and mental capacity of the girls usually selected for this sort of work is considered," wrote contributor H.C. Burdick in a casually derogatory tone, "it becomes immediately apparent that the indexing system must be simplicity itself and fool-proof" (Burdick 1916a, p. 41). Even with a simple and foolproof indexing system, operating a mailing list was a labor-intensive undertaking.

Office workers

The development of the field of direct-mail advertising was integrated with larger trends in the evolution of office work. Through the decades on either side of the turn of the twentieth century, many businesses were expanding in informational complexity. Growth in the employment of clerical labor out-paced overall employment growth. Growth in the scale of the office came with a transformation in the occupational structure of the office. And the trans-formed structure of the office was deeply gendered (Saval 2014; Davies 1982; Strom 1989; Beniger 1986). It was no accident that Burdick referred to "the *girls* usually selected for this sort of work."

Women, especially US-born white women, were a ready supply of clerical labor: with increases in average years of schooling, by late in the nineteenth century many US-born white women had competent reading, writing, and arithmetic skills. Women as a whole were effectively barred from the higher paid, more highly respected professions. US-born white women were culturally resistant to, and often had better options for economic support from their families than, the domestic service, manufacturing, or agricultural work that black and immigrant women did. Employers of clerical labor found this supply useful and attractive: they had the necessary skills along with the race and class markers of respectability; at the same time, they were constrained in their employment options and so they could be paid low wages and given no advancement opportunities (Davies 1982; Strom 1989). In short, an early cost-saving practice in direct-mail operations was the employment of women. Bates' 1896 promotional pamphlet for his multi-service advertising agency includes a photograph of the "addressing department." Rows of white-bloused, black-skirted, bun-haired white women sit at desks, pens in hand (Bates 1896).

Mechanized information processing

Drawing down the cost of labor by drawing in women is not a comprehensive plan for cutting unit costs, however, especially as the demand for women's clerical labor grew. Technological innovation was an indispensable complement to employment practices. An extraordinary flurry of office machine invention worked in concert with changes in the social organization of the office. Direct mail operations were a key site at which technological obstacles were identified, and technological solutions were developed.[4]

By 1905, it was technologically feasible for a well-equipped office to mechanically reproduce identical sales letters with some sort of office printing machine and then address each one of them with an addressing machine, such as the Elliott Addressing Machine or Addressograph (Beach 1905). Each entry in the card file would need to be supplemented with a stencil compatible with the addressing machine. Then, when the recipients were selected, the name-and-address stencils could be fed into the addressing machine and in an hour 2,000 to 3,000 addresses could be applied to envelopes. Even at women's low wages, there were savings from having one addressing machine operator accomplish what would have required a much larger team to accomplish by hand. An invention to ease creation of the stencils was patented in 1909; the patent was granted to "James Sinisi, of New York, N.Y., assignor to Cosmopolitan Addressing Company, a corporation of New York," for a type-writing machine for producing "stencil cards employed in addressing machines" using a "keys and operating means . . . on the order of the standard typewriting machine, so that they can be operated by any one having a knowledge of such machines" (Sinisi 1909).

The increased mechanization of the office was a good cultural fit for the feminization of the office. Office machines are not intrinsically gendered. However, contemporaries constructed a gendered understanding of who should operate those machines using an analogy between what was new – multigraphs and addressographs and so on – and what they knew – light manufacturing. Textile work, beginning in Waltham and Lowell, Massachusetts, in the 1830s, was distinctly understood as women's work. By the end of the century, US-born white women had largely withdrawn from northern textile factories and immigrants had entered; for the US-born, the office became the new mill. By classifying clerical labor using the new office machinery as a kind of light manufacturing, operating those machines with women's hands was quickly accepted as entirely appropriate (Strom 1989).

Women's role in the clerical work of direct mail indeed came to be so universally assumed that a 1924 floor plan showing the recommended physical setting for a direct mail operation included filing cabinets, worktables for dozens of minutely specialized clerical workers, and a women's bathroom but no men's bathroom. Presumably, the one male overseer of the work in the room could be trusted to walk down the hall to the men's room on his own recognizance (Beardsley 1924, p. 14).

Audience control

Those promoting direct-mail advertising promised that this advertising medium of the mail could deliver messages into the field of vision of the desired audience. But they promised more. They promised that the form and content of a well-executed direct-mail advertising campaign would influence buyers' behavior.

The direct-mail medium reached its modernization take-off as a new view of the relationship between expert and audience came to prominence. Merle Curti's content analysis of the prominent advertising professionals' journal *Printers' Ink* found that authors were split between two views of human nature. Some took the view that humans, especially men, are basically rational and will make reasoned decisions about their purchases. Advertising, therefore, should present a well-supported, logical argument that explains how purchasing the advertised product serves the consumer's self-interest. This genre of advertising came to be known as "reason-why" advertising. Others took the view that although humans are self-interested, most, including men but especially women, are not rational. They respond to emotional cues, particularly to anxieties about their social status. From the time *Printers' Ink* was founded in 1888 until sometime around 1905, the first view predominated in its pages and the second was a minority dissenting view. After 1910, the second view predominated (Curti 1967).

As the advertising professionals' estimation of audience's rationality fell, their estimation of their own rationality rose. Just as they were reaching the conclusion that the average man was mistaken in his belief that he knew his own mind and could self-consciously exercise his own will, they reached the conclusion that an expert schooled in the newly distinct academic discipline of psychology could know the audience's minds better than audiences knew themselves and deliberately exercise his will over them. Walter Dill Scott's *The Psychology of Advertising* sold briskly enough for new editions to be issued regularly from its first publication in 1903 through the 1910s. The designers of advertising campaigns described their work less and less as informing or persuading audiences on the basis of facts about the qualities and costs of the products. Instead, they wrote about establishing in audiences an unthinking habit of consuming the advertised product. Herbert Casson wrote, for example, that "the aim of the farseeing advertiser is to make the public buy his goods, not from choice, but from habit" (Casson 1911, p. 70). Consumption habits can be formed, Walter Dill Scott claimed, by tapping into an understanding of instinct (Scott 1910, p. 79). An advertising campaign has been a success, he explained, if audiences "attribute to our social environment that which in reality has been secured from the advertisement which we have seen so often that we forget the source of the information" (Scott 1910, p. 84).

This changing view of the manipulability of audiences overlapped with the emergence of a new language for talking about workers. Scientific management, associated first with Frederick Winslow Taylor and other celebrity efficiency experts, suffused much business thinking. The scientific manager's view of workers is that they weren't that bright and couldn't be relied upon to find the best way of performing their own job. An expert, however, could determine the best way of performing any task, and then could shape the work environment to induce (or coerce) workers to do the task in that expert-determined best way (Taylor 1911). Some advertising professionals imported Taylor's "scientific" label. Herbert Casson introduced his 1911 book *Ads and Sales: A Study of Advertising and Selling from the Standpoint of the New Principles of Scientific Management* by stating, "This book is the first attempt, as far as I know, to apply the principles of Scientific Management to the problems of Sales and Advertising" (Casson 1911). Advertising industry giant Claude Hopkins published a book entitled *Scientific Advertising* in 1923 (Hopkins 1966 [1923]). Instead of workers, Casson's and Hopkins' intended subjects of scientific control were audiences.

The gap between advertising professionals' assessment of their own rationality and audiences' dimwittedness was reinforced by a gender gap. Advertising professionals were overwhelmingly male. Many heavily advertised products were advertised to women, who were understood to be their household's purchasing agent. A handful of women made careers in advertising as specialists in the female perspective. More often than not, however, consumer goods advertisements were written by men who assumed they were talking to women. Often, they overtly talked down to their audiences. Or they flattered them by casting the household as a business-like site of production where women were the scientific managers (though reliant on the expertise of the advertisers supplying them with efficiency-enhancing appliances and ingredients). To maintain their own gendered sense of self, advertising men were apt to refer specifically to women when talking about consumers' malleability (McGovern 2006, pp. 36–42). (Interestingly, famed copywriter Helen Woodward, while agreeing that the average woman consumer had little aptitude for logical thinking, argued that male consumers were no more reasonable. She believed male audiences had to be flattered into thinking they were making rational decisions with copy that looked like reason-why advertising but was really more emotive than rational. "To sell articles to men it is often wise to appear to reason with them, but you must be careful to merely appear to do so – never actually to be logical" (McGovern 2006, pp. 39–40).)

This new scientific management orientation pervaded all advertising media. In direct mail, the audience control mechanisms professionals sought to exert began with the physical circumstances of receiving mail. "The most persistent unasked-for advertising – the little imp that *will* worm its way into the hands and minds of its victims – walks boldly under the protection of Uncle Sam," wrote Isabel Woodman Waitt (Waitt 1916, p. 38). Beyond the moment of first contact achieved by the mail carrier, direct-mail advertisers had to rely on psychological control. Seemingly all worked from the premise that audiences were resistant. As Waitt suggested, target audience members were not eagerly awaiting receipt of advertising material, but instead had built psychic defenses against the intrusion on their attention. Some writers used strikingly militaristic analogies and imagery to describe advertising's assault on these defenses. The analogy inheres in the consensus term, advertising "campaign." But more elaborate analogies expound on the parallels between violent struggle over geographic territory and text-and-image based struggle over attentional territory. Truman DeWeese wrote of a direct-mail advertising recipient, "Just how quickly he surrenders depends very largely upon the sort of follow-up warfare that is waged. The first follow-up letter may make little impression. If ingeniously, tactfully and cleverly pursued, however, he may wave the white flag of truce after about the third follow-up letter" (DeWeese 1908, pp. 126–127). Robert Ramsay titled an article in *Postage* "Like a Modern Machine Gun." (World War I was raging in Europe, but the US had not yet entered, so perhaps the analogy was distant enough not to hurt.) As a general principle, Ramsay wrote, "It is the shots that hit that win the battles." In the particular case study presented in the article, "they hit their mailing list of 1547 names, *nineteen times in twenty-three days*" (Ramsay 1916b, p. 34). Walter Dill Scott cast audiences not as enemy combatants, but as prey. When there is plenty of game and few hunters, he explained, "any marksman may be successful in bagging game." But where there is strong competition, the successful marksman, "plans his method of approach according to the habits of the game" (Scott 1910, pp. 131–132).

Given the assumption that audiences were resistant, the moment at which the mail is received was tremendously important. The Post Office would deliver accurately addressed material into the home or office of the intended recipient. Someone connected to the addressee, even if not the addressee him- or herself, would have to hold the piece of mail and make a decision about what to do with it. Discard it immediately? Spend a second or two or three assessing it? Skim it? Read it thoroughly and attentively? In his encyclopedia of matters pertaining to publicity, Nathaniel Fowler recommended postcards over sealed envelopes because "if the matter upon it is sufficiently brief, he has a chance to absorb it, even though it may pass from his hands directly to the waste basket," whereas a sealed envelope could be discarded unopened, the contents entirely unseen – and Fowler's assumption of audience indifference to mailed solicitations came at the end of the 1890s, before the volume of direct mail really took off (Fowler 1900 [1897], p. 235).

If an envelope was to be used, physically forcing the envelope into the recipient's home or office would not be enough. After that initial moment of contact, direct mail had the least capacity for physical coercion. Whether or not they were attended to, billboards *had* to enter the field of vision of anyone using the street. An advertisement that sidled up next to a magazine article *had* to enter the field of vision of anyone reading the article. (Over time, magazines integrated an increasing proportion of advertising into the editorial pages and left less in the easily-skipped advertising-only section.) The recipient of unasked-for mail had to be either cooperative enough or confused enough to open the envelope.

Having little expectation of audience cooperation, many direct-mail advertisers tried to generate a moment of confusion, so that recipients would open the envelope to resolve their uncertainty about what was inside. (Though some suggested using the outside of the envelope to announce their purposes, for the same reason Fowler advocated postcards.) In contrast to the postcard strategy, in which the intentions of the mail piece were trumpeted in plain view and instantly assessable, an enclosed mail piece often hid its intentions. Innovations in office machinery expanded the range of ways of imprinting an address on an envelope, and as new means of addressing came into use, new social norms and communications practices linked particular technologies to particular social uses. The medium itself signaled meaning: handwriting meant something different than typewriting, which in turn meant something different than the envelope addressed by addressograph and containing a multigraph-duplicated letter. Generally, the more attention and labor were required to produce the address, the stronger the signal of a personal letter. Handwriting first, and eventually typewriting as well, were associated with personal, or at least individualized business-related mail. It wouldn't make sense to engage the office machinery that was designed for runs of hundreds or thousands of pieces to address a personal letter to your friend or to address an individualized business letter to an associate.

Direct-mail practitioners, however, continuously worked to subvert the meaning carried by the medium and in doing so destabilized those meanings. If a recipient had some doubt about whether a letter might in fact be a personal letter, he was more likely to open it. Office machinery producers often promoted their addressing devices on the basis of how convincingly they could imitate the look of handwriting or typewriting. The frequency with which the subterfuge was used, however, weakened it. Nathaniel Fowler wrote that facsimile handwriting in a sales letter "is of the most questionable value . . . because it is over-used and frequently illegitimately" (Fowler 1900 [1897], p. 711). (He thought it more effective in a postcard.) The degree of deception needed depended on the gullibility of the audiences sought. Direct-mail advertising professionals classified intended audiences according to how difficult they were to deceive. "In sending these imitation letters to a class of people who will think them real letters, they should be written in the letter form and the name may be filled in at the head. This makes them even more personal. But in sending them to a class of people who are too sophisticated to be fooled, there should be no attempt to make them seem real letters," wrote Frank Farrington (Farrington 1910, p. 86). They ranked the gullibility of audiences not only by gender, but also by geography. Urban audiences, they assumed, were more jaded than rural, and so getting an urban recipient to open an envelope required more sophisticated subterfuge.

The Post Office mail classification system also signaled content. Beginning with the postal reform of 1863, advertising material was categorized as third-class mail, subject to lower postage than personal correspondence (Post Office Department 1956). One means of inducing a recipient to open the envelope was to pay the higher postage for personal correspondence. No matter how convincing the imitation typewriting of the addressograph, a third-class stamp could give away the game. Charles MacFarlane explained the advantages of using first-class postage, writing, "A 2-cent stamped circular letter, in other words, gets a chance to be 'heard,' which is all that any advertisement can claim. Having gained an audience because of its appearance, perhaps by masquerading as a personal communication, it will be read attentively enough if the introduction is interesting." He then comments, "A house of recognized standing may occasionally allow PRESTIGE to take the place of POSTAGE" (MacFarlane 1915, pp. 161–162). (Also, convincing imitation typewriting could add to the transaction costs of persuading the Post Office to accept the material as third-class mail. If the formats and fonts were too persuasively like personal correspondence, the postmaster might have doubts about the postage classification and require more evidence to apply the lower third-class rate.)

Once a recipient is holding the mail piece and has come to understand that it is an advertisement, what then? Promoters of direct mail argued that a piece of mail would encounter less resistance than a live salesman. Confronted with a live salesman, a resistant hoped-for customer would rather shut down interaction immediately rather than become engaged in a social interaction that gets harder to exit the longer it goes on. A direct-mail promoter sketched a scene of a prospect confronted with a salesman, writing, "[T]he thought uppermost in the mind of the prospect is to get rid of this salesman, a tempter . . . by giving an answer that will get the salesman upon the other side of the door as quickly as possible" (Direct Mail Advertising Association 1916d, p. 23). In comparison, there is little risk of social discomfort in reading the first paragraph of a letter. Even if a letter is uninteresting, throwing it away is less resented than having to interrupt an unwanted salesman's pitch. A salesman may be dismissed because his arrival is poorly timed; a letter will patiently sit and wait until the time is right to read it. The intrusion is less aggressive and so the hoped-for customer's resistance to at least starting to hear (that is, read) the sales pitch, they claimed, would be lower. "*Direct Advertising arouses interest without arousing opposition*," claimed a promoter of the medium (Direct Mail Advertising Association 1916d, p. 24).

Advertising professionals claimed the expertise to craft the sales letter's content and layout in such a way that recipients would, once the envelope was open, become engaged with the sales pitch. The first few sentences had to arouse curiosity. The points needing the most emphasis could be set off with distinctive fonts, colors, or spacing. When an "important paragraph was written in red ink," it "[stood] out from the rest of the letter, it commanded attention, and, needless to say, brought home the bacon." Similar results were achieved by setting the important paragraph apart from the main body of the letter as a postscript (Lewis 1916, p. 27). Never, the pros advised, end a paragraph at the end of a page; it would be too easy to stop reading and never turn the page, whereas a page break in mid-paragraph – or better, midsentence – draws the reader along to the next page (MacFarlane 1915, pp. 75–76).

Having delivered their message, direct mail advertising pieces had to make it very clear what an interested recipient should do next. Any friction or barrier to making a reply lost some respondents. Preprinted reply cards designating a space for each piece of information the seller wanted from the customer, already addressed to the appropriate sales office, channeled responses much better than simply providing an address (or a telephone number, when that became more common) for inquiries.

Such preformatted replies also became a source of new, readily analyzed consumer behavior data. Market research was not exclusively confined to the direct-mail medium, but direct mail was a prominent component of nascent market research practices. An initial approach could be via letter or via an advertisement in a print publication, or both. Whichever medium carried the initial message, advertising professionals recommended running experiments. In variations of the advertisement, try a different headline, a different image, or some other difference in the appeal. The reply coupons could be keyed to correspond to a particular version of the advertisement; this allowed for tracking response rates. Did one publication generate a higher response rate than the other? Did the sales letter with the larger image generate a higher response rate than the version with the smaller image? Knowing the cost of placing an advertisement (in a publication or in the mail) and the number of inquiries generated made it a matter of simple arithmetic to figure out the cost per inquiry. Sometimes it was even possible to link the communications history (and its costs) with final sales (Cody 1916, p. 19; Cruikshank and Schultz 2010, pp. 59–61). More than any other advertising medium available before World War I, direct mail facilitated the continuous refinement of advertising content and targeting in response to continuously collected consumer response data. If you are looking for the origins of commercial data mining, look here.

Approaching the supply chain as supplicant or disciplinarian

Many users of direct mail were small- or medium-scale manufacturers using the medium to promote their goods to jobbers and retailers. Not-so-large manufacturers making consumer goods still carried out their own business in accordance with the push marketing model that so advantaged jobbers before the Civil War, but they were now doing so in competition with nationally promoted branded goods. The large manufacturers of nationally promoted branded goods gained an advantage over jobbers when they approached consumers directly through advertising – primarily print media and billboards. A successful advertising campaign recruited consumers as allies. Brand-name manufacturers encouraged shoppers to "accept no substitutes" and cast retail clerks as untrustworthy characters who would try to pass of inferior goods for their own benefit at their customers' expense (McGovern 2006, p. 81). Advertising agents and national advertising media found national brands to be their most profitable clients. When a brand was promoted nationally, the fixed costs of designing the advertising content were divvied up over many more placements, and the advertising agents received commissions on all those media placements. National brand-name manufacturers, placing orders via advertising agents, were a ready market for print-media advertising space, especially in magazines that could deliver audiences to advertisers in packages that were differentiated by consumer type and integrated geographically. Even as the cost per eye fell, the leading magazines' circulations grew and the prices for prominent placements in those high-profile magazines soared to thousands of dollars per placement, out of reach of the smaller manufacturers (Cruikshank and Schultz 2010, pp. 42–43; DeWeese 1908, p. 26; Ohmann 1996, p. 26). A smaller scale manufacturer didn't need to and couldn't afford to advertise in a magazine with a circulation of half a million. In order to get their goods before final customers, the smaller manufacturers still relied upon jobbers and retailers to call attention to their goods and push them, link by link, to final users. While national brands instructed consumers to accept no substitutes, smaller manufacturers pleaded with dealers to become their allies in an attempt to persuade consumers to accept a substitute after all. Local retailers did have the advantage of being personally known to their customers and generally enjoyed higher margins on sales of the less prominent brands (Strasser 1989, pp. 21–28), so they were likely recruits to the cause of smaller manufacturers. (And local retailers were also inclined to use direct mail to maintain continuous communications with their customer base.)

At the scale of operations of the national brands, a placement in a national magazine made more sense than mailing a first unsolicited sales pitch to final customers. But national brand-name manufacturers could make use of direct mail to communicate the strength of their alliance with consumers to retailers. The biggest players on the scene approached retailers as disciplinarians, not supplicants. Their letters to retailers warned that brand-loyal customers would shop elsewhere if their preferred brands were not in stock, as when the B.J. Johnson Soap company mailed letters to grocers showing the manufacturers' coupon for their Palmolive brand soap that was soon to appear in local newspaper advertisements, with the implied threat that if the grocers didn't stock Palmolive their customers would go elsewhere to redeem their coupon (Cruikshank and Schultz 2010, pp. 105–106).

There was not necessarily a firm boundary between supplicants and disciplinarians. An informational folder from the Advertising Club of Saint Louis explained the complementary uses of direct-mail advertising addressed to dealers and general advertising addressed to customers. "In many instances," it explained, "Direct Advertising is a forerunner of General Publicity, and paves the way for a newspaper or magazine campaign." First, get the goods placed with dealers "through the medium of Direct Advertising sent to the dealer and the efforts of . . . salesmen." Once that is accomplished, "general demand created through General Publicity is promptly met by the dealer and every call becomes a sale" (Direct Mail Advertising Association 1916h, p. 57). We can imagine variations on this idealized scenario. The way the scene played out would depend on the relative bargaining strength of manufacturer and dealers, on the dealers' expectations of the efficacy of the manufacturer's planned general advertising campaign, and, in the final reckoning, on consumers' actual response to the general advertising campaign.

Manufacturers of intermediate and investment goods also made use of direct mail to negotiate their place in the supply chain. Makers of specialized equipment or intermediate processors of raw materials had very narrowly defined markets. Advertisements in general circulation newspapers and magazines were guaranteed a high level of waste circulation. Specialized trade journals that neatly packaged a narrowly defined class of potential buyers were able to charge much higher rates for ad placements, perhaps two to five times the rate charged by a general circulation magazine (MacFarlane 1915, pp. 13–14). Meanwhile, the information accessible from commercial directories or purchasable from credit rating agencies brought down the cost of assembling a package of potential buyers directly. Direct mail was therefore a reasonable choice of medium. The assumed irrationality of consumers didn't apply to business-to-business marketing in quite the same way. Buyers of intermediate and investment goods, like the manufacturers who wanted to reach them through advertising, were businessmen, and so manufacturers assumed such targets were, like themselves, more or less rational thinkers.

Some manufacturers' business-to-business campaigns were aimed at becoming the preferred supplier for a component of an existing production process. But this was also a period of rapid technological change. For innovative manufacturers, direct mail allowed the scope for fuller explanations of the new materials and equipment than could fit in a trade journal advertising placement. Those promoting a new way of doing things, however, had to contend with resistance from those whose livelihoods were rooted in the established way of doing things. J.H. Patterson was an early innovator in direct-mail selling when he used the medium to sell cash registers in the 1880s. His sales pitch emphasized the role of the cash register in combatting clerks' carelessness and dishonesty. The clerks who handled the mail before it reached their employers were insulted (or perhaps *were* dishonest and saw a source of supplemental income threatened) and made sure the letters didn't reach their employers' desks (Harder 1958, pp. 47–48).

The choice of direct mail as a medium had implications not only for relations up and down the supply chain, but also for horizontal competition among those competing to secure the same niche in the supply chain. One of the advantages of direct mail touted by the Direct Mail Advertising Association was the privacy of the mails. An advertisement in a print publication would be visible to all your competitors, allowing them to strategize a counterstrategy immediately. A direct-mail campaign would not be seen, so a marketing push through the mail would not be countered as quickly by competitors (Direct Mail Advertising Association 1916e).

Disciplining the profession

Advertisers and advertising professionals in every sector began their modernization process with a reputational problem. Patent medicines dominated print advertising; doubts about the safety and efficacy of patent medicines – and doubts about the honesty of patent medicine purveyors – cast doubt on the entire genre of print advertisements, pressuring advertisers of less sketchy products to organize and self-police themselves on truth in advertising standards (Goodrum and Dalrymple 1990, p. 29; Ohmann 1996, p. 97). The logo for the Associated Advertising Clubs of the World placed the word "TRUTH" in bold, capital letters in the center (see, for example, the frontispiece of Cherington 1920 [1916]). Some of the most successful publishers, who could afford to be choosy about accepting advertising placements, refused to run patent medicine advertisements at all, thus granting an aura of greater legitimacy to those advertisements they did run (Laird 1998, p. 223). Advertisers and advertising media didn't police themselves as thoroughly as government policy could, however; a 1905 exposé of the patent medicine industry in *Collier's* followed by the 1906 passage of the Federal Food and Drug Act choked off what was still a major source of business for advertising agencies (Cruikshank and Schultz 2010, pp. 98–99). Billposting, meanwhile, was heavily associated with circuses and theaters, which weren't generally considered respectable, and were especially off limits to middle-class women. Billposters' organizations, eager to use the medium to reach aggregations of consumers that prominently included middle-class women, endorsed standards for poster content – standards that would exclude images of scantily clad chorus girls. This had reputational benefits for the advertisers who did choose to make billboard placements, and also reputational benefits for the billposters in their political efforts to gain support for their land-use practices.

Direct-mail marketers, too, had to distinguish themselves from nefarious users of their chosen medium, the mail. Especially after letter postage fell in the mid-nineteenth century, the mail was used for all manner of swindles and frauds. These were often understood to be an instance of urban corruption taking advantage of rural naïveté; many swindles did indeed operate out of

New York City. Whether advertising professionals acknowledged the similarity or not, some of their own sales techniques resembled long-standing swindle techniques. Richard Popp writes, "Indeed, swindlers operated something of an alternative mail order trade that in many ways exploited the same aspirations and desires as agency outfitters like Allen" and the legal (if morally dubious) trade in mail-order inquiry letters was shadowed by a black market in the names of marks (Popp Forthcoming). The direct-mail marketers seeking to establish their legitimacy, like swindlers, designed their mailings to deceptively imitate personal mail, and, also like swindlers, they classified targets by degree of gullibility. The Mail Fraud Act of 1872 had given postal inspectors authority to pursue perpetrators of fraud through the mails, but it was a Sisyphean task (Henkin 2006, pp. 155–157; Gallagher 2016, pp. 151, 210).

When direct-mail advertisers established their own professional organization in 1915, reputational concerns were a key motivator. They had to concern themselves with the climate of justifiable skepticism recipients held toward letters received from strangers. They sought to establish standards for what kinds of advertising clients they would serve in order to distinguish their "truthful" advertisements for "legitimate" products from the unsolicited letters seeking to part people with their money on fraudulent pretenses. In a colorful letter to the inaugural conference, Victor Eytinge wrote, "We must emit and vomit out the nauseous masses that have been swallowed in our swift growth. The public is awake and still looks *too much* with suspicion on anything offered through the mails. We must clean up our department as the better papers and magazines have cleaned up their columns" (Direct Mail Advertising Association 1916a, p. 10).

The mail fraud problem made consumers mistrust sales letters and therefore raised advertisers' doubts about mail as a medium. Compounding those doubts, advertisers had reason to be skeptical of the quality of service offered by self-proclaimed direct-mail advertising professionals. Direct Mail Advertising Association organizers wanted to distinguish their professional work from fraudulent work-from-home schemes that promised the credulous that they could make a lucrative living preparing advertising mailings from home – once they sent in a few dollars for a training booklet. (This was a variation on E.C. Allen's recruitment of sales agents who would hit the road.) They wanted to educate direct-mail professionals so as to raise the efficiency of the medium and thereby raise its standing in advertisers' eyes. And, not incidentally though more circumspectly stated, they wanted to erect exclusionary barriers to entry. "It is not at all helpful to the advertising world," Eytinge charged,

> that any stenographer buying a duplicating machine, may spread a 'Letters Experted' shingle. It is a smirch on the good name of the printing craft, when some shop boasts a 'service department' and the managers know nothing of merchandising, advertising or service. We must raise our standards of work and our standards in men
>
> (Direct Mail Advertising Association 1916a, p. 10).

In specifically calling out stenographers who overstep their bounds, as much as in his call to raise "our standards in *men*," Eytinge was policing a gender barrier – stenography was overwhelmingly a female field (Davies 1982, p. 52).

A two-part series in the inaugural two issues of the new professional journal *Postage* discussed several of direct mail's credibility problems under the title "Fools and Their Money." It ended with a plea for broad participation in self-policing:

> The Associated Advertising Clubs of the World is at the present time engaged in compiling a list of known crooks who are operating through the mails. But this will scarcely be found to be enough if the whole mail order business is to be sweetened, purified, and made as clean as possible for the protection of reputable concerns. May the Editors of *Postage* ask for the assistance of those who are interested in this work?
>
> (Direct Mail Advertising Association 1916c, p. 60).

Conclusion

In certain respects, direct-mail advertising was a backward sector of the advertising industry, especially before about 1910. (Before, that is, it acquired the name "direct mail advertising," still going by terms that named the materials mailed: circulars, sales letters.) The grouping of advertising's component tasks into the purview of particular businesses did not standardize to the same extent as it did for other advertising sectors. The brand-name manufacturers, whom Pamela Walker Laird identifies as the most innovative modernizers among advertisers (Laird 1998, p. 35), "aggressively and deliberately developed advertising techniques to wrest control of the marketplace away from retailers and wholesalers" after 1870 (Laird 1998, pp. 30–31), and their preferred media for consumer-oriented advertising were periodicals and billboard posters rather than the mail. As a late modernizer, direct-mail advertising wriggled into the niches that periodical media advertising and outdoor advertising did not already dominate, or found the gaps where it could serve as a complement to periodical media. "[M]ass marketing and target marketing developed as reciprocal practices, rather than alternatives to one another, and . . . the trade in personal information was integral to the rise of industrialized forms of marketing" (Popp Forthcoming). Direct mail was employed by those still facing or seeking to preserve the older conditions of market control. Manufacturers in less brand-dominated lines used direct mail to approach dealers as push marketing supplicants, seeking middlemen to move their goods a step closer to final consumers. Retailers used direct mail to cultivate their local customer base, hoping consumers would grant their loyalty to their retailer first and to brands only secondarily. When retailers were secure in their position as their customers' point of contact with the market, they could push the products on which they earned the highest mark-ups; when heavily promoted branded goods persuaded customers to "accept no substitutes," retailers were forced to handle products on which the manufacturers' profit margins were higher and their own were lower (McGovern 2006, p. 81). Given the state of late nineteenth-century information technologies, managing a target audience individual by individual was cumbersome and subject to diseconomies of scale. Even the emerging mail-order retailers with national reach did not make their first contact with customers through an individual letter; they advertised in print media, then received and fulfilled inquiries and orders by mail.

Viewed from another angle, however, direct-mail advertising made an extraordinary leap into the information economy and could be ranked the most innovative advertising medium of all. In contrast to the prepackaged audiences offered to advertisers by billposters and publishers, direct mail allowed the audience to be custom selected for each appeal. Magazines' production of the audience commodity was analogous to the continuous process mass production that sent high and steady volumes of rolled oats and white flour and cigarettes streaming onto the market. By contrast, direct mail offered just-in-time flexible batch production of audiences. From the moment mail-order retailers realized the ongoing advertising potential of the customer contact information generated by inquiries and orders, and print media advertisers systematized the "follow-up system" for handling inquires prompted by their ads, direct-mail advertising was linked with data-driven market research and the construction of customers' individual commercial histories. Direct mail's potential for individual-by-individual tracking of responses led to its adoption as a complement to print-media advertising. Keying print-media advertisements allowed advertisers to assess which responses came from which print-media advertisement. Tracking follow-up letters let them determine which approaches led to final sales. They could then calculate per-unit selling costs more precisely. They were not limited to doing their calculations in the aggregate (total advertising expenditures divided by total units sold). Instead, they could try varied approaches, calculate the per-unit selling costs of each variation, then discontinue the underperforming advertising venues and pitches while expanding the more successful. The information-processing needs of direct-mail marketers put them into a call-and-response relationship with information technology innovation. Information-processing bottlenecks called forth new technologies to increase the speed at which data could be collected, stored, filtered, and replicated. New technologies opened up new possibilities for how much and what kinds of data could be brought to bear on the advertisers' marketing practices.

Direct-mail advertising belonged to a larger movement into the information economy, joined by businesses such as credit rating agencies and clipping bureaus. In the hands of a "list house," thousands of individuals' personal data – name and address at a minimum, but sometimes also far more extensive data about their work histories, households, and consumer behavior – became salable intellectual property. That intellectual property did not belong to the people the data described. Individuals have never had full control over their own personal narrative – gossip is probably as old as human language and a person could always find that their reputation preceded them – but the commercialization of personal information was new. Gossip may have been social currency, but it could only be converted to cash through blackmail, charging a fee to the person described in exchange for suppressing information about them. List houses converted information about other people into cash as their overt daily business, charging fees for sharing information. With the trademark laws of the 1880s, the public's knowledge of brands became the basis of the value contained in businesses' intellectual property. With this first explosion of data mining, what data miners knew about the public, individual by individual, also became businesses' intellectual property. An average individual member of the public owned neither what they knew of the businesses they dealt with nor what those businesses knew of them. With increasing frequency, attempts to sell a good *to* an individual potential customer were preceded by the purchase of data *about* that potential customer. (And customers' response to each sales pitch generated yet more data.) As early as the 1880s, the courts recognized marketers' property rights in the names they had compiled and punished those who accessed those names without payment to the owner. (Paying a bribe to a clerk instead of the business owner was a way to gain illegal access to the data.) The people whose names were listed, however, had no recognized property rights (Popp forthcoming). Common turn of the twentieth-century usage omitted the preposition we now use to describe the relation between buyer and seller; the phrasing then was that a business, when successfully persuading someone to buy, "sold the customer." For the early innovators in commercializing personal data and for their contemporary heirs, the phrasing need not change for twenty-first-century usage. The customer is in fact what is being sold.

Notes

1 Translation: "stuff in non-refillable bottles" = alcohol; "W. C. T. U." = Women's Christian Temperance Union.

2 In 1918, Dun was experimenting with crowdsourcing credit information. That year, each edition of their weekly publication *Dun's Review* ran a full-page announcement on the back page promoting their new Credit Information Ledger Interchange, which allowed subscribers to the general report to submit credit information on businesses they have dealt with in exchange for additional, more detailed reports on specific businesses at no additional charge (*Dun's Review* 1918).

3 In 1880 there were 54,000 telephones in the country. The number passed a quarter of a million in the early 1890s, passed a million and a half in the early 1900s, passed six million by 1910, and passed 12 million by 1920 (Cruikshank and Schultz 2010, p. 42; Strasser 1989, p. 25).

4 See, for example, US Patent No. 808,191, granted in 1905 to Joseph P. Bryan of the Automatic Addressing Company of Wilmington, Delaware, for an addressing attachment for printing presses (Bryan 1905); US Patent No. 924,198, granted in 1909 to James Sinisi of the Cosmopolitan Addressing Company of New York City, for a type-writer for producing addressing machine stencils (Sinisi 1909); US Patent No. 1,060,679, granted in 1913 to John Edward Hanrahan of the Chesapeake Addressing Company of Baltimore, Maryland, for a single-type-casting attachment for linotype-machines (Hanrahan 1913).

Bibliography

Associated Billposters Association of the United States and Canada. 1902–1903. *The Billposter-Display Advertising.*

Bates, Charles Austin. 1896. *Good Advertising and Where It Is Made.* New York: Bates.

Beach, Elmer Henry. 1905. *Tools of Business: An Encyclopedia of Office Equipment and Labor Saving Devices.* Detroit, MI: The Book-Keeper Publishing Co.

Beardsley, W.W. 1924. *The Circular Advertising Department.* New York: The Ronald Press Company.

Beniger, James R. 1986. *The Control Revolution: Technological and Economic Origins of the Information Society.* Cambridge, MA: Harvard University Press.

Bryan, Joseph P. 1905. "Addressing Attachment for Printing-presses." US Patent No. 808, 191, filed July 28, 1904 and issued December 26.

Buckley, Homer J. 1916a. "The Possibilities of the Mailing List in Modern Business Building, Article 1." *Postage* Volume 1 Number 1: 54–56.

Buckley, Homer J. 1916a2. "The Printer and His Advertising." *Postage* Volume 1 Number 1: 37.

Buckley, Homer J. 1916b. "The Possibilities of the Mailing List in Modern Business Building, Article 2." *Postage* Volume 1 Number 2: 36–37.

Buckley, Homer J. 1916c. "The Possibilities of the Mailing List in Modern Business Building: The Jobber and his Mailing List." *Postage* Volume 1 Number 3: 15–16.

Buckley, Homer J. 1916d. "The Possibilities of the Mailing List in Modern Business Building, Fourth Article." *Postage* Volume 1 Number 4: 58–60.

Burdick, H. C. 1916a. "How to Compile a Mailing List." In *Sales Promotion by Mail: How to Sell and How to Advertise.* New York: The Knickerbocker Press.

Burdick, H. C. 1916b. "You Can't Grow Orchids on a Mulberry Bush." *Postage* Volume 1 Number 2: 17–18.

Casson, Herbert N. 1911. *Ads and Sales: A Study of Advertising and Selling from the Standpoint of the New Principles of Scientific Management.* Chicago, IL: A. C. McClurg & Co.

Chandler, Alfred. 2002 [1977]. *The Visible Hand: The Managerial Revolution in American Business.* Cambridge, MA: Belknap Press.

Cherington, Paul Terry. 1920 [1916]. *The First Advertising Book.* New York: Doubleday, Page & Company.

Cody, Sherwin. 1916. "Direct Advertising as a Means of Testing All Advertising." *Postage* Volume 1 Number 5: 19–20.

Cruikshank, Jeffrey L., and Arthur W. Schultz. 2010. *The Man Who Sold America: The Amazing (but True!) Story of Albert D. Lasker and the Creation of the Advertising Century.* Boston: Harvard Business Review Press.

Curti, Merle. 1967. "The Changing Concept of 'Human Nature' in the Literature of American Advertising." *The Business History Review* Volume 41: 335–357.

Davies, Margery W. 1982. *Woman's Place Is at the Typewriter: Office Work and Office Workers 1870–1930.* Philadelphia: Temple University Press.

DeWeese, Truman. 1908 [1906]. *The Principles of Practical Publicity,* 2nd Edition. Philadelphia: George W. Jacobs & Co.

Direct Mail Advertising Association. 1916a. "A New Movement and Its Meaning." *Postage* Volume 1 Number 1. January: 9–11.

Direct Mail Advertising Association. 1916b. *Postage* Volume 1 Number 2. February.

Direct Mail Advertising Association. 1916c. "Fools and Their Money, Article 2: Casting the Line." *Postage* Volume 1 Number 2. February: 55–60.

Direct Mail Advertising Association. 1916d. "The Why of Direct Advertising." *Postage* Volume 1 Number 3. March: 23–25.

Direct Mail Advertising Association. 1916e. "Eight Big Advantages of Direct Mail Advertising." *Postage* Volume 1 Number 4. April: 48–49.

Direct Mail Advertising Association. 1916f. *Postage* Volume 1 Number 5. May.

Direct Mail Advertising Association. 1916g. "Shortage of Paper Material." *Postage* Volume 1 Number 5. May: 16.

Direct Mail Advertising Association. 1916h. "Direct Advertising." *Postage* Volume 1 Number 5. May: 57.

Dun's Review. 1918. Published weekly by R. G. Dun and Co. The Mercantile Agency.

Elgutter, Maurice. 1916. "Direct Advertising for Retail Stores." *Postage* Volume 1 Number 2: 31–33.

Farrington, Frank. 1910. *Retail Advertising*. Chicago, IL: Byxbee Publishing Co.

Fay, Robert C. 1916. "The Psychology of Business Letter Writing." *Postage* Volume 1 Number 5: 13–16.

Fowler, Nathaniel. 1900 [1897]. *Fowler's Publicity: An Encyclopedia of Advertising and Printing, and all that Pertains to the Public-Seeing Side of Business*. New York: Publicity Publishing Company.

Fuller, Wayne E. 1991. "The Populists and the Post Office." *Agricultural History* Volume 65: 1–16.

Gallagher, Winifred. 2016. *How the Post Office Created America*. New York: Penguin Press.

Goodrum, Charles, and Helen Dalrymple. 1990. *Advertising in America: The First 200 Years*. New York: Henry N. Abrams.

Greer, Carl Richard. 1925. *The Buckeye Book of Direct Advertising*. Hamilton, OH: The Beckett Paper Company.

Hanrahan, John Edward. 1913. "Single-type-casting Attachment for Linotype-machines." US Patent No. 1,060,679, filed August 31, 1910 and issued May 6.

Harder, Virgil Eugene. 1958. *A History of Direct Mail Advertising* (Doctoral thesis), University of Illinois.

Henkin, David M. 2006 *The Postal Age: The Emergence of Modern Communications in Nineteenth-Century America*. Chicago, IL: University of Chicago Press.

Hopkins, Claude. 1966 [1927 and 1923]. *My Life in Advertising and Scientific Advertising*. Chicago, IL: Advertising Publications, Inc.

Kielbowicz, Richard B. 1989. *News in the Mail: The Press, Post Office, and Public Information, 1700–1860s*. New York: Greenwood Press.

Kielbowicz, Richard B. 1990. "Postal Subsidies for the Press and the Business of Mass Culture, 1880–1920." *The Business History Review* Volume 64: 451–488.

Laird, Pamela Walker. 1998. *Advertising Progress: American Business and the Rise of Consumer Marketing*. Baltimore: The Johns Hopkins University Press.

Lanston Monotype Machine Company. 1916. "The Why of Direct Advertising." *Postage* Volume 1 Number 3: 23–25.

Lauer, Josh. 2017. *Creditworthy: A History of Consumer Surveillance and Financial Identity in America*. New York: Columbia University Press.

Lewis, Norman. 1916. "Dollars and Details." *Postage* Volume 1 Number 3: 26–28.

MacFarlane, Charles Alexander. 1915. *The Principles and Practice of Direct Advertising*. Hamilton, OH: The Beckett Paper Company.

MacNichol, Kenneth. 1916. "The Business Morgue: An Incubator for Hatching Profits." *Postage* Volume 1 Number 1: 30–36.

Mahin, John Lee. 1900. "The 'Follow-Up' System in Securing Business." *System Monthly*. December 1900. Muskegon, MI: The Shaw-Walker Co.

Mahin, John Lee. 1916 [1914]. *Advertising: Selling the Consumer*. New York: Doubleday, Page and Company for The Associated Advertising Clubs of the World.

Mahin's Magazine. 1902–1903.Volume 1 Numbers 1–12.

McGovern, Charles F. 2006. *Sold American: Consumption and Citizenship, 1890–1945*. Chapel Hill, NC:The University of North Carolina Press.

Ohmann, Richard. 1996. *Selling Culture: Magazines, Markets, and Class at the Turn of the Century*. London and New York:Verso.

Paper Makers Advertising Club. 1915a. *We Vote to Work with the Printer*. No.1 in a series of Direct-by-Mail Advertising pamphlets.

Paper Makers Advertising Club. 1915b. *Direct-by-Mail Advertising: The Plan, A Booklet that Tells How to Sell Printing Jobs in a Series*. No.2 in a series of Direct-by-Mail Advertising pamphlets.

Paper Makers Advertising Club. 1915c. *The Manufacturer's Direct-by-Mail Advertising Plan*. No.3 in a series of Direct-by-Mail Advertising pamphlets.

Paper Makers Advertising Club. 1915d. *A Selling Cost for Printing*. No.4 in a series of Direct-by-Mail Advertising pamphlets.

Paper Makers Advertising Club. 1915e. *The Reasons Why for Direct-by-Mail Advertising*. No.5 in a series of Direct-by-Mail Advertising pamphlets.

Poesche, Hermann. 1901. "Bookless Accounting:The History of the Card Ledger." *System Monthly*. January 1901. Muskegon, MI:The Shaw-Walker Co.

Popp, Richard K. Forthcoming. "The Information Bazaar: Mail-Order Magazines and the Consumer Data Trade in Gilded Age America." In *Surveillance Capitalism in America: From Slavery to Social Media*, ed. Josh Lauer and Kenneth Lipartito. Philadelphia: University of Pennsylvania Press.

Porter, Glenn, and Harold C. Livesay. 1971. *Merchants and Manufacturers: Studies in the Changing Structure of Nineteenth-Century Marketing*. Baltimore: Johns Hopkins Press.

Post Office Department. 1956. *United States Domestic Postage Rates, 1789–1956*. Fishkill, NY: The Printer's Stone.

Ramsay, Robert E. 1916a. "The List Makes or Breaks Your Mail Campaign." *Postage* Volume 1 Number 1: 20–21.

Ramsay, Robert E. 1916b. "Like a Modern Machine Gun." *Postage* Volume 1 Number 3: 34–36.

Saval, Nikil. 2014. *Cubed: A Secret History of the Workplace*. New York: Doubleday.

Sawyer, Samuel. 1900. *Secrets of the Mail Order Trade*. Waterville, ME:The Sawyer Publishing Company.

Schumpeter, Joseph. 1942. *Capitalism, Socialism, and Democracy*. New York: Harper and Brothers.

Scott, Walter Dill. 1910. *The Psychology of Advertising: A Simple Exposition of the Principles of Psychology in Their Relation to Successful Advertising*, 2nd Edition. Boston: Small, Maynard & Company.

Sinisi, James. 1909. "Typewriting Machine." US Patent No. 924,198, filed July 24, 1907 and issued June 8.

Slemin, H. C. 1916. "Filing the Follow-Up." *Postage* Volume 1 Number 2: 40–42.

Strasser, Susan. 1989. *Satisfaction Guaranteed: The Making of the American Mass Market*. New York: Pantheon Books.

Strom, Sharon Hartman. 1989. "'Light Manufacturing': The Feminization of American Office Work, 1900–1930." *Industrial and Labor Relations Review* Volume 43 Number 1: 53–71.

Taylor, Frederick Winslow. 1911. *Scientific Management*. New York: Harper & Brothers Publishers.

Tuttle, Martin. 1916. "The Possibilities of Direct Advertising in the Automobile Field." *Post-age* Volume 1 Number 2: 46–48.

Waitt, Isabel Woodman. 1916. "Unasked-For Advertising: A Woman's Viewpoint." *Postage* Volume 1 Number 1: 38–42.

Wolf, Leonard J. 1916. "Finding Your Prospects." *Postage* Volume 1 Number 1: 57–61.

Zenner, A. H. 1900. "How the Zenner Disinfectant Co. Go After Business." *System Monthly*. December 1900. Muskegon, MI: The Shaw-Walker Co.

5   Conclusion

Multimedia demands on the resource of attention

Advertising of all sorts

The maturation of an audience attention market put a collection of dissimilar activities into competition with one another. For example, streetcars and billboards competed with newspapers and magazines. On the face of it, these appear to be completely distinct businesses, but they all sold access to audiences' eyes and advertisers made decisions about the allocation of their advertising among all those options. Kodak at first declined to use streetcars and billboards at all because they believed the "better class" of consumers they targeted could be better reached through magazines (Strasser 1989, p. 102). (Later on, Kodak did include outdoor advertising in their sales strategy.) By contrast, the makers of Sapolio household cleaners thought their target audience, which included domestic workers, could regularly be found on the streets and on the streetcars and their campaign focused predominantly on these public space placements from the get-go (Laird 1998, p. 180).

Initially, different advertising media were handled by different firms. An advertiser wishing to advertise in multiple media had to contract with multiple firms to negotiate the multiple routes to audience attention. Conversely, an advertiser choosing an advertising firm to work with was necessarily choosing a medium – when patent medicine manufacturer Lydia Pinkham fired her advertising agent in 1889 (he had been lying to her about the size of his commission), print media dropped out of her advertising budget entirely and she relied exclusively on trade cards for a year. (She also spent less overall.) Dissatisfied with the results, she hired a different advertising agent and returned to print media (Laird 1998, pp. 19, 87, 176–178). An advertiser choosing how to allocate their budget among the available media was determining an allocation between different firms, not an allocation within a diversified firm.

Publishers, billposters, and direct-mail marketers (and providers in other, smaller attention market sectors) each had to worry about their close horizontal competitors within their sector. They each, especially the first two, had to worry about how large a share of the advertising pie would be skimmed by the middlemen who connected them to the advertisers. But they and their specialized middlemen also had to worry about their entire sectors' share of total advertising spending. Horizontal competition among publishers created incentives for publishers to pursue their own gain at one another's expense. The same was true of horizontal competition among agents. Vertical competition between publishers and agents created incentives for publishers to ally with one another to strengthen their bargaining position with agents; agents had mirror-image reasons to form alliances among themselves. Meanwhile, especially before 1900, publishers and agents together had a shared interest in promoting print as an advertising medium over other options. Billposters and their solicitors were in a comparable set of relations. Direct mail was a little different as it was most heavily used by different advertisers than the first two, had high per-unit costs that restricted its use to a narrower subset of selling applications, and did not have the layer of middlemen that other media had. Unsurprisingly, given the complex Venn diagram of shared and conflicting interests, alliances were unstable and the strength of cooperation waxed and waned.

In the print-media sector, publishers and agents were fairly evenly matched in vertical competition. Publishers' associations were strong enough to keep agents' commissions in check, but agents dominated communications about the advertising industry and selling practices through periodical publications such as *Printers' Ink* and an entire library of mostly agent-authored books about advertising aimed at businessmen, many of which were published under the auspices of the Associated Advertising Clubs of America (AACA) or of the World (AACW). (And many of which you can now read in digitized, open-access form.) By contrast, the Associated Billposters' Association dominated their sector. It was the Billposters, not the solicitors, who published a journal and pamphlets for businessmen. Eventually, the agent-publisher alliance to promote print above billboards broke down and advertising agents who had started with print began to expand into billboard placements, as well, displacing the specialized billboard-only solicitors. Some such multimedia agents also offered direct-mail service. (The Bates agency was already touting their direct-mail department in the mid-1890s.) Diversification of agency intermediation, along with the expansion of agencies into a range of market research and creative services, offered great convenience to advertisers. They could work now with one provider to coordinate an overall marketing strategy.

Billboards vs. newspapers

Decade of conflict: the 1890s

The 1890s was transformative both for publishing and for billposting. Modern magazines burst onto the scene and the publishing industry as a whole flipped from majority-subscription-financed to majority-advertising-financed. Billposters organized nationally to secure local monopolies, constructed new wooden, then iron billboards, standardized the "listed and protected" billposting contracts through which they rented out the billboard display space, used their pricing power to set fees in proportion to local population size, then used those monopoly rents to further expand and upgrade their billboards. Both media were proliferating and modernizing. In this formative stage, competition between these two groups of sellers of gazes took place at two levels simultaneously. Billposters along with the solicitors specializing in outdoor advertising and publishers along with the agents specializing in periodical placements competed *within the structures of the market* as they existed at any given moment, and they also battled over the *construction of market infrastructure* and the rules of play.

Within the market structure at a given moment, purveyors of gazes competed on price and quality of product. Billposters were fond of price-per-gaze comparisons as they had the edge by that measure. A modest number of well-placed posters could intercept the eyes of just about every resident of a given city at rates considerably lower than the rates necessary to place a newspaper advertisement in periodicals with a similar reach. For example, in 1900 *The Billposter-Display Advertising* ran an article explaining that an advertising expenditure of $3,000 would buy the advertiser a full-page color ad inserted into the three largest New York City daily newspapers for one day; the same $3,000 would purchase a billboard display reaching at least the same proportion of the New York City population, and probably greater, for *thirty* days (Associated Billposters Association of the United States and Canada September 1900, p. 5). Billposters also frequently questioned the reliability of newspaper circulation as a measure of how many readers really saw the advertisements. Not only were publishers known to pad their reported circulation numbers in those years before the Audit Bureau of Circulations was established, but even actual readers who were not figments of publishers' faulty accounting could easily skip over the page on which an advertisement was printed without ever seeing it. It is much harder for a pedestrian or streetcar passenger to avert her eyes from a large billboard at a busy intersection.

Publishers and advertising agents who specialized in print denigrated outdoor advertising and touted their own virtues as an advertising medium in turn. They claimed (though this was hard to demonstrate rigorously) that newspaper advertisements were more effective, making the selling cost lower. They promoted periodicals' ability to sort audiences by social class and interest. They contrasted the long, detailed copy newspaper advertisements could accommodate with the extremely simple sales pitches required by the poster medium. The advertising agents remained tightly allied with publishers for most of the decade because they were certain of their print-media commissions and uncertain of their prospects for securing income through other media. Laird writes, "[A]dvertising agents generally discouraged advertisers from using non-commissionable media – such as posters and trade cards – which they attacked as 'misuse' of expenditures. In this way, advertising agents tried to block the use of certain types of advertising forms that had, in some cases at least, proved to advance the progress of business." Agents' interest in the advertisers' business success did not supersede their own. Theme with variations: a few decades later, advertising agents opposed radio advertising until they found a way to earn commissions on it (Laird 1998, p. 158).

At the same time, the rules of the advertising game were continuously contested. Outdoor advertising's greatest arena of action was newly burgeoning cities. City residents and their municipal governments were engaged in a continual rearguard struggle to solve the problems of urban life. What activities could be accommodated and where? As sites of production, sites of household provisioning, and sites of residence became increasingly separated, how would people move through urban agglomerations to get from one site to another on a regular basis? One of the fiercely fought battles over the uses of urban space was over outdoor advertising. Professionalizing billposters and sign painters wanted to establish property rights that would recognize their right to construct, maintain, and place advertising on billboards and painted signs and their right to restrict anyone else from posting over or defacing their legitimate ads. They needed government action to accomplish this. Progressive reformers wanted a different kind of government action, not so compatible with the interests of the billposters. They wanted sharp restrictions on size, placement, and content of billboards, taxes and licensing fees levied on billposters, or even the elimination of outdoor advertising altogether (Warner 1900; Woodruff 1907). Newspapers, fearing a loss of market share, were reformers' eager allies in efforts to block the conversion of the urban landscape into an advertising medium.

Indeed, billposters saw the nefarious influence of periodical publishers behind *all* restrictive efforts. According to their power analysis, periodical publishers felt threatened by billposters' potential to attract advertising expenditure away from the page and onto the billboard. Municipal leaders feared the ability of the newspapers to shape public opinion and so felt compelled to work in the newspapers' interests by restricting billboards. (The billposters' argument implicitly agrees that newspapers are persuasive in the realm of political opinion, even as they were claiming to potential clients that newspapers are no more and probably less persuasive as a sales tool.) Billposters accused some purported citizens' groups of being fronts for the publishers' interests, an accusation of what we would now call astroturfing. They were probably at least partially right, though not entirely. "Scenery" advertising *was* attacked by advertising agents and newspapers; "defamation of the landscape" was one of the most frequent ad-related topics covered in the *New York Times* in the second half of the nineteenth century. But it was also attacked by those who were critical of advertising in general (Laird 1998, p. 214). Inter-sectoral competition in the attention market is not the only reason to want some limits on billboards – the audiences themselves may have wanted their eyes back.

Détente: after 1900

The competition between billposters and periodicals did eventually soften from both sides. A number of developments contributed to the détente. Newspapers found they could successfully advertise themselves in the outdoor medium. Although the cross-sector competition over advertising dollars remained, within-sector competition among newspapers for readers and hence advertising dollars spurred newspapers' need to advertise themselves in multiple media. Once they took up billboard advertising of themselves, the high visibility of publishers' own posters damaged the persuasiveness of their claim that *other* advertisers should use newspapers exclusively and forced them to retreat from attempts to totally discredit outdoor advertising (Associated Billposters Association of the United States and Canada January 1903, p. 31).

A growing number of advertising agents made placements in both periodicals and on billboards for their clients. The N.W. Ayer and Son agency was already one of the most famous and prosperous media advertising agencies in the US when they expanded their business into billposting contracts and became an official solicitor for the Associated Billposters in 1899, a reversal of their earlier policy of trying to steer clients away from posters. In 1900, Ayer offered for the first time to assist with designing posters. Within a few years they were actively pushing a both-and message to clients rather pushing an either-or choice regarding billposting and periodical media (Laird 1998, pp. 158–159; Associated Billposters Association of the United States and Canada March 1902, p. 3). In 1905, major Chicago agency Lord & Thomas added an outdoor advertising department (Cruikshank and Schultz 2010, p. 63). (Charles Austin Bates, another famous media advertising agent of the day, was also an early official solicitor for the Associated Billposters. His designation did not last long, though. Whereas Ayer was widely respected, Bates was a polarizing figure. Over the course of his career he experimented with turning audience attention into personal income every which way and when he tried to monetize his attention-gathering experience by selling a directory of outdoor advertisers in direct competition with the Associated Billposters' own official "big list," he was dropped from the list of official solicitors (Associated Billposters Association of the United States and Canada April 1902, p. 26, June 1902, p. 17).)

As agents diversified and fewer advertisers of any size tried to forego the agencies, the publishers and billposters both needed the agents' intermediation to get business. The agents' ability to intermediate was damaged by the vocal and vicious attacks, so competing suppliers of gazes eventually found it to be in their best interests to tone it down. Also, the cumulative precedent-setting effect of all the prior hard-fought legislative actions, judicial decisions, and business practices was to make rules of the game clearer and more settled. Despite publishers' control of the only mass medium in which extended public debate could take place, billposters won most of their legislative and judicial battles: their property rights in display spaces were increasingly secure. When the rules were up for debate, there was always a chance that a small temporary advantage could be leveraged into a large permanent tilt in the playing field. Once it was clear that neither combatant would permanently vanquish the other and they would have to continue to play for incremental gains, the stakes were not so high and hyperbole gave way to more measured pitches.

Indeed, there were even gestures toward an alliance. The *Milwaukee Sentinel* put up posters with the slogan, "Advertising of all sorts helps all sorts of advertising," and as a result the Associated Billposters held up the *Sentinel* as an example of a good newspaper. It may not be necessary to choose sides between billposting and newspaper advertising, billposters and publishers concluded; both may be on the same side. Rather than battling over shares of a fixed pie, newspapers and billposters could act on a shared interest in increasing the volume of all sorts of advertising (Associated Billposters Association of the United States and Canada October 1903, p. 16, January 1903, p. 39).

Direct mail enters the fray

Direct-mail advertising came late to the standardize-and-professionalize game. Their professional organization was established in 1915 and the first issue of their professional journal came out in January 1916. Though growing, they earned a far smaller share of advertisers' selling costs than the publishers and billposters. Advertisers in the mid-1910s spent about \$350 million annually on newspaper placements, for example, but only \$150 million on direct mail (Paper Makers Advertising Club 1915). Direct-mail advertising was a complex undertaking with many contributors, each of whom strived for a cut of the total payments made for direct-mail operations as a whole. The absolute size of any one contributor's share could increase by expanding their slice of the existing direct-mail pie or by enlarging the entire direct-mail pie. Direct mail, in turn, could grow by drawing advertising dollars away from other advertising media, or by expanding total advertising expenditures on all advertising media. Advertising professionals participating in the direct-mail sector (exclusively or in combination with other sectors of the advertising sector) and makers of the intermediate and investment goods required for direct-mail advertising campaigns (papermakers, printers, office machinery manufacturers) all worked to argue for the mail's efficacy as an advertising medium.

The promoters of direct-mail advertising had to measure the potential gain of bids to win market share away from more established media against the potential gain of securing a complementary role and riding the rising tide of overall advertising expenditures. They had great hopes of growing their sector of the attention industry, but concluded that they had little hope of supplanting other media. They simply couldn't risk alienating the major advertising industry players. In their bid to persuade advertisers to spend more on direct mail, they carefully presented their services as a *complement* to other forms of advertising. By the time direct mail began its steep ascent, publishers and billposters had eased up in their denigration of one another, many advertisers treated different media as complements rather than substitutes, and advertising agencies were increasingly willing and able to manage integrated multimedia advertising campaigns. Direct-mail promoters fit themselves into this context. While certainly touting the distinct advantages of direct mail, they also consistently presented direct mail as one medium in a multimedia strategy. (Historically, too, direct mail had roots in the "follow-up system" connected to print-media advertising.) "Let me make clear, first of all," Maurice Elgutter cautiously qualified his promotion of direct mail, "that I am not belittling any of the other forms of advertising you are using, certainly not newspaper advertising" (Elgutter 1916, p. 31). Elgutter was following his professional association's party line: The Direct Mail Advertising Association was formed under the existing umbrella of the Associated Adverting Clubs of the World (AACW), not as a competitor to it.[1] (Direct Mail Advertising Association 1916a). Their association journal *Postage* was founded with a statement of policy including the clause, "*Postage* will not enter into any controversies or discussions regarding the relative merits of various mediums (Direct Mail Advertising Association 1916b unnumbered page).

Direct mail was indeed often applied to selling problems that other advertising media didn't address or used in conjunction with other advertising media, especially general circulation print media. Direct-mail advertising campaigns could begin with a newspaper or magazine advertisement that included a mail-in form – when a potential customer mailed in the form requesting more information, their name and address entered the mailing list and the individual mailings began (MacFarlane 1915, p. 8). Along with name and address, the most important piece of personal data an advertiser could have about a target was an indication of their interest in the product and responses to print-media advertising provided just such an indication. Nevertheless, direct-mail promoters did sometimes present head-to-head cost comparisons that could easily be read as recommending the substitution of direct mail for other media. Direct-mail advertising did the most refined sorting of target audiences and undertook the most labor-intensive route to interception of audiences' eyes, making their cost per eye the highest of the early twentieth-century media. But that does not imply that the cost per inquiry or cost per final sale was the highest. The refined sorting, direct-mail promoters claimed, allowed waste circulation to be trimmed to the absolute minimum. Furthermore, the individual-level data collection of a direct-mail campaign provided stronger evidence for their response-rate claims than the newspapers could provide. Even direct mail's special niche of being most testable could, however, be cast as complement rather than substitute to other forms of advertising. The ability to test response rates and experiment with variations of a planned ad campaign raised the possibility that using direct mail as a testing ground could improve the effectiveness of advertising in *other* media as well (Cody 1916).

Publications with specialized audiences were closest to being a substitute, more so than general circulation newspapers and magazines. Trade journals, in particular, were a means of narrowly targeted business-to-business advertising. They promised advertisers targeted delivery of their advertisements to precisely those people whose line of business would make them plausible buyers for the product being promoted. For their precision, they charged a premium. Since a trade journal's circulation was sharply limited by the size of the trade they served, the total advertising revenues depended on the ability to charge a precision-targeting premium. As advertising agencies diversified the range of advertising media they worked in on advertisers' behalf, *Printers' Ink* diversified their coverage of the advertising industry (despite keeping the print-media-specific title). In 1913, F.J. Low took to the pages of *Printers' Ink* to defend trade journals against direct mail, but also to call trade journal publishers to task for any dissembling about their circulation. "Circulation is really a mailing list, plus the services of a printing-addressing-and-mailing company, plus the services of Uncle Sam," he wrote. For an advertiser to assess the value of a trade journal's advertising space, he must have detailed information about their circulation. If they are transparent about their circulation, Low wrote, trade journals offer a significant cost advantage over direct mail (Low 1913, pp. 72–73).

By 1916, when the direct-mail advertising professionals were working to increase their visibility and their market share in the Associated Advertising Clubs of America, selling costs had reached a higher share of total costs than ever before. In part this came from greater productivity in manufacturing; even if selling costs had remained level, selling costs as a share of total cost would have risen as the goods got cheaper because of the falling contribution of per-unit production costs to the denominator. At the same time, mass producers felt an urgency about managing demand in the hopes of avoiding overproduction or price-cutting and so devoted more resources to advertising than their predecessors had. The selling costs of advertising and distributing on a national scale were still a net gain for those who did it and national-scale manufacturers captured an increasing share of the market. Nonetheless, advertisers were eager to find productivity gains in the selling process to complement the productivity gains in the manufacturing process (Tipper 1914, pp. 25–30). Equipped with new office machinery, new data management techniques, and a pool of low-cost female clerical labor, the direct-mail advertising professionals held out the promise of a rationalized, waste-less sales effort. As the population approached the urban-rural tipping point to become majority town- and city-dwellers, billboards held out the promise of intercepting more eyes with fewer placements than ever before. And print media remained the largest sector of the attention market, splitting the difference between billboards' low-cost advantage and direct mail's precision targeting advantage while wrapping the advertising in attractive attention bait that readers asked for and paid to receive.

New media since 1920

The main chapters of this study leave off about a century ago. In the years between 1920 and 2020, new media technologies opened up new possibilities for attention interception, and each was incorporated into the attention market in turn: radio, television, the internet. Of course, each new communications technology carried other possibilities, as well. Any medium of communication could in principle be used by all sorts of different message senders to reach all sorts of different recipients for any number of purposes. Yet most media outlets were turned decisively toward the purposes of advertisers and advertising professionals; just as periodical publishers did before them, those in control of the newer media turned their audiences into the source of commodified attention to sell to those who wanted to sell goods.

In the early 1920s, radio was the new communications medium, its many possible futures not yet foreclosed. David Sarnoff of the Radio Corporation of America (RCA) initially suggested that the expenses of creating and broadcasting radio content should be covered by fees charged on the sale of radio receivers and, if more were needed, from public funds and philanthropists. He likened radio stations to public libraries. AT&T tried to operate a radio station like they operated their telephone service, inviting anyone to make use of the station for a fee. They had trouble finding takers, however, until a real-estate enterprise called the Queensborough Corporation became their first customer and broadcast the first commercial advertising over the American airwaves on August 28, 1922. Despite some audiences taking offense at the intrusion of advertising and RCA's fears that advertising would lose the goodwill of listeners, the commercial model quickly came to predominate (Archer 1939, pp. 31–33, 54–55, 64–65, 71, 230–231). The first business books about radio advertising were published in 1927 (Cruikshank and Schultz 2010, p. 271).

The technology of radio transmission could have been used for widely dispersed access, but commercial broadcasters wanted to secure control of the airwaves; RCA, NBC, and CBS influenced the Federal Communications Commission's decision to allow manufacture of radios as receivers only so that most users would only receive, not send messages via radio signal. With the FCC's collaboration, commercial broadcasters dominated the new medium. From 1928–1935, educational broadcasters who had taken up 40 percent of the airwaves in the medium's early years were reduced to 4 percent. "In the process," writes Lee Artz, "radio in the United States became less a medium of citizen mass communication and more a system for commercial broadcasting" (Artz 2006, pp. 20–21). Major advertising agencies temporarily resisted dealing in radio placements and newspaper publishers tried to steer advertisers away from radio, but radio had taken on a recognizably modern commercial character by the late 1920s. NBC named Frank A. Arnold as director of development. In 1927 Arnold went on the business conference circuit, touting the virtues of radio advertising and NBC claimed over $2 million in advertising revenue. In the early 1930s the agencies found mechanisms for collecting commissions and began brokering radio placements and incorporating radio advertisements into the multimedia campaigns they designed for clients (Archer 1939, p. 303; Laird 1998, p. 158; Cruikshank and Schultz 2010, p. 271) – just as newspapers editorialized against billboards and as advertising agents who had initially resisted billboard advertising later insinuated themselves into the already-mature bill-posting business around 1900. To compete in the attention market, radio broadcasters submitted to audience size measurement but fought against constraints on their pursuit of attention. At least some radio listeners were self-aware about their conversion into a commodified audience and resisted by means such as boycotting products that advertised aggressively on the radio (Newman 2004).

A generation later, television began working its way into US households. By the 1960s, television was pervasive enough that Arvidsson describes it as having become an "ambience for life," not a separate sphere distinct from everyday life

(Arvidsson 2006, pp. 26–27). Like all of its predecessors (once the reception-only model was imposed on most radio users), television was an oligopolistic medium with "centralized production, mass distribution, and one-way communication" (Hardt and Negri 2000, pp. 298–299). For its first few decades television followed the attention capture-and-sale model that radio had already settled into: consumers buy the receiver but pay nothing for the programming while the programming is paid for by advertisers wanting to reach the audience. Ratings played the role for television that the Audit Bureau of Circulations played for print media, counting up viewers so advertisers knew how many eyes they were buying and broadcasters could charge accordingly. The high minimum cost to produce and place a television ad and the diminishing marginal cost of additional ad placements once the spot is produced and initially placed create economies of scale and barriers to entry (Durlauf and Blume 2008, p. 33). Like the leading magazines of the turn of the twentieth century with their enormous packages of eyes, sold only in bulk, television became and remains both out of reach for small sellers and indispensable to national brands. Also analogous to print, television coupled extensive strategies for intercepting large numbers of eyes with intensive strategies for selecting audiences strategically and making the most of the time spent in that audience's field of vision. During the 1970s and 1980s, the cost of producing television ads surged upward faster than inflation. The most expensive ads produced in 1970 cost about $70,000 (just production, not placement); the *average* ad produced in 1990 cost $168,000. During the 1980s, the number of stations proliferated and advertisers and advertising professionals responded with a greater emphasis on selecting the correct combination of more narrowly-targeted placements. The advertising agency department responsible for buying media placements became a center of creative strategic planning staffed by "the wiliest tacticians and the toughest negotiators" (Rothenberg 1994, pp. 228, 305). Cable briefly appeared to be a way for viewers to purchase programming and thus buy their way out of exposure to advertising, but cable stations quickly adopted the magazine financing model, receiving income from both subscriber fees *and* advertising placements.

At the same time, while advertisers were selecting audiences more precisely and wooing or wowing them with high production values, the certainty of interception was fading. Audiences had never committed on moral principles to the regime in which the sale of their attention funded the production of the shows they wanted. The manufacturers of television sets and related equipment helped create the conditions for audience attention to be captured (one or more televisions in almost every American home), but also developed and sold products that made audiences' advertising-evasion easier. Remote controls allowed viewers to mute the advertisements or change the channel without leaving the couch. VCRs allowed people to record shows and speed through the ads when watching later. Cable packages coerced higher subscription payments from subscribers by bundling channels rather than allowing à la carte selections, a disservice to viewers, but then cable providers also made viewers a more difficult quarry for advertisers to catch when they started including

DVRs and on-demand services, which made it easier than ever to choose when to watch a show and to skip ads – without even having to watch the ad blur by to know when to release the "fast forward" button! (And even if watching in real time, when an ad comes on, having a hundred cable channels provides more alternatives to flip to.) On the other hand, while on demand makes it easier than ever for the TV viewer to skip the ad, it also makes it easier than ever for the TV service provider to collect data about viewing behavior, and even steer viewing behavior with algorithms suggesting which should be the next show in your queue.

And of course, the internet happened. Like the long-standing communications system retroactively renamed snail mail, the architecture of the internet allows any user to both send and receive content. (Radio, remember, could have developed that way, too, if the FCC had been swayed by different interests during the critical period in the 1920s.) In the closing years of the twentieth century, which were the early days of rapidly-expanding internet connectivity, plenty of internet users and observers and commentators were excited about the democratic potential of widespread access to a medium in which, like the mail, transmission was multidirectional and, unlike mail, the recipients were open-ended. But there was no reason for attention harvesters to voluntarily refrain from expanding their operations into the digital realm and there were no policies or practices that would prevent them from doing so. By the early 2000s, it was becoming clear that the primary means of financing the construction of online digital spaces would be the sale of the attention of those spending time in those spaces. The internet would be "the biggest attention harvest since television." Just as advertisers became the primary customers of print publishers a hundred years before, advertisers became the primary customers of digital-content producers, aggregators, and gatekeepers (Wu 2016, pp. 213, 267–275).

In 2007, the first iPhone was introduced. Less than a decade later, a significant majority of US adults and teens already had smartphones. Digital spaces became not a virtual place to travel to from real life, but an additional dimension of the spaces we live in, no less real than and fully integrated into the rest of life. Widespread adoption of smartphones, which many users carry on their person almost continuously and look at reflexively throughout the day, opened up a vast new expanse of attention to interception. As Mara Einstein insists, your phone is not a magical device; it is an advertising medium. Like the direct-mail advertisements of a century ago, advertisements designed to target audiences online are crafted with the express intention of confusing recipients about the source, a practice Einstein calls "black ops advertising" (Einstein 2016). Also like the mailing list compilers of yesteryear, only with more powerful tools, advertising professionals working online see audiences as links to other audience members and mine data about social contacts as eagerly as they mine data about individual behavior. Meanwhile, the multidirectional transmission of the internet turned out to facilitate uses just as undemocratic as unidirectional broadcasting media. Because data flows both to and from users, every move a user makes is visible to data miners (Einstein 2016; Zuboff 2019).

With unidirectional advertising media it was fairly easy to get a close estimate of the number of eyes (or ears) intercepted, but it was cumbersome, often to the point of impossibility, to discover how a recipient responded. Advertisers could not know what the purchased audiences did with the magazines delivered to their mailboxes, how they moved through city streets and perceived the billboards, whether they opened their unsolicited mail, what they did with their televisions and radios. With the two-way flow of data online, much more can be known about audience responses: how long each audience member spends with a browser window open, which links they click, what content they share and with whom, and more. Much more can be known about a wide and expanding range of audience behaviors, establishing the context in which they receive an advertisement, so delivery of advertising can be micromanaged to a degree previously out of reach.

The newness of the digital medium obscured how much was not new. The phrase "attention economy" entered the lexicon with Michael Goldhaber's 1997 article in *Wired*. He wrote as though the attention economy were new (Goldhaber 1997).[2] The volume of information in circulation now overwhelms our capacities for attention by an even wider margin than before. But attention scarcity was already a concern of advertisers at the turn of the twentieth century. The information technology available now is orders of magnitude more powerful than the card files of the 1890s, so the scale and scope of data gathering and data analysis are new. But these unprecedented data-processing powers have been put to uses that have long been in the sights of attention-market operatives. Smartphones fill crevices of audience time that were previously inaccessible to attention interceptors. But attention interceptors have long been searching out new routes to eyes and ears. The internet combines the extensive reach and low per-unit costs of billboards (and then some) with the intensive custom-assembled precision and response-testing of direct mail (and then some). Advertisers are engaged in a quest for greater certainty about consumer behavior and attention-market behemoths like Google and Facebook promise to deliver. The granular detail of the data they collect on every user allows them to put very sophisticated products up for sale on the "behavioral futures market," to use Shoshana Zuboff's phrase (Zuboff 2019). But the contradiction between the socialization of production and the anarchy of the market has always inhered in capitalism. Capitalists bring together workers and materials on a massive scale, but, noted Frederick Engels in 1880, "No one knows whether his individual product will meet an actual demand, whether he will be able to make good his costs of production or even to sell his commodity at all. Anarchy reigns in socialized production" (Engels 1880). This contradiction has always launched the knights of business on the quest for certainty. The effort to systematically control consumer demand through branding and advertising goes back to the late nineteenth century. Advertising practitioners then, as now, articulated a goal of influencing consumer behavior without audiences' awareness of who exerted the influence or how. Digital tools may get advertisers closer to their goal of creating predictability for themselves through extensive access to and intensive manipulation of audiences. The goal itself was articulated long before this particular set of tools. Just as advertisers' interests exerted tremendous influence on the development of the publishing industry, radio broadcasting, or television, advertisers' interests have exerted tremendous influence on the development of the architecture of the internet. It should not be surprising, then, that the internet does what advertisers have long dreamed of.

Contested property rights in attention

Attention ownership claims of the interceptors

The precedents set between about 1870 and 1920 – the focus of this study – continue to matter. (As do the specific media developed in those years: print media, billboards, and direct mail are not extinct!) By 1920, business practice, legislation, and case law had together established attention as the salable property of the interceptor, not the intercepted and personal data as the property of the miner, not the mined. This is still so. This property rights regime grew out of the use of advertising as a weapon in the competitive struggles among manufacturers and distributors, the necessity of a mass media if advertising were to be delivered to audiences on the scale required, and a tendency toward specialization that placed intermediaries between advertisers and their target audiences. Many of the competitors seeking to profit in the attention market have changed and some of the tasks that are part of the advertising process have been reassigned or regrouped. The basics are still recognizable, though. There are advertisers, there are audiences, and there are intermediaries intercepting and selling audiences' commodified attention to the advertiser. The new automated technologies for assembling custom-made audiences should logically lead to greater efficiencies in the tasks of intermediation, which could in principle shrink the share of the economic pie captured by attention merchants. Instead, attention intermediaries have taken their place among the largest, most powerful corporations in the economy.[3]

Commodification of the attentional and informational aspects of our selves is contested, not absolute. Audiences readily abandon the advertising inserted as interruptions to television programming when technology makes it convenient. In 2007, when DVRs were still fairly new and only present in a quarter of households, Nielson estimated that use of DVRs to record shows and skip past ads allowed watchers to evade $600 million worth of advertising, about 1.5 percent of all television advertising (Conley 2008, pp. 100–101). Many computer users set their web browsers to block pop-ups and install ad-blockers to eliminate, or at least reduce, the barrage of advertisements appearing in the main content window – and, when possible, the amount of data collected about them. Advertisers and advertising professionals respond with subterfuge: advertising that hides its origins (Einstein 2016), coercive user agreements for all kinds of online services that obscure, rather than reveal, the extent of data collection and the uses the collectors and their clients make of that data (Zuboff 2019).

Also as a result of contestation, some attention-commodification practices are constrained by law. So far, the constraints are fairly minor. Some specific audiences or specific venues for intercepting audiences are withheld from sellers of specific products. For example, the late-twentieth-century wave of laws aimed at reducing tobacco use included bans on advertising to children; children's attention is still a commodity but there is a class of buyers not permitted to purchase it. "Do Not Call" registries restrain telemarketers from imposing on our attention through our telephones to some degree. It's notable that the registries are constructed as an opt-out, not an opt-in; telemarketers have a claim on your attention by default unless you refuse the claim. And other means of attention interception either have no opt-out mechanism or require you to pay a ransom to reclaim your attention from advertising. Attention interceptors can get a cash payment for your attention but there are vanishingly few circumstances in which *you* are in a position to get a cash payment for your attention. (You could consider the entertainment or information you get mixed in with the advertising that is delivered to you to be a payment-in-kind, but such payments are a value-circulation dead end. You can consume the entertainment or information but can't exchange it for anything else.)

Attention as a common resource

If we are in any sense "owners" of our attention, our ownership rights are weak. Economists have a technical term for a good whose owner cannot prevent use by another or, from the perspective of the user, a good that can be accessed without payment: such goods are *nonexcludable*. There may be costs involved in extracting, processing, using, or transporting a nonexcludable good, but there is no cost for the good itself. For example, to convert sunlight into electricity, you *do* need to pay for a solar panel, but you do *not* need to pay for the sunlight itself. If you use well water, it will probably cost you something to dig and maintain the well, but you do not have to pay for the water itself. Similarly, there are costs involved in laying the traps that intercept our attention. Magazines pay for writers, illustrators, paper, printing, and mailing, but they do not pay us for our attention itself. Billposters pay for the leasing of space, the construction of billboards, the pasting of posters, but not for our attention. Direct-mail marketers pay for mailing lists, writers, paper, printing, and mailing, but not for our attention. In the case of sunlight and water, no one in particular owns those resources, so there is no one in particular *to* pay. In the case of our attention, it is much clearer who in particular could in principle make an ownership claim, but we have not collectively established property rights in our own attention and have not been in a position to demand payment or refuse sale. Our attention is nonexcludable.

What of the experience of having our attention consumed, depleted? Economists have a technical term for goods that can be used up, those which, when used by one person for one purpose become less available to any other user for any other purpose: such goods are *rival*. Once you eat a sandwich, no one else can eat that same sandwich. Once you burn a log, no one else can burn that same log. Similarly, if you are paying attention to one thing, you are not paying attention to something else. Multiple studies have concluded that when there are multiple draws on our attention, our brains cannot handle them all simultaneously. Instead, we switch rapidly among them, but the switching itself is a drain on our cognitive resources and reduces our success with whatever tasks we were trying to attend to. One of my favorite experimental results showed that even successfully resisting a temptation to task switch drains our cognitive resources: people attempting to complete tasks that measured cognitive capacity while their phones were sitting next to them on the table were less successful than those who kept their phones in their pockets, who were in turn less successful than those who stored their phones in a locker in another room while working on the puzzles *even though all notifications were turned off and no one interrupted their work on the puzzles to use their phones.* The effects on cognitive performance of having a phone nearby were comparable to the effects of being short on sleep (Duke et al. 2018). The period of widespread iPhone adoption also saw a 10 percent increase in injuries among children under the age of five. The 3G network was expanded in phases, with service introduced in different regions of the country at different times, which created the circumstances for a natural experiment. Region by region, the local introduction of 3G service and use of iPhones was quickly followed by an increase in young children's hospital visits (Palsson 2015). Caregivers' attentiveness to their new phones meant inattentiveness to the children in their charge. Our attention is rival.

Resources that are both nonexcludable and rival are extremely vulnerable. If there are few barriers standing in the way of use and whatever is used is used up, depletion is a likely result. It is especially likely when there are significant monetary rewards for appropriating and selling the resource. We have a term for this, too: the tragedy of the commons (Hardin 1968). Any one fisherman can have more to eat and more to sell by catching more fish; if, collectively, all the fishermen in aggregate catch fish faster than fish can reproduce, the fish population collapses. Any one cattle rancher can have more to eat and more to sell by setting more cattle out to graze on the grassland; if, collectively, all the ranchers in aggregate keep so many cows that they eat the grass faster than grass can regenerate, the grassland turns to dust. Anyone who devises a way to get in our faces can sell that space in our visual field to advertisers and the more they get in our faces, the more they have to sell; if, collectively, all the attention merchants in aggregate assault our senses beyond our capacities to process, all of their messages get lost in the din and our brains get jittery.[4]

Living in the attention commons

Commons – systems of shared, rival resources – don't have to be tragic, but avoiding tragedy requires strong mechanisms for governance. Elinor Ostrom's research, for example, documents many examples of users of common resources successfully managing those resources for long-term sustainability (Ostrom

1990). Still, the environmental news, from deforestation to biodiversity loss to plastic pollution to climate change, shows that tragedy wins too often. Industrial capitalism's tragedy of the commons is natural resource depletion and degradation; information capitalism's tragedy of the commons, layered over the accelerating environmental crises, is human attention depletion and alienation from information about ourselves (Zuboff 2019). We have many discussions about how to cope as individuals with the overload of claims on our attention – mindfulness practices, web browser ad-blockers, social media fasts, software that will block your internet connection entirely for a time period of your choice, evasion of social interactions – but have hardly begun to articulate the problem of collective governance.

Polanyi theorized, based on past observations, that when the market mechanism overwhelms other, non-market dimensions of social life, societies react by finding ways to put boundaries around markets and by developing compensating mechanisms to limit the depredations that pure market logic inflicts on the social body. He called this the double movement: one piece of the movement is the tendency of markets to expand their reach and the other piece is the tendency of societies to bar markets from specific social spaces, or at least to restrain and corral markets to social ends (Polanyi 1957 [1944]). Margaret Jane Radin's language of the "contested commodity" speaks to the same tension between market expansion and social restraint of market logic. She argues that we should think of commodity status not as a yes/no characterization, but as a continuum. At the "yes" end of the continuum are things that can be traded between a willing buyer and willing seller on any terms the two agree to between themselves. After the sale, the seller has no lingering property rights in the item sold and the buyer has the full range of property rights in the item purchased. At the "no" end of the continuum are things that cannot legally be exchanged between a buyer and seller on any terms, either because no one has legally recognized property rights or the only legally recognized property rights are inalienable.[5] In between the two extremes are contested commodities: things that can be bought and sold but only on terms within a range determined collectively through the political process; the property rights ceded by the seller and gained by the buyer in the exchange are not absolute (Radin 1996).

Fictitious commodities, those items that are treated as commodities even though they were not created for the purpose of exchange, can be contested. Indeed, they are likely to be contested. Polanyi argues that letting the market mechanism loose on fictitious commodities is particularly destructive, so we should expect the double movement to take the form of contesting their commodity status. When the expanding reach of market logic converts land (broadly construed to mean environmental resources) to a fictitious commodity and ecological degradation follows, we know we need collective governance to manage the crisis. Land and the resources extracted from it can be privately owned and can be exchanged between one owner and another for a price but use of the land is subject to a thicket of restrictions: zoning laws, building standards, environmental standards. Sometimes we succeed in at least partially mitigating the problem we are trying to address, too often we don't, but we at least know that the topic of discussion is environmental policy. When the expanding reach of the market converts labor into a fictitious commodity and consumes workers' lives in ways that fray the social fabric, we have seen labor movement responses that seek to set some bounds on the hours and conditions of labor, ban child labor, and set more equitable parameters for the distribution of the fruits of that labor. As with land, sometimes we have partial success, sometimes we fail, but we at least know that the topic of discussion is labor policy.

The expanding reach of the market is consuming the fictitious commodity of attention and we are struggling to mount a coherent double movement response. Medium by medium, we have haphazardly erected obstacles on certain attention interception routes, while leaving others entirely unguarded. Local land-use regulations can put restrictions on billboards, for example, and in some places this power is exercised more than it is in other places. A speed bump or even a significant barrier on any one particular attention interception route does not necessarily limit the overall size of the attention market, however. It could just displace the attention grabbing into other known media or send attention miners on prospecting missions into not-yet tapped venues (Conley 2008, pp. 103–104). There is no constraint on the scale of the attention market as a whole.

The extreme demands on our attention are conjoined with the strip-mining of our personal information. Shoshana Zuboff's *The Age of Surveillance Capitalism* details the accumulation by dispossession process that opens ever more arenas of our daily lives up to digital data miners' operations. Her questioning refrain is, "Who knows? Who decides? Who decides who decides?" Right now, the answer is that the surveillance capitalists know – they collect data *from* you that they do not share *with* you. They go to great lengths to obscure the extent of their collection from you while touting the depth, breadth, and detail of their data to their customers. They decide what to do with your data; at the very most you might have an opt-out choice, but only at the cost of the product or app's functionality. In principle, our political system should provide a deliberative process that could let us decide who decides, even if our decision is to evict the surveillance capitalists from their position of knowing and deciding. But data miners are big political donors, electoral campaigns are big users of secretively appropriated personal data and the interventions such knowledge enables, and in the post-9/11 era government officials have been more inclined to leverage private surveillance in their security operations than to restrain data appropriation, so the apparatus of government has done more to enable surveillance than to democratize data (Zuboff 2019).

If we untether our imaginations from what we conceive to be politically possible and allow ourselves to gloss over the implementation details in which the devil resides, we could sketch the broad outlines of policies that would treat management of the social resource of attention as a collective, public responsibility. We have conceived of environmental policies that limit the total quantity of a resource that can be used. Within the overall cap, allocation may be determined sometimes by negotiated agreement, sometimes by permits sold at auction. (Fisheries are in trouble, but the situation could be worse without catch limits.) We have, conversely, conceived of environmental policies that cap the total quantity of a pollutant that can be emitted with the allocation of pollution rights to be determined by negotiation or auction. (Sometimes, too rarely but not never, we even enact such policies effectively. Lo and behold, the hole in the ozone layer has shrunk!) We could apply the same principles to commercial sales of our attention and commercial messages inserted into our communicative environment. We could imagine an overall cap on the commercial harvesting of human attention.

What most occupies our attention is the foreground of how we experience our lives. Tim Wu (citing William James) makes this point in his call for beating back the attention merchants' appropriation of our eyes and ears (Wu 2016, p. 344). Similarly, Shoshana Zuboff urges outrage and resistance in the face of surveillance capitalists' constant monitoring of our behavior, their rendition of our behavior into their own proprietary data, and their production of data-based behavioral predictions and behavior-shaping interventions that allow them and their customers, the advertisers (including electoral campaigns), to displace us from authorship of our own futures (Zuboff 2019). Appropriations of our attention and personal data do not occur in a vacuum, however. No one in the commercial attention supply-and-distribution chain treats attention as a final consumption good. Our attention, when harvested and sold at commercial scale, is an input into efforts to mold our behavior. The attention buyers whose interests have most shaped the practices of attention sellers are those who want to sell us things; their primary interest is our purchasing behavior and all other behaviors are interesting to them only in relation to our spending.

The attention market is so intricately interwoven with the rest of the commercial world (on the demand side) and the social world (where we occupy the raw material end of the supply side), that it is impossible to say what will happen if we grab at the thread of our attention and try to pull it back from buyers' purposes and redirect it toward other uses. How hard can we tug? How far can the fabric stretch? If efforts to reclaim our attention from its commodified uses stretch the fabric as far as it will go, maybe the elasticity of the other strands will snap the fabric back into something hardly different from its prior shape. But maybe the assertion of a different locus of control over attention could begin a tear that sets off a wider unraveling of the power relations embedded in the consumer culture whose basic outlines were sketched in the closing decades of the nineteenth century (Strasser 1989).

At stake in determining the locus of control over attention is not just the experience of paying attention, but also the experience of being attended to (or not). Payment as the basis for access to attention, as the market for audience attention currently allows with few fetters, has troubling consequences. But if not on the basis of payment, on what basis and by what means *can* we seek attention? Attention is, after all, not only a resource that arises from us and may be appropriated from us. Others' attention is also something each of us needs to receive. Reciprocity of attention is the stuff of social connection and social connection is a human need, even for the most introverted among us. Loneliness manifests itself in our bodies, not just the abstractions of the mind. The lonely die sooner (Cacioppo 2008). Like intimate social relations, collective political action requires attention.[6] If we reclaim the raw resource of attention from the market that deals in attention as a fictitious commodity, what might occupy our attention instead, and whose attention might we occupy? How will we decide?

Notes

1 After well-attended sessions on direct mail during the 1915 Associated Advertising Clubs' national convention in Chicago, Homer Buckley and other organizers worked to establish a permanent organization that would be dedicated to matters of direct advertising and that would be recognized by the National Commission as a department of the AACW.

2 Goldhaber posited that attention was *replacing* money as the most desirable currency. This is a mistake. Attention is only valuable to the attention dealers when it can be monetized. Attention is a route to money, not a replacement for money.

3 Mariana Mazzucato makes a comparable point about finance. If financial institutions were really using new information technologies to get more and more efficient at their task of intermediating between lenders and borrowers, finance should require a smaller and smaller share of the total value generated in the economy to complete their work. Instead, finance's share is growing (Mazzucato 2018).

4 To be fair, not all demands on our attention come from commercial sources. We all make attention claims on one another. But noncommercial social claims on attention can sometimes be hard to disentangle from the commercial interests of the attention dealers. Certainly, in the case of social media, many ordinary users make claims on one another without commercial intent, but they share the platform with commercial attention dealers and the platform itself is continually monitoring and manipulating the digital setting to capture as much attention as possible for their real customers, the advertisers.

5 For example, apples are as pure a commodity as you are likely to find. They can be sold for any price agreed to between buyer and seller. Once sold, they belong fully to the buyer, who may eat them raw or cook them first, allow them to rot, juggle them, or resell them to someone else. At the other extreme, since 1865 in the US, no one has had legal property rights in another human being, not even a baby, so there can be no legal market exchange in ownership of humans; it is not even legal to sell oneself into slavery. (Some people do still labor under coerced conditions that deserve the name slavery but it does not take the exact same form as chattel slavery.)

6 Even now, while access to commodified attention and personal data play such a large role in the pursuit of electoral politics, not all political fights over attention are about commodified attention. Other routes to attention are also contestable. Consider struggles over whether, where, and how anti-abortion protesters can make claims on the attention of those seeking or considering abortions, or struggles over what should be brought to the attention of children through school curricula, or struggles over whether, where, and how someone panhandling may make claims on the attention of passersby who may, perhaps be able to spare some change.

Bibliography

Archer, Gleason Leonard. 1939. *Big Business and Radio*. New York: The American Historical Company.

Artz, Lee. 2006. "On the Material and the Dialectic: Toward a Class Analysis of Communication." In *Marxism and Communication Studies: The Point Is to Change It*, ed. Lee Artz, Steve Macek, and Dana L. Cloud. New York: Peter Lang.

Arvidsson, A. 2006. *Brands: Meaning and Value in Media Culture*. London and New York: Routledge.

Associated Billposters Association of the United States and Canada. 1899–1904. *The Billposter-Display Advertising*.

Cacioppo, John. 2008. *Loneliness: Human Nature and the Need for Social Connection*. New York: Norton.

Cody, Sherwin. 1916. "Direct Advertising as a Means of Testing All Advertising." *Postage* Volume 1 Number 5: 19–20.

Conley, Lucas. 2008. *Obsessive Branding Disorder: The Illusion of Business and the Business of Illusion*. New York: Public Affairs.

Cruikshank, Jeffrey L., and Arthur W. Schultz. 2010. *The Man Who Sold America: The Amazing (but True!) Story of Albert D. Lasker and the Creation of the Advertising Century*. Boston: Harvard Business Review Press.

Direct Mail Advertising Association. 1916a. "A New Movement and Its Meaning." *Postage* Volume 1 Number 1. January: 9–11.

Direct Mail Advertising Association. 1916b. *Postage* Volume 1 Number 1. January.

Duke, Kristen, Adrian Ward, Ayelet Gneezy, and Maarten Bos. 2018. "Having Your Smartphone Nearby Takes a Toll on Your Thinking." *Harvard Business Review*. March 20. https://hbr.org/2018/03/having-your-smartphone-nearby-takes-a-toll-on-your-thinking

Durlauf, Steven N., and Lawrence E. Blume, eds. 2008. *The New Palgrave Dictionary of Economics*, 2nd Edition. New York: Palgrave Macmillan. ("advertising" entry pp. 31–34 by Richard Schmalensee 1987, revised for 2008 edition by Richard Genesove.)

Einstein, Mara. 2016. *Black Ops Advertising: Native Ads, Content Marketing, and the Covert World of the Digital Sell*. New York: OR Books.

Elgutter, Maurice. 1916. "Direct Advertising for Retail Stores." *Postage* Volume 1 Number 2: 31–33.

Engels, Frederick. 1880. *Socialism: Utopian and Scientific*. www.marxists.org/archive/marx/works/1880/soc-utop/index.htm

Goldhaber, Michael. 1997. "Attention Shoppers!" *Wired*. December 1. www.wired.com/1997/12/es-attention/

Hardin, Garrett. 1968. "The Tragedy of the Commons." *Science* Volume 162: 1243–1248.

Hardt, Michael, and Antonio Negri. 2000. *Empire*. Cambridge, MA: Harvard University Press.

Laird, Pamela Walker. 1998. *Advertising Progress: American Business and the Rise of Consumer Marketing*. Baltimore: The Johns Hopkins University Press.

Low, F. J. 1913. "Why He Uses Trade Journals Instead of Mail Lists." *Printers' Ink* Volume 84. September 25: 72–73.

MacFarlane, Charles Alexander. 1915. *The Principles and Practice of Direct Advertising*. Hamilton, OH: The Beckett Paper Company.

Mazzucato, Mariana. 2018. *The Value of Everything: Making and Taking in the Global Economy*. London: Allen Lane.

Newman, Kathy M. 2004. *Radio Active: Advertising and Consumer Activism, 1935–1947*. Berkeley, CA: University of California Press.

Ostrom, Elinor. 1990. *Governing the Commons: The Evolution of Institutions for Collective Action*. Cambridge: Cambridge University Press.

Palsson, Craig. 2015. *Smartphones and Child Injuries*. www.palssonresearch.org/wp-content/uploads/2015/12/Palsson-Smartphone-11-2015.pdf

Paper Makers Advertising Club. 1915. *We Vote to Work with the Printer*. No. 1 in a series of Direct-by-Mail Advertising pamphlets.

Polanyi, Karl. 1957 [1944]. *The Great Transformation*. New York: Farrar and Rinehart.

Radin, Margaret Jane. 1996. *Contested Commodities*. Cambridge, MA: Harvard University Press.

Rothenberg, Randall. 1994. *Where the Suckers Moon: The Life and Death of an Advertising Campaign*. New York: Vintage Books.

Strasser, Susan. 1989. *Satisfaction Guaranteed: The Making of the American Mass Market*. New York: Pantheon Books.

Tipper, Harry. 1914. *The New Business*. New York: Doubleday, Page & Company for The Associated Advertising Clubs of the World.

Warner, John DeWitt. 1900. "Advertising Run Mad." *Municipal Affairs* Volume 4: 267–293.

Woodruff, Clinton Rogers. 1907. "The Crusade Against Billboards." *The American Review of Reviews* Volume 36: 345–347.

Wu, Tim. 2016. *The Attention Merchants: The Epic Scramble to Get Inside Our Heads*. New York: Alfred A. Knopf.

Zuboff, Shoshana. 2019. *The Age of Surveillance Capitalism: The Fight for A Human Future at the New Frontier of Power*. New York: Public Affairs.

Index

Printed in the United States
by Baker & Taylor Publisher Services